BUILDING
HEALTHY
GARDENS

A SAFE AND NATURAL APPROACH

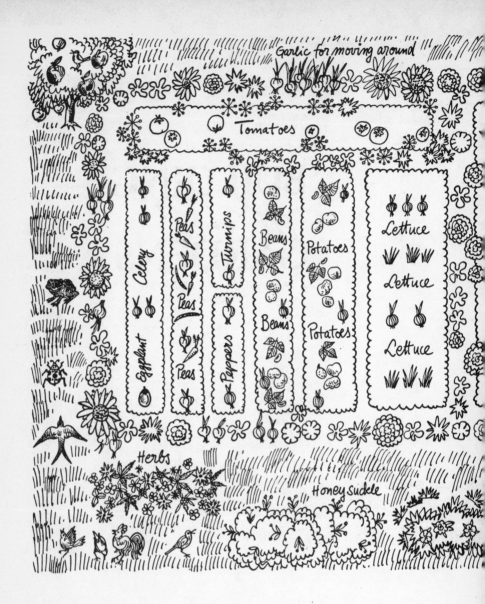

A Garden Way Publishing Book

Storey Communications, Inc.
"America's Garden Publisher"
Pownal, Vermont 05261

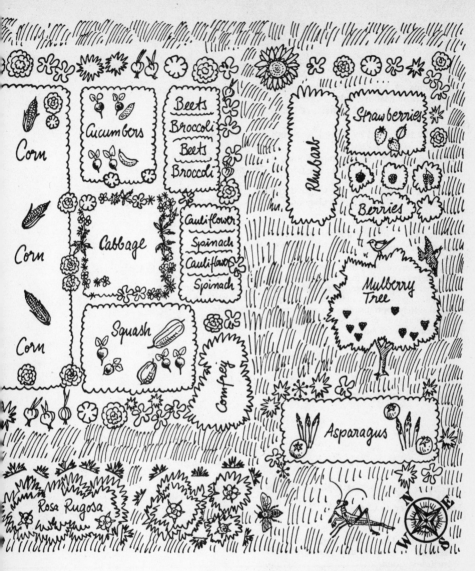

BUILDING *HEALTHY* GARDENS

A SAFE AND NATURAL APPROACH

Illustrations by
Karl W. Stuecklen

by
Catharine Osgood Foster

Front cover photograph by Gary Mottau/Positive Images
Illustrations by Karl W. Stuecklen
Production by Mallory Lake
Edited by Jeff Silva and Constance Oxley

Originally published by Alfred A. Knopf, Inc., 1972 as
  The Organic Gardener
Vintage Books Edition, Vintage Books, A Division of Random
  House, New York, 1972 as *The Organic Gardener*

Printed in the United States by The Alpine Press
First Printing, January 1989

Library of Congress Cataloging-in-Publication Data

Foster, Catherine Osgood, 1907–
  Building healthy gardens.

  "A Garden Way Publishing book."
  Rev. ed. of: The organic gardener. 1972.
  Includes index.
  1. Organic gardening. I. Foster, Catherine Osgood,
1907– . Organic gardener. II. Title.
SB453.5.F669   1989   635'.0484   88-45486
ISBN 0-88266-527-8 (pb)

Grateful acknowledgment is made to Rodale Press, Inc. for
permission to quote from J.I. Rodale's *The Organic Front*,
copyright © 1949 by J.I. Rodale

iv

For
Barbara,
Jill,
Linda,
Bob,
Fred, and
Tom—
good helpers,
teachers, and
gardeners

CONTENTS

1

2

3

4

5

6

7

APPENDIX

Rich Soil, Few Pests, and a Varied Environment

Gardeners who want to create a healthy garden aim for one that is, as completely as possible, in harmony with the natural forces of growth. Since they want the garden to benefit their own health, they must respect the balances of nature which control the plants, animals, insects, and microorganisms whose interactions create the healthy balances. Therefore, they cooperate with nature rather than attacking its basic harmonies.

Many of the methods of cooperation have been studied and practiced during most of this century by organic gardeners. The first edition of this book was written for them. Though this edition has been drastically revised, my belief in gardening for the sake of the garden's entire population of living things has remained steady. If there happens to be a buildup of one element that upsets the balance, there are natural ways to counteract it. Among the most interesting are ways to control insect buildups, and many are suggested in this book.

When I was first asked to write the book, it dawned on me that my husband and I had been "organic" gardeners all along, without ever using such a name for the ways we did things. It was obvious to us that we should aim to have a healthy and thriving garden, and that it would therefore contribute to our own health. Over the years we have learned more and more about nutrition, and have added vegetables to our gardens which are especially noted for high vitamin and nutrient content. I plant edible flowers now, also, and use the basic healthy methods in the flower beds, as well.

Our farm at that time was varied—with an orchard here, hen yards there, a big barn, several gardens, berry patches,

1

hedges, a running brook, a swamp, and fields beyond, stretching to pastures on the lower slopes of a wooded Vermont mountain. There was no monoculture anywhere. But we did have a lot of chickens. With variety like that there is an entire population of nature's controls alive and working all the time in the air, around the plants, in the soil, and in the healthy interchange of nutrients and antibiotics in solution in the water of the soil. The soil structure and the soil solution, I know now, were continually replenished by the organic matter put out on the ground from the henhouses, the vegetable garbage, the mown grass, the autumn leaves, and the weeds we threw out. We had plenty of wasps, bees, ladybugs, a few praying mantises, and many birds who ate lots of insects and weed seeds. Whenever the hens were let out in the proper season, they may have gobbled up a hundred asparagus beetles an hour. We had no Japanese beetles then. And ducks and geese and goats were the only weed-killers we knew about.

The gardens were on slopes, well drained and well aired. They were well-nourished gardens, too, especially the one we put on the spot where we tore down an old henhouse. The organic matter there, after a winter under a thick blanket of snow, was entirely composted by the time we got ready to plant. Organic gardeners who compost systematically create heaps and maintain a routine of composting. In those days we just put manure out whenever we had it. And we wouldn't have thought of paying a garbage man, for we trusted the land to take care of the wastes we put on it. Besides, we were busy. There was teaching to do, articles to write, research or lessons to work at, the hens to take care of, and birds to watch. We gave time and thought to protecting the birds, feeding them and enticing them into the garden with places to nest, bird feeders, and wild berries to eat, which they actually prefer to the less tangy cultivated cherries, blueberries, or raspberries. In fact, protection of the birds was a principal reason for our refusal to use poisons. Once in a while I'd get an urge to spray, but my husband wouldn't permit it. He'd remind me that we wanted to protect our dogs, and the other animals, and the birds; and we wanted clean fruits, chickens, and vegetables for our own use and for the neighbors who were our customers.

We had never heard of aldrin, dieldrin, DDT, or other

hard chlorinated hydrocarbon pesticides. When they came on the market, I believed the ads and bought some sort of mixture with DDT in it, but my husband forbade that, too. Ever since, the magazines and journals and a good many of the books that have come into our house have revealed with increasing alarm what these poisons are made of, what they do, how they accumulate in the environment instead of breaking down, and how they affect biological systems, threatening the entire food chain from bacteria to eagles. A decade ago we saw one article reporting that in a certain New York City restaurant there was not one item on the menu except the black coffee that did not have DDT in it, according to lab tests done on all foods served there. That demonstrates how pervasive and persistent DDT was, and how unbiodegradable modern pesticides can be.

I began to learn new ways to do things because I had to. I read a great deal about organic gardening, visited gardeners who used organic in preference to chemical methods, and saw that many of them, too, were learning new ways because they had to—and wanted to. Many remembered, as I did, the dust bowl in the Midwest and deplored the loss and exploitation of good topsoil throughout this country. Many were reading, as we were, about the dire, unforeseen side effects of the hard pesticides.

Some, like neighbors of ours on a gravelly, shaly hill, were challenged by the problems of building a whole new soil. They discovered that using manure, compost, and the newly made soil which they created themselves was considerably easier and cheaper than buying tons of topsoil to be brought in. The previous owners of their place had bought some topsoil for the lawn, but the area where the new family wanted to put their vegetable garden was so gravelly it was impossible. The minute you start scavenging for a compost heap you become expert at finding sources for the organic matter you want to use for it. These gardeners found a goat farm, the dump where the town's street department put autumn leaves, neighbors who did not want their lawn clippings, and a chicken farmer who would let them have all the litter and manure they'd take away if they'd gather it themselves and pile it in their truck. Like everyone else, they had plenty of weeds to add to the pile, and in the fall some old mulch from their first little garden. I watched all this process with great interest, and when the wife, who is a

member of our garden club, gave a talk on "Conservation, Backyard Style," I learned a lot of new tricks. Now, after several years, that garden in the backyard looks fine.

When we moved to a new place, we were glad to find that the previous owners had been careful gardeners who built up an excellent soil. In fact, it was so good that Japanese beetles had moved right in. They were getting pesty on the asparagus and grapes, but that year our county agent asked members of the garden club to try out the newly discovered milky spore disease which parasitizes the larvae of the beetle and puts them out of commission. It has nothing to do with milk; it just makes the larvae look white.

This was my first experience with a biological control that was called by that name, though birds and wasps, ladybugs and ants were always helpers in maintaining populations that would get out of hand completely if not preyed upon. And the beneficial bacteria, fungi, and antibiotics in the soil are certainly biological controls all the time, whatever you call them. So is garlic and the curious antibiotic that is discharged from it, and so are many herbs, including the tansy that fends off the pesty insects called aphids. So are what are called trap plants, like the dill which attracts tomato worms away from tomatoes, and the white roses which, if you can bear to think of such a thing, will distract your Japanese beetles away from your grapes and corn and asparagus and zinnias. Well, so are the zinnias. Even more distracting is the knotweed that will come up among your zinnias if you let it.

Maybe it was luck or maybe it was the right day for me, but at just the right time I heard a lecture which introduced me to organic sprays made of garlic, onion, and red pepper, and even plain soap and water. The aphids had come, so I tried these sprays. They worked—the soapy water on the lupines, and plain water followed by garlic and onion on the string beans. (See page 77 for recipes.)

The next year I began taking classes in plant physiology to discover what really happens when plants grow, and how good and bad practices affect them.

Now, if trouble strikes, I don't have to reach for the bottle or aerosol can to cure the ill with medicine, or rather poison. Nor do I dream of telephoning for an airplane to spray the entire place or of buying one of those little tractors shown in ads with pretty models who are supposed to be riding up and down their yards spraying everything in sight. I go out and spread wood ashes, or transplant nasturtiums or marigolds to the plagued area, or get out the hose and give infested plants a good washdown. My husband likes to think up ways of outfoxing the woodchucks and rabbits—by sprinkling blood meal around their holes or along a row of lettuce—or of trapping insects like earwigs in dark lengths of rhubarb stem, and fending off snails and slugs with a three-inch barrier of sharp sand, which they'll refuse to come through with their soft, tender bodies. He will not get out the gun, and he won't spray poison or treat the corn seeds with poison. The crows he keeps tame and well fed year-round, and they come to one of our feeders on a table beside a pine tree five at a time. We call them and they answer. Then after we put down the food we hit the box we use as a container for a second signal and they fly right in. They are eating by the time we get back to the house. They have only bothered our corn once. (See entry on corn.)

People who garden by these ideas cook by them, too. I had many practices that were those of a so-called natural foods cook. From some home economics class I took in school, or from some article in one of the farming magazines, I'd learned that you poured nutritious vitamins and minerals down the drain if you strained your vegetables without saving the water they were cooked in. I didn't always use this liquid for soups and gravies, so I invented other ways to use it. You can put it in biscuits and muffins as part of your liquid ingredient. You can save it for cooking the next vegetable, if the tastes don't swear at each other. If it won't be used for a day or so, put it in an ice tray and freeze it. In the summer, when you blanch vegetables for freezing, you can use the same water over and over, and afterward thin mayonnaise, white sauce, or cottage cheese with it. Use what's left for a blender-drink of herbs and greens.

I have learned some of these tricks in recent years, but in the days when I didn't get home from work till nearly six o'clock, I mostly used the pressure cooker, which takes hardly any water anyhow. I learned not to put salt in until after the cooking. If you stand over the pot and watch it, you can boil that little bit of water away at the last minute and have no problem at all about what to do with it. Gradually

7

you learn to use for organic purposes all those nutrients that used to be wasted.

Soften the dogs' dry kibbles with the extra cooking liquid. Put it in the pail of stuff that goes to the chickens or goats if you keep them. Put it on the compost heap, or right on the garden. Use it for making organic sprays, herb teas (if mild enough in taste), and to water your houseplants. You might even dribble it out of the watering can onto their leaves, in the hope that its nutrients will make a foliar feeding. You could run an experiment to find out. (See chapter 2.)

The cooking I did was simple, somewhat lazy, and parsimonious, and reflected the fact that my edition of Fanny Farmer is very ancient. I cooked with what happened to be around, and a lot of it came from the garden, henhouse, or hedgerows. We did not have a TV, so I was never tempted to try out all the newfangled, adulterated, souped-up timesavers that other women have been inveigled to try. I did try a few I saw on the shelves at the market, but there was resistance again from my Yankee husband, so I went right back to the natural ways I'd learned before. Besides, we both like the taste of foods prepared on the spot, of whole grain flours, pure maple syrup, fresh fruits, fresh vegetables, fresh eggs.

We had farmer friends up and down the road where we lived, and an expert old German nurseryman as a neighbor at the top of the hill who gave us suggestions about when to plant, when to harvest, what varieties were good for our zone, and good tricks for cultivation. These farmers all used fresh or home-canned foods and stuck to the old ways of gardening, too. What I know now is that their gentle conservative old ways were, for the most part, organic gardening ways. So I believe that it is perfectly natural and easy for people wanting to grow their own vegetables to use traditional methods. In those days many of us used superphosphate as a fertilizer because it worked fast and we could see results. Organic gardeners of today, preferring natural, untreated materials, use rock phosphate instead. It works all right, but more slowly, and it avoids leaving any residue.

As I see it, the only real difference between a pure organic gardener—a disciple of Sir Albert Howard of Indore, India; or Ehrenfried Pfeiffer, of the Bio-Dynamic gardening group;

or the Rodales of the Organic Gardening and Farming Press in Emmaus, Pennsylvania; or any of the other old-time founders of Friends of the Land and the organic gardening movement—and a plain old conservative Yankee farmer is just this: That the organic gardener has a philosophical and scientific conviction against using chemical fertilizers and pesticidal poisons while the Yankee has doubts and suspicions, a deep satisfaction and certainty about what he has already done with success, and a respect for the wholeness of nature which he never verbalizes the way the disciples do.

As long as the old-timer was feeding himself and his family, his stock and his chickens, he stuck to the good old ways, just as the organic farmer did. At our farm we knew that minerals in the heap of scraps to go out to the chickens were good for the chickens, and for the soil, too, when they again became available in manure to dress the land. We also knew, with or without a detailed knowledge of why, that it is good for the soil to manure it. We also knew that humus was good, whether or not we understood the structure of the soil and what makes for good nutrients for plants and for the animals and people who eat them. Whereas confirmed organic gardeners have carefully run compost heaps, farmers have dung heaps or whatever their state's milk laws will permit.

After we moved from the farm to the rather suburban place where we live now, we did feel the pressures to switch to chemical gardening more acutely than ever before. People up and down our road were starting patios or putting in swimming pools and beginning to talk about getting rid of mosquitoes. The organic gardener wouldn't think of using any but herb sprays (see page 77) on areas where mosquito larvae breed. The best is a garlic spray, as determined by the scientists at the University of California at Davis, who reported that a few parts per million could kill the larvae. And we have observed that those at a picnic who eat plenty of garlic are the ones who don't get mosquito bites. The insects simply stay away. Now most garden club members and conservationists wouldn't spray for mosquitoes either. We'd rather bring in young toads, and do, for they eat up mosquito larvae by the hundreds and even by the thousands. They have to be moved very young, for they don't like change after they grow up—a good thing, for once they are at your place, they do not want to leave. You

9

can entice swallows by leaving your barn or garage door open, and watch them dart over mosquito areas and consume those insects in quantity. Dragonflies eat mosquitoes, and so do frogs and fish.

Many suburban people, and now many newly rural people, have only recently lived where nature and its rough ways are a daily encounter. When they go outdoors and find mosquitoes and other creatures sharing the environment they want for themselves, that puts them in a fighting mood. The organic gardener does try, I believe, to have a less belligerent way of dealing with things, and to try to fit in with the patterns that exist without man's interference. We stay outdoors more, at more times of day, and I've even advised complainers to stay indoors—or at least way away from where the mosquitoes are. And a lot of us are learning that nothing is perfect. I find it pleasant to know that the only thing perfect in nature is the total, overall design whose exquisite interlacing intricacy is beyond comprehension and beyond compare.

An artificial violet, a paper rose, or a plastic ear of corn can be changeless and spotless. Also ugly and utterly lifeless. Any live leaf or live string bean may have spots on it or bites taken out of it. I have heard a young homemaker say *hurray* when she discovered that the carrots she was buying had some bumps and imperfections. I've said it myself, and hoped that the imperfections meant that here were some vegetables that had not been drenched with pesticides to make them smoother and unbitten.

We don't want our vegetables to look as smooth and flawless as plastic, and we wish the public relations people and chemical company salespersons would stop saying that we do. The more organic gardeners learn about gardening, the more we realize that not only the use of pesticides, but also the plant breeders' and truck-garden farmers' preference for vegetables that ship well or last long on the shelf, are subjecting us to stringy cabbage, rubbery lettuce, huge peas, and all the other vegetables that are tasteless and tough. Now we grow our own.

I've talked to any number of people—including gardeners— who think they cannot grow unsprayed, or rather unpoisoned, gardens without expecting something to come and ruin them. There are lots of answers to this fear.

The first is: There are dozens of other preventives if you

get a shortage of water, a crop that won't grow, or an insect invasion—from plain hosing down the plants to replanting or fertilizing to setting traps, including trap plants and companionate plantings of tomatoes and cucumbers, for example. Plants such as tomatoes, marigolds, garlic, and mint release toxins of some sort to repel insects coming in to lay eggs. Plants such as daisies and marigolds have pollen which attracts beneficial predator insects such as lacewigs and sylphid flies. You can also use black lights to catch egg-laying moths, gooey tanglefoot to trap caterpillars, or a little beer in an almost-empty can to entice snails and slugs to do themselves in.

Another point is: What if you do have to replant here and there, or what if you do have bugs? A few bugs won't hurt you. Pick them off and drop them in a jar of water with a film of kerosene over it. Or let some of them eat up a few plants—the ones they choose will be weaklings, anyway, which you would pull out later. Unless you have a great big farm operation, you won't get a huge invasion such as those that sometimes come to large fields of a single crop, where the feasting is all too favorable. Monoculture invites trouble.

One of the organic gardener's best retorts to objectors is that if you have a very good, rich, healthy soil, your plants will be rugged and healthy and unattractive to insect predators. It works. I've seen it over and over in many home gardens, and home gardeners do not practice monoculture. In my own garden I've noticed that the lowest, senescent leaves on the runtiest plants are the ones that get bitten and attacked first. Those worst leaves on the smallest of the squash vines or cucumber vines are the ones the cucumber beetles will go right for. Pick the predators off and pickle them in that kerosene brine. If the weather is dry give the plants a good watering, too, (especially at the roots). Plants also need lots of water at pollination time.

The healthy soil and garden will be in top form in a yard full of creatures and plants that live at your place with you. Do what you can to keep them that way, discouraging few of the living creatures who come, and allowing the patterns of coexistence to settle as many problems as possible. This is the organic attitude.

A last answer is: You know you don't want to mess up such marvelous patterns with poisons, and you know you don't want to interrupt the food chains of all the creatures in your yard, or to eat lettuce that has been spattered with some sort of synthetic pesticide. If some of it washes into the ground, it may reach the bacteria, fungi, actinomycetes (little microorganisms of a kind between fungi and bacteria), as well as molds, earthworms, shrews, perhaps mice and moles, and all the other life forms that keep the soil in condition and the cycles in operation. A few people, and very thoughtful many of them are, are still worried about whether the United States should try to be the breadbasket for the world. They worry whether or not American large-crop monoculture is possible without pesticides (which they call economic poisons), and whether chemical fertilizers are an inevitable part of that way of farming, too.

We are in a dilemma, they fear, and they overestimate the role the United States can play. Some aspects of the problem they sometimes neglect: the question of the water shortage looming ahead; the appalling malnutrition and starvation in our country alongside our affluence; and the fact that we have mountains of compostable refuse of a hundred or so kinds, millions of gallons of high-nitrogen effluents, billions of tons of rock phosphate we could put to use.

We have passed laws (though they are not very effective) to control the misuse of pesticides and herbicides. We have found many new sources for other kinds of pest control. And as a happy note, 75 percent of the agricultural research at the Bethesda, Maryland, labs of the U.S. Department of Agriculture was for a time devoted to developing more and better biological controls for the economically important pests. Good progress, to be sure.

When I was first asked to write this book, my reaction was that all the practical things that could be said about organic gardening had already been said. There was a spate of books, pamphlets, and magazines published by Rodale Press and Garden Way Publishing, and in England by the people at Henry Doubleday and by the pioneer Lady Balfour. Then I began thinking about all the young people I knew who were boldly launching out into a new style of living, with gardening as one of their main occupations. There are hints that can help any beginner, and there are some cautions and reassurances to give. Also there are all the fascinating explanations for the various methods you use. When I made up my mind to write the book, I found it very exciting to review suggestions from other experienced gardeners and to comb through books by plant physiologists and soil experts. It was fascinating to read about the roles of organic matter in the soil and the way nutrients are taken up into the plants, and about the predation patterns among plants and animals which keep the cycle going.

When I wrote the first edition of this book, few seed merchants offered special supplies for organic gardeners. Nowadays most offer compost makers and compost materials, including packets of the bacteria needed to convert the raw materials of a compost heap into the fine, black substance we use as fertilizer. Mail-order companies offer any number of biodegradable and biological pest controls. From many you can get the famous *Bacillus thüringiensis*, which paralyzes the gut of the corn worm, cabbage worm, and most other caterpillars. You can buy various predator insects, including ladybugs, praying mantises, lacewings, and also botanicals for nonchemical sprays of rotenone, pyrethrum, sabadilla, and ryania. It seems obvious that the requests of organic gardeners for these natural supplies have been listened to. The seed companies wouldn't carry them unless there was a widespread demand from gardeners.

Today's organic gardeners can start out with a good backing of seed merchants and suppliers, plenty of printed materials including government pamphlets, and can even get untreated seeds upon request. The important thing is for all gardeners to know as well as possible what they are doing and why.

The chapters that follow are addressed to several kinds of readers: to anyone appalled by the effects of poisons on their own food, on the whole food chain; to old-time gardeners looking for biological controls; to enthusiastic but inexperienced natural-foods gardeners looking for ways to get started and for practical things to do; to those still undecided about the kind of gardener they want to be. I hope to persuade those who are looking for better arguments than they have already heard, for gardening without pesticides and for using a composting method in preference to a chemical fertilizer one. It is natural to want valid reasons for switching to a different way of gardening, and I hope to supply some.

For the most part I want to reassure those still wondering

whether a change of method might involve a lot of extra work. I believe that in the long run organic gardening methods are labor-saving and thoroughly satisfying to people who want gardening and farming to be free from a fixation on chemicals and pesticides, and to encompass again the natural riches available everywhere—from the banana skin in your garbage pail to the monumental and potentially recyclable wastes from our big cities.

After some suggestions about ways to get ready to garden, there are chapters on composting or making your own nutrient mixtures, on the soil and what it does for us and for our gardens, and on the garden itself, its vegetables and other gifts.

When you are ignorant, you fall for what the ads or garden centers tell you. With an inquiring mind you are glad to know why experienced gardeners advise the use of manure, compost, lime, and biological controls. With some know-how, enthusiasm, and the attitude that a few failures are not going to hurt things much if you stick to natural methods, you will find you can be your own judge and have in your garden what you want in it. I hope everything at your place will be blooming with good riches, delicate fresh foods, and a sense of well-being, because all that you'll have there belongs there.

Getting Started With Indoor Gardening and Basic Botany

G ardeners always learn that nature is not a plaything of people. Even though some still ride over their fields in big machines and fling chemicals and pesticides onto the land, many of us have made up our minds to cooperate with as many natural forces as possible, and leave out the dubious chemicals. Gardening organically is a way of taking part in the cycles of nature's overall garden and of sharing in its basic harmonies.

As organic gardeners we take positive steps to see that the capacities of nature are not overexploited and polluted, and to do this we need to learn as much as possible about what these capacities are. The practices of gardening show you what they are; a knowledge of the natural processes behind the practices will show you why organic gardeners choose to do what they do. The purpose of this book is to enlarge your acquaintance with both, and to help you over the humps, especially when you want to take things too seriously, or consult too many experts, or when you go into a panic. I want to give you some hints and some facts I've found that appear to be pretty good explanations about the soil and the growth habits of plants; most of all I want to make the enterprise of gardening rewarding, relaxing, and exciting.

Start on Any Scale, Any Place, in Any Season

Start in as small a way as you like—on the kitchen counter with a few radish seeds on a wet blotter, or with plans for making over a suburban yard with new methods free of pesticides and dubious chemicals. You can set up a small greenhouse under fluorescent lights, a place to start flowers and vegetables in organic peat pots for later transplanting to the garden, window box, or terrace planter. You can begin small-scale composting by saving your vegetable garbage and hunting around your neighborhood for humus-making materials like leaves, grass clippings, or wood chips. Such materials can be put in a plastic bag or in the bottom of a compost bin you build out of wood or concrete blocks. You can study seed catalogs, draw up layouts and planting schedules for a small city yard, park-allotment plot, or big south-sloping field on a new homestead. However you begin, look forward to a lush, pest-free, well-composted, and -fertilized garden controlled without poisons or additives, organically nourished and blooming with clean, bright flowers and ripe, delicious vegetables and fruits.

You can enter the yearly revolving cycle of nature's twelve-month garden in winter, spring, summer, or fall, and do things for the sake of a garden of your own that are appropriate to any of those times of year. If it is spring, you hurry to prepare a place, order seeds, and get right out to plant—and it is all rather hasty and may raise some difficulties if you haven't taken time to plan properly. If it is summer, you can travel around and see from other people's gardens what you'd like to do the following year, watch what grows well on different parts of your land, make plans, start composting, and prepare for fall plowing and perhaps a cover crop. You might also try some small quick crops like cress, beans, and radishes on cleared ground. If you start in the fall, composting might be your main effort, since this is the season of plentiful leaves to include in your pile; again, plan on fall plowing and a cover crop. In either of these seasons you can study your land for drainage or irrigation needs, for the best locations for the garden and fruit and nut trees, and perhaps try to start growing or transplanting materials that you can use to make organic sprays for use the following year.

Winter, in most areas of the country, is a period of lull; there is time to spend away from the outside chores that demand constant attention other seasons. But once a full-fledged organic gardener, you will find your summer chores—such as weeding and spraying, very much reduced—though you will still need to do some early-morning trap inspecting and bug gathering. Many of the suggestions I am going to make for the winter can, of course, apply to other seasons, from running experiments to learn what plants do under certain lights and heats to trying your hand at plant propagation.

All my suggestions are intended to get you started with experiments with which you can teach yourself about the principles of plant growth and the plant structures that make them function. Your aim will be to find out what happens when plants grow, and why. You will remember what gardening practices are best because you will have done things for yourself on a small enough scale so that every step and detail were clear. You will have successes and failures, but no error or loss is tremendous—though you will discover that after you have gotten to know your plants, you will feel a sadness when something goes wrong with them. During winter you can usually make amends if something does go wrong indoors, and you will have plenty of time to meditate about what is happening, and what can happen. You will always be learning how much more there is to learn.

Plant Radishes on a Blotter

To learn about seeds, how they take up water and open up to grow, plant some radishes. All they need at first is continuous water. Put them on a wet piece of towel or a wet blotter, or in a saucer with water; the blotter is best, for it controls the moisture. A plastic or glass cover of some sort is needed. A petri dish like those used in labs is good, because it is glass and you can watch what is happening. Keep the blotter moist so the seeds will germinate, sprout, and send out a root with root hairs. At this stage no nutrients need be added. Besides water, warmth, and oxygen, all the nourishment and carbohydrates for energy that the little plant needs is stored in the endosperm body of the seed. The radish, like many other plants, has two seed leaves, or two halves to the seed which separate when the embryo sends forth a root in one direction and then a stem in the other. These plants are called *dicotyledons*; those with a single seed leaf (such as lilies and corn) are called *monocotyledons*. The shortened names are *dicots* and *monocots*.

After the separation you can watch this fairly easily— especially if the seed coat has slipped off. The root is oriented toward the earth and will grow down, if possible;

the stem goes up, toward the light. On a horizontal petri dish the roots seem to go out and around. Once you get used to this radish and the way it grows, it might be a good idea to start some bean seeds. They are larger, and their structure is slightly different. When the seed coat has absorbed enough water to be soft and easily pushed off the core of the seed, gently open it and watch how the young plant growing from the embryo or germ gets going when it, too, has absorbed enough water to initiate the change. Once they're started, be sure not to let your seeds dry out. Try anything around the house—orange, lemon, and grapefruit seeds, avocado, squash, wheat berries.

After radish seeds have been growing a little while, the root hairs look spectacular. Though none are more than a half-inch long, there are so many of them, and their surface exposure is so extensive, that each of these little plants is already on the way to its miles of surface exposure to the soil solution which would nourish it if it were in the ground. When in the ground, the root hairs form close bonds with the soil particles that yield nutrients to them. Each hair is a rounded protrusion of a single surface cell on the root. Most plant cells are squarish or oblong, but these root-hair cells have this extra protrusion. It is so small that it can squeeze between clay particles in spaces of .002 microns. The wonder is that it is all part of one T-shaped cell, and that each root-hair cell is an efficient device for drawing nutrients directly into the plant.

Both in the kitchen and outdoors in the garden, the materials you supply to help your plants must be scaled for entry into these tiny root-hair cells. These cells are the agents for transforming mineral matter into organic matter. Life is being created at every moment. And the process, even on a very small plant, operates on a vast scale. The rest of the miracle is that plants, unlike animals, create their own food.

You will see, as the root grows, that its zone of root hairs changes—for they do not grow out from every part of a root. Old root-hair cells die and new ones are formed in the part of the root that is growing fastest: the zone of maturation, so-called, near each root tip. A rye plant studied by H. J. Dittmer had fourteen million rootlets with a total length of 380 miles; he calculated that their root hairs ran to the billions, probably fourteen or fifteen billion.

The few hundred you may see on your radishes will be

absorbing water and, later, nutrients for the plant. Since the roots are not buried you could move these whole little plants however you wanted without injuring the root hairs. You can eventually plant them without doing much damage. But if planted in the ground and then moved, they would suffer quite a lot from moving; many of the tiny root hairs would get pulled off because in soil they would have forced their way between the incredibly thin layers of clay onto which nutrients cling.

The little radish plants grow by cell elongation, getting the energy to do so from the stored carbohydrates in the endosperm of the seed. When the leaves form, if they are in the light, they turn green. This means that the chlorophyll-forming structures are now being created, and that photo-synthesis, the making of the plant's own food, has begun. If given some complete plant nutrient, or fish emulsion in water, the growth will go on.

Once in a while you have to expect failures. I've had zinnias growing in a petri dish develop brown rootlets and seem to lose their root hairs. Even so, in the moist atmo-sphere, the early first leaves kept going several days after the roots began to deteriorate. Though most will die, two or three can survive; the question is, how?

You begin to speculate when this sort of thing happens, and then you may plant over again and compare what happens the next time. You can always learn from these failures. In the winter, on your experiment table, they are not serious. You just cross them off, put the ruined stuff on your compost heap, and start again. The difficulty may well have been a fungus disease called "damping off." To avoid this, you can use all clean sand for a planting medium, or sterilize your potting soil in a slow oven (200° F) for twenty-five minutes.

Now Plant Some Seeds
in Potting Soil

This is the right time for planting some seeds in a good potting soil, to see how they grow in that. Mix seven parts loam, three parts peat, and two parts sand. To sterilize the loam mixture heat it for 30 minutes at 180° F. High heat makes the mixture smell awful; that is avoided at the low heat of 180° F, a heat actually hot enough to destroy harmful microorganisms in half an hour. For each twelve cups, add a half-cup of compost or dried cow manure. All these you can buy at garden centers and many chain stores. In order to watch the growth, plant the seeds in a plastic cocktail glass with some holes knocked out of the bottom for aeration and drainage. Since the roots will shun the light, wrap the container in foil to keep the soil dark; then you can simply remove the foil whenever you want to see how the rootlets and root hairs are growing. I started several squash seeds this way last winter in a small amount of good soil, and it was very interesting to watch how rapidly the whole container filled up with roots. This made the plants pot-bound. That is, they were crowded, or the three that survived were. The effect was pleasing in that the competition for nutrients by what must have been yards of rootlets made the stems short, the plants small, and the blossoms come early. The one I transplanted to a slightly larger pot bloomed for two months. (This phenomenon of a plant flowering when undernourished is often used by greenhouse gardeners to force blooming.) Eventually the stem became quite woody, probably at the time it began to develop a nitrogen deficiency, though the blooming itself would indicate a nitrogen deficiency already.

Plant a Potato

In a much larger clay pot I planted a potato in a rich, light potting soil. I didn't bother to cut the tuber in pieces; I just put it in whole and waited. In a few days two sprouts appeared. One was short, and never grew more than a couple inches. The other shot up to a height of almost three feet in a matter of weeks. It blossomed once, and then the delicate white petals fell off and the plant stopped growing and just stayed there as a tall green accent in my kitchen window. This pot, too, filled up with a mat of roots. It required an enormous amount of water, and I kept the feathery-leaved top slice of a carrot pressed into the soil as an indicator. When there was enough water, the little green leaves that grew out of the carrot stood up and looked fine and healthy. When the pot became dry, down they drooped and looked about ready to die. I had waited for weeks for the top to die down as potato plants do in the garden when they are nearly ready to dig. By mid-June the leaves had begun to yellow and drop off. I

Potato and Carrot

pulled up the plant and saw nothing but a nubbin. What could you expect? Then my husband Tom felt around in the soft earth and found two potatoes. One of the two was clean, scabless, and full-sized; the other was very small, also clean and unblemished, and good. Next time I plan to grow potatoes in three different potting mixtures and compare the results.

Plant Several Tomatoes

Whether or not you plan to start your own tomato plants to set out in the garden later, start a few for experimental watching anyway. Try various ways on different plants to encourage them to flower early. Give one plant a cold treatment after it reaches five inches in height; keep it cool for two or three weeks. On another, water scantily for four days to suspend leaf growth temporarily. Take some of the leaves off another—especially the young expanding leaves. Then see whether these practices

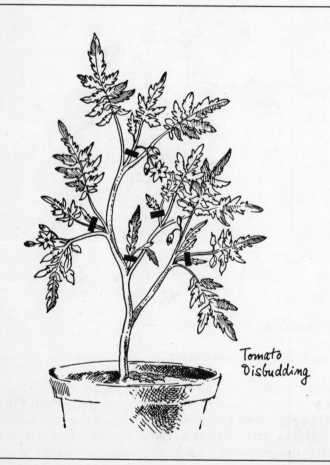

Tomato
Disbudding

improve or inhibit the flowering in any way. "Disbudding" tomatoes has been known to increase the number of flowers, as well as to move up the flowering date from eighty to fifty days (especially if only two or three leaves were left on the plant). Then try giving a plant two or more days in one, by turning on fluorescent lamps during the night for an hour, or by putting the plant in a dark closet during the day for an hour, or both. The best light bulbs to use are full-spectrum ones, which do not deprive the plants of any natural wavelengths. Each of these experiments will not necessarily work, but they are interesting to try. Such factors as intensity of light, degree of photosynthesis in the parts you leave on the plant, the action of various enzymes and pigments, and a hundred other factors you are not thinking of will be influencing the plant all the time. Last of all try watering with a sugar solution or apple juice, or even try putting a fresh, young, cut apple inside a plastic bag tied around a tomato plant. (If those won't induce flowering in a tomato, try the top of a pineapple. And if cold treatment won't induce flowering in a tomato, try it on peas.)

Try Various Soil Mixtures

For anyone just learning about organic plant growing, experiments with adding compost, dried manure, cottonseed meal, or other nutrients to potted plants on the windowsill are well worth the effort. You can teach yourself what nitrogen, phosphorus, and other nutrients do, and compare leaf size and color, sturdiness of stem, and general well-being in pots treated differently. Many discoveries about the needs of plants have been made in laboratory tests in which certain elements were systematically omitted in order to observe the results of the deprivation. Making a new soil mixture and repotting your plants is also instructive. It is a good idea to keep a big pan of potting soil, or a mixture of soil, leaf mold, and compost under a shelf or in some cupboard, so you have it on hand not only to add to when you make a scavenging discovery, but also to use when you need it. Keep experimenting with different mixtures of soil and sand, and with perlite, peat, vermiculite, and sphagnum moss in different proportions to the basic loam. More will be said about what is in the soil and in its components in later chapters.

Plant Marigolds, Mints, and Tangy Herbs

Aside from conducting the experiments, you can begin plants that you will want for your cooking and for your garden later on. Marigolds are important as repellent plants and for use in organic sprays. Nasturtiums are also good to start for outside use later, and if they bloom they will brighten up your kitchen at the time of year you most need it. Use biodegradable peat pots because nasturtiums resent transplanting. Those given a good rich soil and plenty of nutrients at frequent intervals will do well. Those planted in small pots with a poverty of nutrients will be stunted and eventually yellowish.

The herbs you can grow on your kitchen shelf, for use in your cooking and for planting outside later, are those that mind neither the heat when young nor the shock of transplanting. Those to try would include lemon balm, basil, borage, caraway, cress, dandelion, dill, hyssop, lovage, marjoram, parsley, rosemary, sorrel, French tarragon, and woodruff. Parsley and lovage may be moved to a shady spot in your yard, but most of the rest of them should be moved gradually into the sun. Do not try such delicate plants as chervil, or bother with the hardy perennials available wild along so many of our roadsides. (It is, of course, unwise to eat things that have been subject to lead poisoning from auto exhaust.)

Learning About Light

After some of your plants are up, try moving them around to different exposures. A southern window is very useful for giving plants plenty of sun, but since you can never quite achieve overhead sunlight, the plants will stretch out of shape in fulfilling their instinct to grow toward the light. What happens is that a hormone responds to the need and acts on the cells on the side of the stem away from the light. These cells then elongate, enabling the plant to bend and move in the direction it seeks to go. Rotate the plants every day to compensate. Once the stems grow long, they will stay long until the rest of the plant catches up—if it does. A plant needs direct, overhead light to slow down this stretching. If you can rig up a fluorescent light over a shelf (or your kitchen table, where you can also put your plants), try that, too. The kind of light that provides the full spectrum (including near-ultraviolet rays) is the best to use. Both plants and humans are believed to have better health under this full-spectrum light. Some people are having fairly good luck with full-spectrum Vitalite (used even in hospitals and offices now), Gro-Lux, and Plant-Gro. For simulating of full-spectrum daylight, you do not want plain fluorescent bulbs, and certainly not pink ones.

Some of the full-spectrum lights will last for nearly a year, burning night and day. But you shouldn't subject plants to continuous light. Even when forcing spring plants to flower, the custom is to give the plants two nights in twenty-four hours by turning on the lights for an hour at midnight. In this way the plants get short nights, as contrasted to continuous long days (though the two are two ways of looking at the same phenomenon). Chrysanthemums, it is known, bloom only in long-night periods, usually October and November. To get them to bloom, darken your room for some extra hours in months that have longer days than those we get in October.

It is interesting to discover that glass blocks sun rays of certain lengths, and that you need supplementary wavelengths to simulate what the plants would have received in direct sunlight. But leave it to the experts to do the experimenting with violet rays; it is dangerous to fool around with such things.

The radiant energy your plants must have is needed not only for photosynthesis in the green leaves, but also to trigger processes that control stem length, flowering, straightening out a warped seedling, and most enzyme actions. Though seed germination usually occurs in the dark of the soil, radiant energy is needed for that process, too. All the energy used by plants (and animals) comes from the sun. There is no other source.

A reflector is a good light source to use for your kitchen shelf—and under small-growing plants in the garden, too. I use a strip of aluminum foil, sometimes crinkled, to put on the window sill where the sun will strike it, and outdoors between the rows. Some people use even bigger reflector devices outdoors, and if you want this kind of aid for a partly shady place in your vegetable garden, make it in the winter. To see how well it works, try out reflectors on a sunlit shelf where you are growing lettuce, parsley, and cress. The additional heat will also help the plants. Watch to see how good light affects your plants.

Plants ripen to full-blooming maturity in direct sunlight (unless they come from the forest and are adapted to shade). In good light the nitrogen and mineral contents are properly balanced and plants conform most fully to their inherent characteristic type—with optimum root growth, shoot formation, and leaf development. Without enough light you can get them to advance, but they will never have good quality because their proteins will be arrested and many of their simple sugars will not develop into complex sugars. In this unhealthy state they harbor the fungi you do not want, stretch and use up too much nitrogen to reach some light, or stay stunted with small structures, overactive enzymes breaking down the proteins and carbohydrates they do have, and using up their vitamin C. German studies of plant crystals that indicate whether the plants have been grown by organic or commercial chemical fertilizers have revealed that shade patterns and nonorganic fertilizer patterns are sometimes similar. The crystals of healthy, sunlit, organically nourished plants are alike, and are proof to Bio-Dynamic specialists that such plants are normal (and that chemically fertilized ones are not).

Your outdoor garden will need plenty of light to protect it from dampness, slugs, snails, earwigs (which love dark places), and the bacteria and fungi of decomposition that will go to work turning your plants into something for the compost heap long before you want them to. Even so, a lot of plants will grow, for photosynthesis goes on in almost any light—even moonlight.

Plants Require Certain Temperatures

Combined warm and cool temperatures are preferred by most plants, as you'd naturally expect—warm in the day, cooler at night by about 5 to 10 degrees. Most of the houseplants, however, that we have acclimated to our heated houses and apartments can stand a fair degree of heat at night. Anyone who has nursed along a cyclamen after Christmas knows, I'm sure, that a good cool place at night is the only thing that will save it—aside from correct watering, of course. The total range for plant activity in temperate climates is only 60° F: none to speak of below 40° F, and none at all above 100° F.

How to Stretch a Plant's Endurance

If you are growing plants in a northern climate in the winter, you are already stretching their natural endurance. Outdoors, too, there are a few things to be done, and you can make preparations all year-round. In the fall, when early frosts threaten, have protection ready to lay over the plants. In our town during a cold snap in October, you can see old sheets and jackets spread over people's favorite tender flowers and vegetables when you go out early in the morning on the way to school or for the morning mail. In some areas you see smudge pots. In the spring, after a late frost, you can see people out before sunrise hosing down their very tender young plants to melt the ice crystals that may have formed. I do this at least twice each spring to save the tender shoots of asparagus that are up.

Devices for providing artificial heat have been used for centuries, and in our age, electrical gadgets with some new wrinkle come on the market every year or so. Many of these gadgets are very helpful in providing plants conditions that they prefer. One of the handiest gadgets is a seed flat with heat tape inserted in the soil. You can build any size greenhouse, from twenty inches up. You can build hot beds and cold frames outdoors, attached to your cellar window, or up against a south wall. You can fill large plastic bags with warm water to warm up the soil when you lay them on the ground in the sun.

A Heated Flat for Your Kitchen

Any size of flat or planting box or shelf can be given heat by using the heat tapes supplied by seed and catalog companies. The lining of the flat can be wood, metal, or polyethylene, and the first layer can be vermiculite, a very absorbent natural mica material available at hardware stores and garden centers. Use horti-cultural, **not** insulation, vermiculite. Then put in a four- or five-inch layer of soil, mixed with a moisture-holding mate-rial such as peat moss, or the moss from true bogs called sphagnum moss. Some seed companies sell the whole unit, all fixed up for you and ready for immediate use. It is best to have a plastic or glass top of some sort to hold the moisture in the air near the plants. The unit from seed companies often comes equipped with such a top. The advantage of warm soil for seed germination and young plants is that the soil solution which provides nutrients can be kept at the optimum temperature for good growth. If the weather gets too hot, set up a small fan; and if it gets moist and sticky, a hair dryer will do the trick.

Hot Beds and Cold Frames

Whether you live in the suburbs or in the country, you'll have plenty of room outdoors for a hot bed or a cold frame. The advantage of these garden aids is that you can stretch the seasons by starting plants early, and can even grow certain crops for harvest directly from the frames. Plan to face either of these frames to the south, with protection on the north and windy side, but not under dripping eaves. Give them good drainage.

To build a wooden frame, make a structure that is no wider than six feet, no longer than twelve feet, and with a depth of twenty-four inches at the back and fifteen inches at the front.

Do not try to make it wider than six feet, or you won't be able to reach into it to work in it. Do not attempt a length beyond twelve feet because then you'll have difficulty controlling the moisture and temperature, and consequently any pests which might come your way. There is no use enticing them to thrive in damp warmth if you can avoid it.

In the bottom of the frame, for a hot bed dig a two- or three-foot pit and put electric heating coils across it, or some hot-water pipes if you build up against an apartment wall, house, or greenhouse with hot-water heat. Put manure on top of the coils, then add a soil made of two parts loam, one part sand, and one part compost and/or peat and leaf mold. The sand will be of the best quality if you ripen it in the compost heap for a month or so. In perfectly natural hot beds only manure is used to heat up the mass, and the electricity (as with our grandparents') is omitted.

Both hot beds and cold frames must have glass or plastic lids, of a size you can lift up to let in the air if the space inside gets too hot. The usual old-fashioned lid was a window sash, and two of them add up to about the right size for one bed. Put them on hinges so they can easily be lifted and propped up. Double glazing is helpful. Add, for example, a layer of polyethylene inside the glass.

The advantage of a cold frame over a hot bed is that you can plan to raise plants out of season, or let them linger out of season in an environment that is not different enough

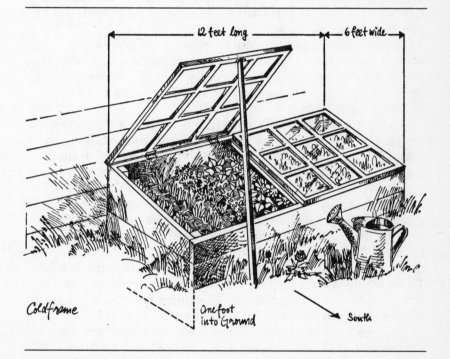

Coldframe — 12 feet long — 6 feet wide — One foot into Ground — South

from the outdoors to let them get tender. In fact, a cold frame, if used properly, will develop especially rugged and healthy plants. You leave them exposed to the weather whenever they can stand it, and protect them only when it is too cold for them to endure frosty nights or cold, windy days.

The length of a cold frame is not so important as with the hot frame because you will air the cold frame more frequently and the moist warmth will be avoided for any extended periods. As for location, it is even more important with a cold frame to use the warmest spot of protected southern exposure you can find. The only source of your heat is the sun. Over the frame you place window sashes or some sort of fiberglass. But never let it get hotter than 80° F. Close the frame at night to preserve some warmth and prevent frostbite. Seed companies sell various kinds of frames, often with automatic devices to open the lids at 80° F and close them at 78° F for plant protection.

Fill the frame with good rich loam, and plant thickly. Rows do not have to be farther apart than an inch or so, for you will watch their growth with an eagle eye, and pluck out all plants but the sturdiest.

There will be rapid transpiration once the plants get started, so water daily, and use only tepid water. Little plants hate to be assaulted by cold water. Therefore, do not use a hose. Use a sprinkler with very fine holes at the end of the spout.

Another advantage of a cold frame—if you are interested— is that you can send away for plants that do not belong in your climate ordinarily and create a climate in which they might survive. Keep the temperature, in any case, at around 70° F.

If you plan to have both a hot bed and a cold frame, separate your vegetables into those that like a cool beginning to their lives as plants, and those that prefer it to be warm all the while. Some with warmer proclivities are tomatoes, peppers, and eggplants, so they go in the hot bed. Those liking it cold include the brassica vegetables: broccoli, cauliflower, and cabbage. The unfussy ones, such as lettuce and radishes, can be started early, too, in either the hot bed or the cold frame, where you can help them adjust to the cool of the outside air every day when you open up the frame. The cold frame can also be used as a transition place to help harden the young plants for final placement in the garden. You can start tomatoes or cabbages in the hot frame, then move them to the cold frame, and finally to the out-of-doors. For this much moving, you might want to plant your seeds in biodegradable pots or flats, so you will never have to disturb the roots while they are growing. This adds to your expense, but it is a fairly safe method, especially if you use sand in the mixture to help drainage, and sink the pots in loose earth and cover the rims to prevent their drying out. If you tend to overwater to compensate for drying out, use clean clay pots, to which little roots will not cling, for a safeguard. You can also buy devices that make tight blocks of potting soil, and thus avoid containers altogether.

If you do not use pots, but just move the plants from one piece of ground to the other, let them establish themselves for several weeks. You may have broken off and disturbed the root hairs, and they need that much time to readjust. To minimize damage, transplant early, when there are two true leaves, and handle only the leaves, easing the plant out of the soil. Be sure to water both the old and the new beds before transplanting, for this helps the little plants to survive the shock.

Organic gardeners who want to feed themselves and their families over as long a growing season as possible will use hot beds and cold frames to stretch the seasons. The main danger, usually avoided by careful watch, is that of losing your plants to the fungus organisms called damping-off, which thrive only in moist warmth. Keep the air moving and your plant won't suffer from them too much. But if you see your plants drooping, or the stems getting rotten at the ground line, thin them out. Also put on a mulch of vermiculite, or even sand. At any stage you can reduce the likelihood of this fungal attack of damping-off by avoiding overcrowding. The lack of air circulation invites the fungus to settle on the plants.

When you start exposing cold-frame plants to fresh air outside, do it slowly. Reduce the usual amount of water for a day or so before you open the lid for a full half hour. Then open it for a whole hour, then two hours, and so on. There will be wind, so your watering schedule will have to vary. In a week, you can probably leave the lid off all day.

In really cold weather cover the frames with blankets. When the sun comes out, take them off again and let the sun get in, but keep the lids on. Plastic bags of warm water put on the soil in the morning will help it to warm up more quickly after a cold night.

Some people also use their cold frames as storage bins for such root vegetables as beets, carrots, turnips, and rutabagas. Even celery can be kept between good layers of straw. Remove a foot or so of soil before putting the lower layer of straw in for all these vegetables. Cover them well, inside and outside the frame. Invert a bushel basket filled with leaves over the latch so you can get at the vegetables under the snow, or when everything is frozen up. If you don't have a cold frame, half bury an old refrigerator with the door side up, but be sure to remove the latch, of course.

One plant protection device you can plan for is an extended homemade hotcap or cloche—which is really a structure like a long, narrow, small greenhouse that you stretch right down the length of the row. You use curved plastic and curved wires that look like croquet wickets. Make the cloches in short sections, however, so that they can be

Hot Caps,
Floating Cover,
Clear Plastic Tunnel,
Shade Tunnel

removed easily if the air suddenly gets hot and muggy inside.

Three-by-five-foot sections are feasible for a structure one foot high. Plan for wadding to stuff the ends on cold nights. Little plants do well in this miniature greenhouse when handled right, and you can expect corn or whatever you put under it to come along days ahead of the corn you plant out in the open.

A window bubble made of plastic can make a tiny hot-house out of your cellar window. An advantage of this is that instead of having to lean over, you can do your winter gardening right out the cellar window. When you want fresh young lettuce on a cold day, you do not have to go outdoors and walk around to a frame to get it. The other

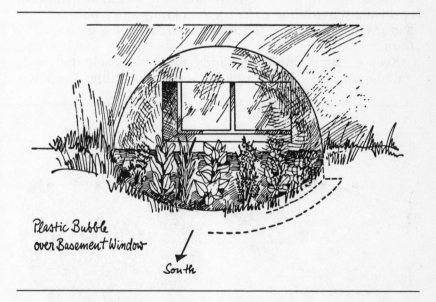

Plastic Bubble
over Basement Window

South

advantage is that when the hot frame garden needs airing, there is a safe source of cellar air, neither too cold nor too hot, to ventilate the plants. Some people buy window greenhouses to use out of upstairs windows. Protective enclosures for individual plants in the garden include hotcaps, paper or plastic tepees, gallon jugs with the bottoms cut off, and green-and-clear-striped Suncaps, which provide both sun and light shade. Also look into Wall-O-Water tepees holding water which heats up and holds the heat overnight. Row protection now available includes a slitted plastic Tunnel-Grow and Floating Row Covers of such lightweight plastic that the plants can push it up themselves.

Discovering Plant Structures

When you get your equipment all set, and your plants begin to grow, you find yourself more and more concerned with what is going on right under your own eyes, and curious about what plant structures are and what they are doing all during the cycle, from seed through growth and flowering to seed again. As you become familiar with the way plants do their jobs, you get a sense of what they require, and develop a skill in giving it to them if you can. Most important, you become aware of the entirety of a plant and of its earth, air, warmth, and water environment. You get to know all its patterns and rhythms, and this is surely the secret of the green thumb.

Keep a magnifying glass handy and look closely the minute your curiosity is aroused about something. Keep a

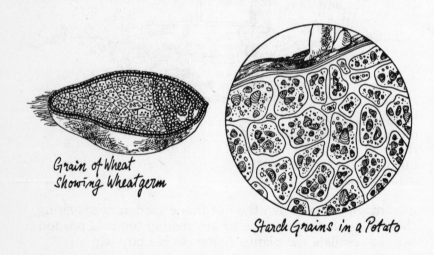

Grain of Wheat Showing Wheatgerm

Starch Grains in a Potato

very sharp knife nearby, too, so you can make a crosscut to examine. You might one day become curious about a potato—what it is, what it is made of, what function it serves on the plant, what its eyes are, and what its sprouts are like. Take one out some evening and start slicing across it to find its structural parts. If there is a microscope in the house, all the better. Find the outer skin, the cork just under the skin, and then the storage cells inside with the starch grains, the parts of the eyes, and, if it is getting toward spring, the sprouts themselves. Slice through a sprout and compare its textures and makeup with the big starchy potato tuber. Even ten minutes looking at a potato this way will give you an entirely different perception from the one you have, especially if you've always thought of a potato merely as something whitish with a brown peel to be cut off and thrown away. A potato tuber grows at one end of an underground stem, and is the storage place for the food which the big leaves of the potato plant make all summer in your garden, or a good part of the winter on your window shelf if you decide to grow one as I did. The eyes and sprouts are for the next generation of plants that use the potato as a storehouse for their food. Human potato eaters are invaders of the plants at the time in their life cycles when they are storehouses.

How Nutrients Go Up and Food Comes Back Down

You might also become curious about a carrot, or about how the nutrients go up and the food comes down into roots or tubers. Make a clean slice across a carrot and see all the layers. Way in the center is the woody part, in carrots as in trees. It is called *xylem*, meaning wood (as in xylophone), and is pronounced to rhyme with file-em. This part functions to bring water and nutrients up from the soil. Its long cells are structured to make it easy for liquids to pass up the root and stem to the branches, flowers, and leaves. These woody cells eventually become strong enough to hold up heavy plants. By the time trees are as big as redwoods, these xylem cells have to sustain tremendous weight.

Next to the xylem is the *cambium*, and then the *phloem* (pronounced to rhyme with Rome). The cambium layer is so thin that you won't see it, but it is the vital layer, because from it generates all the new cells of both xylem and phloem.

The phloem brings back to the plant, for use and for storage, the food that the leaves photosynthesize out of light, air, and water. Its cells are long, thin, and well adapted to their task. These minute structures are invisible to the eye, and quite hard to find under a microscope. But a good, well-illustrated botany book will clarify questions for you, and it will be well worth your time some long winter evening to study the way they look and work.

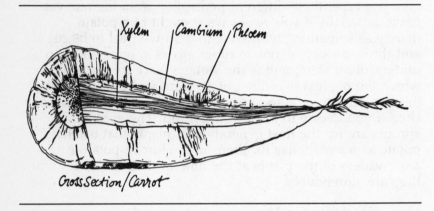

Cross Section/Carrot

It will be worth it, I think, because you will gain an intimate sense of the nutrients going up and the food coming down in a perpetual rhythm. Afterward a plant can never again be something still, upright, and stiff to you, but a tremendously active, productive living organism. You are aware of how sturdy it can be, what enormous jobs it can do, but also of how fragile it can be and how injury to its infinitesimal parts might upset or ruin the workings of the whole living plant—and then perhaps a whole food chain. For you also begin to feel how the life of this plant is interwoven with other lives, and with other structures in the environment and in the soil.

The One and Only Basis of All Food

In the leaves of a plant all the green cells have chloroplasts, or little structures containing the pigment chlorophyll, which makes the plant look green. Only when chlorophyll and light are present can the marvelous event of photosynthesis take place—when the plant transforms carbon dioxide from air and water into simple sugar. That sugar becomes the food for the plant and thus the basis for all other food that exists. It is the most important chemical reaction in the whole world, and is so simple and clear as to be miraculous. Isn't it astonishing that the energy of the sun itself can be transformed into the basis of the whole earth's energy in these tiny cells? Because it is happening in so many billions and trillions of green leaf cells all the time, we get blasé about it and forget that this single first step leads to all food and all energy available to us.

An oversimplified form of the equation is: $6CO_2 + 6H_2O + 674$ kilogram calories $\rightarrow C_6H_{12}O_6 + 6O_2$. You can see that what happens is simply that carbon dioxide plus water plus calories react to yield sugar and oxygen. The oxygen produced with the sugar goes partly to the air and partly to the plant. The actual process is much more complex.

Miles of Surfaces
Inside Leaves

The cross section of a leaf, if we could see it, is rather astonishing, too. On top is a protective cover, then packed cells, then spongy, openwork cells, and on the undersurface holes like mouths to take in the air. During photosynthesis in the leaf, the water that combines with carbon dioxide comes up from the soil in a steady column, the carbon dioxide comes in through the openings, and the calories used in this process come from the sun. Within the layers of cells in the leaf there are millions of chloroplasts; their surface area in a mature tree can add up to as much as 140 square miles. All of those at work making simple sugar amount to quite a production. By the time the energy has been converted to animal and then human food (if you eat animal flesh), the energy has been considerably dissipated.

The veins you see in a leaf are the vascular bundles, all having both xylem and phloem passageways. The cells that store food made by the plant are simple, thin-walled cells found in the tubers, pith, fruits, bulbs, flowers, and unspecialized parts of stems and roots. The plant itself is the best storage facility ever developed. I think it is up to gardeners to take advantage of this and learn how it all happens, and then to try to use plant foods at the height of their food value. Plant foods include, besides the sugars and starches, big protein molecules, nucleic acids, oils, enzymes, and such nutrients as iron, potassium, sodium, sulfates, and others. Plant cells also have pectin, tannins,

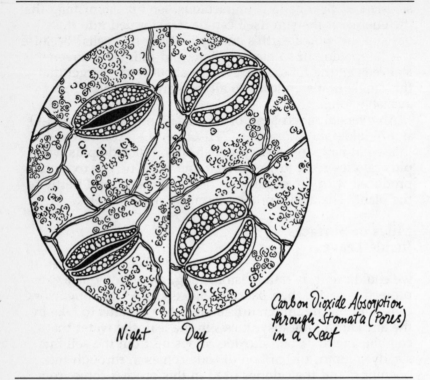

Night   Day

Carbon Dioxide Absorption
through Stomata (Pores)
in a Leaf

cellulose, and lignin. You may have no urge to look into all
of these, but the very list suggests to any gardener the
complexities of the biochemistry of plants. Biogeneticists
work to modify plant contents for adaptability to various
conditions (for example, to withstand freezing).

Tampering
Nutrients and growth sub-
stances of many kinds are available, and you can try some of
them out on your plants to see what happens. If they are
touted in advertisements as miracle substances, guaranteed
to make your plants gigantic, and are based on newly
invented chemicals or newly extracted hormones, enzymes,
and fungus concentrates, I hope you are somewhat suspi-
cious and refuse to fall for the latest appeal to ego and
laziness. If the new products tamper with hormones, you
might recall ugly, warped plants and what has been injected
into the necks of chickens in recent years to plump them

for market, and revolt. There is plenty of evidence that disturbances of organic processes in the outdoors are of dubious value, to say the least. In an experimental laboratory, however, there is justification for using growth substances and other materials that affect plants. You can learn something from controlled comparisons of treatment, and you are not letting loose something into the environment if you confine your activities to a lab or a kitchen shelf. Of course you use caution and burn or properly destroy anything that might contaminate birds, animals, the soil, or the creatures of the soil.

There are nutrients accepted by organic gardeners which you can use to see how your plants respond. These would include fish emulsions, seaweeds, cottonseed or other high-nitrogen meals, granite dusts, and rock phosphate. But again, for indoor purposes of comparison I see no reason why so-called complete commercial mixtures of nutrients containing set proportions of nitrogen, phosphorus, and potassium should not be used. Knowledgeable botanists who count themselves as organic gardeners sometimes use commercial fertilizers outside also, along with their mulches and composts, to achieve even bigger, healthier, and thus even more pest-resistant plants.

Growing plants in plain water, with nutrients added periodically and frequent flushing, is a method used in many labs. Sometimes you can adapt this method by using peat moss to hold the plants in place. Perlite can be used, though it can get moldy; vermiculite, also, though it can get water-logged and become unhealthy for plants. These are both natural substances. Lettuce grown by this hydroponic method is sometimes available in markets.

Auxins and gibberellins are growth substances which many commercial growers use; they also use sprout-inhibiting substances. Seed merchants sometimes use organic and other fungus inhibitors, too, which often shock gardeners with their bright pink color when the dyed seeds come out of the packet.

Organic gardeners are often fussy about using any of these supplements—whether or not they are called organic. They want to be purists, perhaps. A supply of dried manure or compost from the heap or from the store, or the liquid made from steeping it for several days, is more to their liking. Instead of using any other fungicide they'll put a piece of charcoal into the water they use (or bone black or activated carbon used in cleansing processes). Charcoal is very porous and absorbs impurities, as well as oxidizing some of them. Fertrell and Seaborne are trustworthy, widely available organic nutrient supplements. Other nutrients, such as foliar sprays, might or might not affect beneficial bacteria and other soil organisms and their interdependencies, which we don't yet understand.

Begin to Do Soil Testing

To give yourself a good start in learning what you need to know about the biochemistry of the soil and plant growth, I recommend that you do some soil testing. There are several reliable firms that provide soil-testing kits of varying prices, depending on how elaborate you want to be in your search for the exact qualities of your indoor and outdoor soils. Try to find out precisely how acid or alkaline your soil is, and what you may need by way of nitrogen, phosphorus, and potassium—the three main additives in commercial fertilizer, and frequently the three most needed elements in the soil. One company even provides a little guide to organic fertilizers, and a key to what your various vegetables might need by way of nutrients (see Appendix). Practice on your indoor soil, and if you can get hold of a six-inch-deep slice of your outdoor soil in the wintertime, start testing and making plans for outdoor composting, and for your supplies of materials to improve your soil.

These simple testing kits provide a dye which, when mixed with a sample of soil, indicates on a color chart (included) whether your soil is acid or alkaline, and where it is on the pH scale. A soil might test from pH 3 at the very acid end to pH 7, which is neutral, to pH 11, which is at the very alkaline end (actually the scale is 1 to 14). The figures indicate exponential increase—that is, from the neutral 7 to ten times as acid at pH 6, and ten times as alkaline at pH 8, and so on increasing by ten times for each figure. The rain and snow in my backyard in 1988 tested pH 4 to pH 4.5, or somewhere down near grapefruit juice, which made it 100 times as acid as one would consider normal. Thus the term "acid rain."

What pH Means

What is being measured by a pH test is the hydrogen ion concentration and its effect. When the molecules of water in the soil break down to their components, they have electrical charges that attract them to other chemical components, enabling them to join and form new compounds. The positively charged hydrogen component, or ion, is balanced with the negatively charged other part of water, called the hydroxyl. At pH 7, the balance is perfect. When there are more positive hydrogen components, the soil gets acid, and the pH goes down from 7 to a lower number.

On the pH scale, the jump from 7 down to the more acid 6 is not just a one-unit jump, because each point in the scale represents ten times as many hydrogen components as the figure above it. At pH 5, there are a hundred times as many. At pH 8 there are ten times as many alkaline units, and at pH 9, a hundred times as many.

When there are a lot of hydrogen components on the loose, you can counteract the acidity by adding lime to bring back the alkalinity. When the solid becomes alkaline, you can add sulfur and lots of organic matter.

Most vegetables like a neutral or slightly acid soil, with pH 6 to pH 7.5. This is exactly the range in which soil organisms do best. Fungi take over below pH 5.5.

The common range in the mineral soils of humid regions is pH 5 to pH 7, or moderately acid. In more arid areas it runs to moderately alkaline conditions. Peat soils are very acid, with a pH going down to 3, and the extremely alkaline mineral soils going up to pH 9. All this is important because the degree of acidity or alkalinity affects the soil solution, and the capacity of the plant to use it and its nutrients.

If you experiment by adding materials to your soil to make it more acid or more alkaline, you can eventually discover which specific plants like which specific conditions. A lot of study has already been done on plant preferences, however, so you can have the knowledge right away that a range of pH 5 to pH 6 is compatible for growing corn, soybeans, or tomatoes. A range of pH 6 to pH 7 is all right for asparagus, beets, and cauliflower—and even if it goes as high as pH 8, those plants will do quite well. Spinach, lettuce, peas, cabbage, and carrots also do well at this range of pH 6 to pH 8. These tolerances of the pH concentrations on both sides of the neutral point show that the practice of blindly adding lime to soil, without testing to make sure you need to raise the alkalinity, may well be a waste of time, though the lime may improve the soil's structure.

Gardeners who use a lot of organic material should check often to see how their soil is affected in various parts of the garden. Also remember that bacteria do not like it too acid; their range of tolerance is only pH 5.4 to pH 9. Fungi have a range of tolerance from pH 3 to pH 9, so they can tolerate more soil conditions than bacteria can. Since you want both in your soil, you should take care to see that the range is right.

If you don't want to do any testing yourself, you can send a sample to your state university through your county extension agent. Test results can vary considerably, for conditions in your soil can vary from one inch of soil to another. The degree of moisture or dryness can bring on different results, also. Directions with soil-testing kits usually recommend that only dry soil samples be used.

When you learn of an acid condition, try to find out its source. Leaching or the washing away of soil nutrients may have caused acidity to build up. When alkaline bases, dissolved into the soil solution by its acids, are washed away, acids are left behind. The common bases are calcium, magnesium, potassium, and sodium, released from the minerals in the soil. Such nutrients reach the plants via an interchange of ions through the root hairs. A root releases one ion for each one it attains. It is the ongoing, perpetual interchange which makes the life of the plant possible.

If you learn that your soil, as tested, is rather alkaline, as it well may be in the West, try to find the source of that imbalance, too. If, for example, the condition comes from chlorides and sulfates of sodium, calcium, or magnesium, you can flush them out. Your county extension agent can help you with these complicated matters when you happen to run into them.

To make a soil more alkaline, add lime. The preference for the organic gardener is finely ground dolomitic limestone, as will be described later. To make a soil more acid, add pine needles, peat moss, sawdust, or tanbark.

What the Nutrients Are

Though you can't discover all the intricacies of your garden without professional help, your gardening and windowsill experiments will hinge, nevertheless, on the fact that plants—as far as we now know—need fifteen of the elements out of the sum they contain. The elements can enter the plants both through roots and through pores.

These elements are carbon (C), hydrogen (H), and oxygen (O), from the air and soil water. There are also nitrogen (N), phosphorus (P), potassium (K), sulfur (S), calcium (Ca), magnesium (Mg), and iron (Fe)—all of which have been known since the end of the nineteenth century. In more recent years the trace elements—boron (B), copper (Cu), manganese (Mn), and zinc (Zn)—have also been determined to be necessary. The latest to be ascertained is molybdenum (Mo). Plants also take in silicon, chlorine, and sodium, but it has not yet been shown that they need these elements. For phosphorus to enter the plant the pH of the soil solution should be almost neutral (pH 6.8-pH 7). Calcium leaches very easily.

Oddly enough, plants also cycle small amounts of a group of elements that seem to be truly nonessential: aluminum, arsenic, lead, barium, mercury, bromine, tin, cobalt, gold, nickel, and selenium. Some of the unknown factors behind plant vigor might come from one or another of these, though the literature of organic gardening usually attributes that vigor to an, as yet, unidentified vitamin or two or three.

Animals need fourteen essential elements (it is believed) plus three others: sodium, cobalt, and iodine. Almost all of these go into the roots of plants in the ionic form, but nearly all can also go in through the pores in plants' leaves, either as a gas or in water.

Most nutrients in slightly acid soils are readily available for your plants, though some become unavailable when the soil is more than slightly acid. Phosphorus is an element in all soils, and unless the soil is nearly neutral it also becomes quickly unavailable. This element moves very little in the soil, so insert it in areas where roots will be growing, preferably before planting. Bone meal is also a good source of superphosphate. Potassium is very slowly available, but it is plentiful. It leaches easily from the soil, so it is wise to add some every year. Plants can use only a little of what's there. Calcium, a base, is very easily washed away in humid climates, and the soil then becomes still more acid. Conditions which cause leaching of calcium also leach magnesium, an element essential to good plant growth. Use dolomitic limestone as fertilizer to counteract such conditions.

One good way to become versed in these facts is to supply a houseplant with a nutrient mixture deficient in one element, then to see whether the plant gets scrawny, spotty, yellow, or leafless. After that, give it a foliar spray to observe its recovery when the deficiency is made up for through the leaves.

Normal uptake of nutrients depends less on what a plant actually needs at the moment than it does on the rate of root growth and the chemical composition of the interchange surfaces of the soil particles. In fact, nutrients in amounts more than needed can go into a plant, and sometimes even go in at a rate that turns out to be toxic.

If it is nitrogen your plant needs, you might try urea if you apply it as a foliar spray, but it may burn because of the high osmotic concentration of the spray solution. The juice goes out of the cells when you want it to go in. The organic gardener is likely to try cottonseed meal or blood meal on the soil instead, even with the knowledge that urea is made from the natural nitrogen in the air—usually souped up with an additive, however.

If your plant needs sulfur and you live in the city or suburbs, just put the plant outdoors for a while if it's not too cold. It will probably pick up about what it needs from the sulfur dioxide pollution in the air. If it is magnesium you want, use an Epsom salt solution.

Water

In addition to learning about nutrients, you will want to discover how water affects your plants. The best thing to do is get or make half-inch cotton wicks so you can study the movement of water in the soil and plant. Most people know very little about watering, and I've heard that more houseplants are ruined by poor watering habits than by anything else.

Some people just poke the soil in a plant pot, or flat, to see whether it feels wet. This is a poor practice for two reasons. First, daily pressure will eventually compact the soil and make it hard and airless. It's as bad as tramping around on a wet garden. Second, though the soil may feel dry, and actually be dry on top, it may have plenty of moisture below for the roots of the plant.

In our overheated houses we can expect very rapid dehydration of the surface exposed to hot air, so enclose your plant in plastic sometimes for a day or so after watering to give it a chance to live a while in a nice moist atmosphere. Most plants would like that. This trick is used by people going away for a weekend, so their plants won't dry out; the wicks recommended above can be used as well. For weekend watering, just push the wick into the soil at the top of the pot.

To study water uptake, rig up the wick so that one end of

Test to study water uptake

it goes into the soil at the bottom of the pot or flat, and the other end is in an enclosed jar. You can run the wick under the jar lid, and loosen the lid to a point where the osmosis of water is not cut off. Then tape the edge of the lid. Enclose the whole set-up to prevent undue evaporation.

Measure the amount of water you put in the jar, and then note the time. The point is to see what the rate of absorption turns out to be within twelve, twenty-four, and forty-eight hours, for instance. It is best to set up several plants for comparison.

Begin Composting

Ever since Sir Albert Howard invented the Indore method, composting has been the key to organic gardening. When you start on the fascinating processes of composting, you may become a totally converted, and purist, organic gardener overnight. Here are some ways to get started.

If you live in a cold climate, and start in the middle of winter, the place for a bin or box is in the cellar. Because at certain periods there will be a fair amount of juice involved, it is better to use a wooden box and not paper. For safety's sake, you may want to line it with layers of newspapers or with a sheet of polyethylene. Then add a layer of sand, or a layer of peat or sphagnum moss. These serve both for absorption and as materials to help build the compost itself. Compost is old vegetable materials and other old organic materials which have been worked over by microscopic organisms (mostly bacterial plants) until they have turned into a rich, dry, black material. Humus is the same thing, but we usually think of humus as made in the woods and compost as helped along by human hands.

Into this box in your cellar you put all the vegetable residues left over from preparing your meals and from the plates afterward. Never use fat, and that means do not use meats. This is all you need to start with, but there are additions which can help things along: leaves, dirt, manure, blood meal, ground lime, and much more. Some people like to add an "activator" to get the bacteria in there and working. Details and explanations can be found in the chapter about compost. For aesthetic reasons, you will probably want a lid on this box. In such a box or bin the work will be done by aerobic bacteria: those which need air, or rather oxygen, to do their jobs. Make airholes and put coarse, open materials at the bottom to let air in.

Anaerobic bacteria, or those not requiring oxygen, work in

an airless place—best acquired nowadays inside a double thickness of plastic bag, such as those put in garbage pails. You can easily allocate one of your garbage bags to vegetable refuse, and carefully add such animal bits of refuse as hair, fingernails, wool, leather bits, and the like. Some people use meat scraps and cage cleanings, but I don't. There will be a sulfur, decaying smell to this accumulation at times, but it goes away. Organic gardeners put big bags of this sort on the back porch or down cellar, or hang them up in the garage. The fact that the bag is really airtight (and tie it tightly to see that it is) makes the possibility of an offending smell minimal—and only when one opens the bag. In fact, I kept some vegetable leaves tied tightly in a plastic bag on a radiator in my kitchen for two or three weeks last spring, and no one would have known it was there. No smell escaped until I took it outside to put on the earth. Then it smelled vile, but the juice and smell disappeared into the soil almost immediately.

This kind of back porch composting is a very simple matter. You just save your scraps, and anticipate the time when they will be converted to humus. A neighbor of mine in the cold climate of Vermont has a big family and a lot of vegetable residue and refuse to get rid of. She keeps a pile of big plastic bags of the 20- to 30-gallon size near the back door, and fills up one after another all winter long. They freeze, and are no bother to anyone. When the weather begins to warm up, she drags them out to one or another of her compost piles, and either lets the filled bags sit in the sun for a week or dumps them on a pile and adds blood meal, cottonseed meal, the ashes from her incinerator, sawdust, leaves, dirt, or whatever she has handy for the layers. She enjoys this back porch winter activity because, as she says, she has the "pack-rat syndrome." When she sees the telephone company truck go by in March with a load of wood chips after a tree-trimming operation, she runs out after it and begs the driver to leave his load near her compost piles. He always obliges, for it saves him a trip to the landfill site.

I know others who compost indoors by keeping a barrel of earth in the cellar or back hall, and burying the vegetable refuse in that as it comes along. This contraption can be watered. You can also put in some red earthworms to help along the composting action by digesting their soil materials and returning their castings to the earth. Do not put worms where the materials are hot. Worm activity is one of the best examples of cycling you can watch, and everything used and returned makes the soil better and better. If there is any light where you have such a barrel, plant some seeds in it and see how lush they grow.

Those of us who do winter composting feel we are quite a bit ahead with our gardening. Those who have the room and the inclination put their vegetable garbage on an outdoor pile. Out in the cold, bacterial action will be delayed until spring when the sun comes back. Then you will also add sawdust, leaves, and other organic material.

The Crux of the Plant

After all your experiments are performed, and you have plants up and coming into bloom, take time to examine the crux of the plant, the flower. If it has been pollinated, fruits follow. Of course many of our vegetables are really fruits, unless they are seed pods, seeds, or leaves. (Most fruits are true fruits unless they are pomes or berries or nuts.) Few people eat flowers, probably because of ancient superstitions or just plain ignorance. Candied violets have survived, but violets and nasturtiums in salads are rare on American tables. We eat cauliflower, of course, and the buds of broccoli. And an imaginative friend of mine serves chive flowers for their delicate onion permeation of a salad.

It is wonderful enough that we eat plants at all, and that their biochemistry contributes to our biochemistry. It is also wonderful that our ancestors tested them out and found which ones were good for food, which ones good for medicine, cosmetics, emetics, purges, stimulants, poultices, and poisons.

If not often for food, we do take the nectar of flowers for perfumes, though nectar is mostly for bees and other pollinators. We don't take much, and it may have been a shrewd wisdom protecting the life cycle of plants that explains why ancient peoples held back from eating flowers. Plants or parts of plants that have been eaten as aphrodisiacs have had a very hazardous existence. Some, in fact, are extinct, and others are endangered species. The pre-Classic Greeks invented stories about the bad luck effects of pulling up mandragora. By the logic of magic, its man-shaped root (called mandrake) was supposed to advance virility. The root would scream, the old wise men claimed. And that half-scared everyone to death just to think of it. They left the plant to survive. I saw it growing on the Greek island of Delos, which was probably the crossroads of traffic in plant materials, even as it was of human materials in ancient days. Its green rosettes were evident in grassy hollows and among the anemones on the presently uninhabited island.

A flower is a means of facilitating fertilization and making seeds. It is bright-colored to attract the pollinators. The female part, in the pistil, has cells which receive the male cell from the pollen made in the male stamens. Then the eggs are fertilized, the plant fruits, and a new embryo can grow until we have new plants for beans, eggplant, peas, or tomatoes, all growing new seeds for the next round.

It can happen in many ways. For some plants the agents are birds, bees, wasps, flies, butterflies, moths, or other insects (if you haven't already killed them with pesticides) who pick up pollen on their bodies as they move from flower to flower collecting nectar. Many flowers have both the male and female parts in the same flower. Other plants have separate male and female flowers, or even male on one tree or plant, female on the other. Some seeds blow in the wind. Some are carried on dog fur.

At the top of the pistil is a sticky or fuzzy or otherwise attractive and catching surface all set, at the right time, to pick up a grain of pollen for fertilization. Below it, reaching to the ovary, is a passage down which the male cell stretches its pollen tube to do the actual fertilizing of the ovule in the ovary.

In gardens drenched with poison pesticides, a doleful pattern of events can be expected. There are no insects; there is no transfer of pollen; no natural fertilization; there are few developed seeds or fruits or flowers to put in your salads. A while ago I saw a film of apple orchards in Japan, showing avenues of trees so saturated with sprays that all the bees in the area were dead and gone. Pollination of every apple blossom that was to set fruit in these orchards had to be done by hand by conscripted army personnel.

Often there are many eggs in the ovary, and a pollen tube that arrives releases two sperm cells. One unites with an egg and commences the embryo—for example, wheat germ; the second unites with a structure that begins the growth of the endosperm, the sturdy food-storage area, which will support the embryo and eventually the new plant.

Germination has been known about for a long time, although sometimes forgotten. Theophrastus, a pupil of Aristotle, pointed out that different seeds germinate differently and that the root is the first structure to start growing.

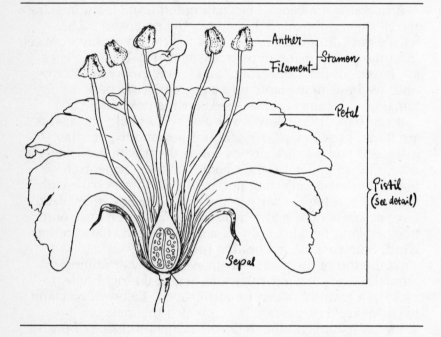

Plant Heredity

It was not until Gregor Mendel's work in the nineteenth century, however, that scientists discovered why plants should not pollinate themselves. To be strong and adaptive, an organism needs two different parents with different genes. Insects, such as the Mexican sleeping sickness mosquitoes, that adapt to new hydrocarbon pesticides have shown how tremendous adaptive vigor can be. Horticulturists who hybridize for blight resistance have also demonstrated that new genetic strains can be stronger and healthier—at least for a while—than some of the previous popular garden varieties that may have been weakened through inbreeding or overspecialization somewhere along the line. This need for genetic vigor is one of the reasons why botanists and ecologists are so anxious to preserve primitive, long-lived species, which might turn out to be exactly what are needed to breed new hybrids in times of bad crops or a corn blight. A gene pool of this sort was in great demand during the period when corn blight threatened the crops in the Midwest. Farmers in Iowa that winter bargained and bartered furiously to get nonhybridized seed they felt they could trust.

Exchanging Information

The suggestions in this chapter—and dozens of other activities and preparations that will occur to you—are among the ways a gardener can

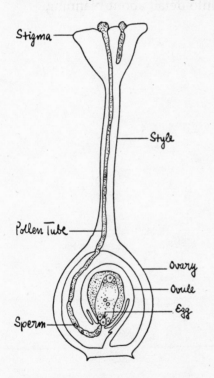

begin to use time indoors to get used to the ways of gardening, to get prepared to do it, and to develop a feeling for growing things. I am convinced that the more ways of relating to plants and gardening that you can develop, the better.

In our town (and it has happened in many others, I imagine) we started an organic gardening club during the winter months to exchange ideas, addresses for sources of materials, and the names of farmers who would sell aged manure, or let persons come to clean out the henhouse for a supply of fresh manure. In the spring we were all too busy to get around to visiting each other, but in the summer we had fine, fascinating trips to each other's gardens and got ideas about putting nasturtiums with cucumbers, for instance, if we never had—or about how to get a really superior crop of edible weeds (lamb's-quarters) among the beans (or beans among the lamb's-quarters) by cavalier neglect.

We also swapped information about raising fish and frogs in farm ponds, and we heard great accounts of how many earwigs a frog would eat if you'd catch them for him.

I don't mean to imply that all the suggestions I've made are essential to the would-be organic gardener, but I know they can add a new dimension to the life one can lead with plants. All I want to stress for the beginner is that there are three things of special importance to do: begin composting; begin to know the growing habits of plants by intimate acquaintance in your own house, in a spot where you can watch what is happening; begin to make plans, buy equipment, order seeds, and, as far as possible, practice ahead of time what you are going to be doing outdoors later. The next chapter goes into detail about planning.

Get Ready,
Get Set, Plan

If you are already on the mailing lists, your seed catalogs begin arriving in January. It is a welcome change from other studies and activities to settle down on a winter evening to select which seeds you will need for your garden in the spring. Though it is an enormous temptation to get too much, and tricky to figure the right proportion of vegetables, flowers, and herbs to plant for good garden health and pest deterrence, careful planning will keep things under control.

But be bold. Plan to do some outside experimenting to follow your indoor experimenting. Select herbs and vegetables you have never grown before—or never heard of before. Try out some you have never thought you'd like and see whether this food, eaten fresh, young, and tender, is actually something you never really tasted before. And be sure to include enough pungent, pest-free, or at least pest-repellent flowers and herbs to intermingle with your vegetables and to surround the garden.

When you have studied up on these matters (consult chapter 6 often), make a layout. One is diagrammed on pages 62–3, but you will have to figure out your own, of course, to suit the terrain and exposures you have, as well as the space.

Plan Your Whole Garden

During the long winter evenings you should map out your entire garden, not just the vegetable part of it. Always keep in mind that you aim to create a garden that is a total living environment—not only for vegetables but also for trees, shrubs, grasses, and flowers, and for all the beneficial (and instinctively marauding) bacteria, fungi, actinomycetes, mice, shrews, moles, chipmunks, squirrels, skunks, gophers, and helpful frogs, toads, ladybugs, lacewings, and lots of birds who will frequent your place if it is well balanced and adjusted to the foods these creatures require. They keep themselves under control if given half a chance, so you may never have an unmanageable population explosion of any species. The ideal location for a vegetable garden is in the sun, or mostly in the sun, on a south-sloping site and not in a valley. It may need a windbreak or wall around it, but it must have good air circulation, too.

Vitamins Involved

If you approach your garden planning from the point of view of nutrition, four vitamins will be of importance. For vitamin A, consider carrots, chicory, dandelion, string beans, peas, kale, parsley, spinach, turnip greens, broccoli, chard, collards, endive or witloof chicory, lettuce, peppers, pumpkins, squash, and sweet corn. For vitamin C plan to select any of the following: beets, broccoli, Brussels sprouts, cabbage, cauliflower, kale, kohlrabi, parsnips, peppers, potatoes, tomatoes, mustard, parsley, radishes, spinach, and sweet corn. If you live in the right climate, include avocados, bananas, lemons, oranges, grapefruit, muskmelons, and berries such as strawberries and raspberries. For vitamin B_1: green lima beans, Brussels sprouts, peanuts, green peas, potatoes, tomatoes, globe artichokes, asparagus, and beets. And for vitamin B_2: avocados, carrots, chicory, green peas, spinach, green lima beans, kale, and turnip greens.

Turnip greens, kale, tomatoes, and parsley are high in nutrients. For healthful herbs try anise, balm, basil, chervil, dill, marigold, marjoram, parsley, nasturtium, summer savory, sage, and thyme—all suitable for indoor growing also.

Winter Storage

To plan for vegetables you can store in pits or cold cellars, consider especially those you can sow in the summer and harvest at top quality in the fall. Plant late turnips, carrots, beets, cauliflower, cabbage, rutabagas, and also late cabbage, broccoli, celery, kohlrabi, onion sets, winter radishes, chicory, Chinese cabbage, winter squash and pumpkins, potatoes, and beans and peas to dry. If you have no place to partition and insulate in your cellar to make a cold-storage place for your winter vegetables, you should make plans for pits in which to bury them in moist sand under leaves. Others that can be stored include Brussels sprouts, parsnips, and such fruits as apples and pears.

The vegetables best to freeze include asparagus, lima beans, string beans, broccoli, cauliflower, chard, corn, kale, peas, cooked pumpkin, spinach, New Zealand spinach, rhubarb, and such berries and fruits as blackberries, blueberries, cherries, currants, gooseberries, raspberries, and strawberries.

Those to can in Mason jars are peppers and tomatoes—don't forget tomato juice and grape juice—asparagus, lima beans, beets, chard, sweet corn, spinach, and such fruits as cherries, peaches, pears, and rhubarb. Under no circumstances should you try to can cabbage (except sauerkraut), cauliflower, celery, cucumbers, baked beans, eggplant, lettuce, onions, parsnips, turnips, or vegetable mixtures, because there is danger of bacterial contamination. All precautions should be taken to avoid the deadly germ of botulism. If the directions in your cookbook say 75 minutes for sweet corn at 10 pounds pressure, leave them in the cooker for 85 minutes, not a minute less. Any contaminated foods must be boiled for at least 15 minutes to kill the dangerous bacteria.

Vegetables to dry include lima beans, shell beans—right on the vine—carrots, corn, peppers, pumpkin, and winter squash. I used to have a little cloth and wooden contraption for drying vegetables, and it worked quite well, but I liked it better for herbs than for vegetables that could be easily stored in other ways. Dried fruits, because they are so delicious, are something else again. Try cherries, grapes, blueberries, currants, and pears. Plums, too, of course, to make your own prunes.

How to Read a Seed Catalog

Send away for as many seed catalogs as you think you'll have time to read, but in general, deal with seed companies in your own zone. The names of many are given in the Appendix, but read the newspapers and garden magazines for other ads and addresses. Occasionally a specialty nursery like White Flower Farm in Litchfield, Connecticut, will ask you to pay a couple of dollars, but they will deduct that amount from your first order. Send to different parts of the country—Wayside Gardens in Ohio, and Parks in South Carolina, Farmer Seed and Nursery in Minnesota, Veseys in Canada, and to such old, established firms as Stokes, Harris, and Burpee. There are a few out-and-out organic gardening houses like Nichols in Albany, Oregon; Johnny's Selected Seeds of Albion, Maine; and Walnut Acres in Penns Creek, Pennsylvania. In the organic gardening books and articles there is not much stress on organically grown seeds, perhaps because it is felt that pesticides cannot penetrate the hard seed coats into the endosperm of the seeds, so that seeds remain fairly clean. In recent years many seed companies have informed their customers whether or not their seeds have been treated, and with exactly what. Sometimes it is a mild fungicide like Captan; sometimes it is merely a heat treatment. If you ask a house like Harris for untreated seeds, they'll send them to you. I tend to feel good about a catalog that tells you just what the company does, and to trust that company to be reliable. Also, look to see what fertilizers are being advertised. Practically all seed catalogs now offer some organic fertilizers and pest controls. One seedsman, Udo Scholiz of Ringers in Eden Prairie, Minnesota, offers no other kind. If, as in this catalog and some others, the only fertilizers offered are organic composts and dried manures, again you feel good.

Carefully scan the garden aids to see whether the company offers sensible ones in accord with the gardening principles you are learning. In recent years, for instance, small indoor table greenhouses have been advertised in the garden-aid sections of various reliable companies. One from Burpee's has a plastic cover which, if too tight, would make the little 14-inch house get moist and cause the disease of damping-off. But the ad says it has a ventilating adjustment, self-watering saucers, and an air space between the plant tray and the outside container, all excellent precautions. What's more, the cost is low. A heating mat, of course, costs more.

Less reliable companies claim magical results with unspecified substances, or unfailing success for exotic plants and unusual, freaky specialties that are supposed to appeal to

56

your eye for novelty, and not to your liking for solid gardening and the ordinary hard work it involves. The only timesavers and worksavers you want to fall for are mulches, some of the quick compost aids, certain harmless tools, very rugged, disease-resistant, fast-growing plants, and clean seeds.

Think twice about those catalogs with gaudy pictures of ever-blooming rose trees, hibiscus blossoms twice as big as a child's head, and blueberries as large as apricots. Why be enticed by promises about fairy-tale cascades of three or four kinds of roses, or nuts, or fruits on one tree, or potatoes and tomatoes on one vine? Such oddities are possible, but they may not suit your needs at all.

Be sure to study planting zones and learn what can and cannot be grown in your area. It can be hard to resist temptations to grow some plant in your zone which is not hardy there, or not suited to your climate or soil condi-tions, even though a company promises success. I am greatly tempted to try growing artichokes, though I know better. Yet I persist in hoping that some smart plant breeder will come up with a new hybrid which can endure the rugged conditions of Vermont. The rosy come-on of catalog copy usually includes appeals like "lavish crops" and "flowering glory." Then it states: "Successfully grown as far north as New York," and my better judgment checks me because I know artichokes like a moist temperate climate, preferably not far from the sea, and I know specialists recommend trying artichokes only in seaside areas—not as far inland as we are.

The vocabulary of all catalogs is apt to be excessive in one way or another, but as a clue, look for quiet claims like "heavy crop," or "bears well for several weeks if kept picked," instead of the glamorous promises. Look also for a full, logical collection of offerings, not a haphazard spotty one.

One sign of a good catalog is that the company gives you planting hints. Down in the corner of a page on corn, for instance, will be a box telling you how to grow sweet corn, how far apart, how deep, what kind of soil, how much a packet will plant, special nutrients needed, and when to pick. The catalog provides such information for each vegetable. A company like this never advertises fertilizers as "instant action," or says "one spray kills all." And it never advertises Venus flytrap or the magic carpet of flowers which you just unroll and keep watered. Or ceramic cats and toadstools. Or plastic grass.

Cheap trees and shrubs will be just cheap, though I do know organic gardeners who have such good soil and such green thumbs that they are able to remake them into valuable plants. A Russian olive at fifty cents will, yes, eventually grow to be a fine bush, but at this price it will be such a spindly little thing when it arrives that you will hardly see it for several years in the hedge where you put it.

There is one thing to say for cheap plants. They are often cheap because they are of a variety that does very well in all kinds of conditions, spreads fast, and is so rugged that the plants are fast multipliers, hard to control. Sometimes you can find bargains in pachysandra for ground cover, or other ground covers like lily of the valley and ajuga; or sometimes bargains in multiflora roses for hedges; or for sedums or vetch. One perennial plant called crown vetch is a winter-hardy legume that will fill up banks and gullies. Twenty-five plants will cover 100 square feet in three years and it may take you over in four years. Paying fifty cents a plant, in five years you would surely have your money's worth—if you want to be swamped, that is. I'd avoid all such plants, especially multiflora roses, which are actually outlawed in some states as nuisances in fields and meadows. Ajuga can get into your lawn and spread all over.

Sometimes these glamour-appeal catalogs do, however, offer good gadgets that appeal to organic gardeners. Moles can be repelled by vibrating devices, they say, and adjustable cloches and row covers can be useful as rabbit and insect deterrents. I have had good luck repelling moles by planting Crown Imperial bulbs. Other fairly good bargains are nets, strips of plastic for mulching or compost protection, small birdhouses, and bird feeders. So are some of the hoes, shredders, augers for deep feeding, and staples like flower pots and hoses. Most of the reliable and trustworthy old houses sell these extras also, of course.

When you settle down to look over the catalog of a reliable company, first scan the features of the year in the front of the catalog, but don't make any decisions yet. Just keep your eyes open for suggestions particularly useful for you and your needs—such as a new bush variety of squash that will save you a lot of room, or a well-proven, disease-resistant variety of pepper or potato, or a long-season one of lettuce which will increase your harvest, or a variety of tomato that gives you a better vitamin supply than any of the others. Just take note of these and then compare the features with the extended descriptions in the body of the catalog. Compare prices; sometimes there are savings advertised in the front pages. A special called "A Family Garden Collection," for example, may offer all the vegetables you plan to grow, and in varieties with just the qualities you seek. It may be a very good bargain—and after the soil at your place has built up, you can count on your rich, composted, and well-mulched garden to make these vegetables yield well. Consider pelleted seed and seed tapes as convenient aids to planting and spacing, and dwarf varieties as space savers.

In the main part of the catalog you should read every direction and plant description, and also every box with pertinent information. You will discover how many packets to order, how much one of the packets will sow, and specific difficulties to avoid. All too many catalogs still recommend hard chemical sprays made out of chlorinated hydrocarbons. Learn to disregard all such things, and pay attention only to the biological- or botanical-oriented suggestions concerning rotenone, pyrethrum, sabadilla, and other organic preparations. These products are now more widely available than in the past. Then read every description under a certain vegetable to see what qualities the company finds pertinent enough to stress, and judge whether it is addressing the commercial grower or the home gardener. Some may stress size and shape, others color or firmness, or sturdiness and flavor. You can also see by the amounts offered (100 pounds, bushel, etc.) whether the seeds are intended for commercial growing. Think twice about such aspects as sturdiness or the ability to stay tender until large size. These comments hint at durable market quantity rather than home-garden quality. If it is a variety of string bean you are choosing, for example, turn down a bean praised for an ability to stay tender. You already know that if you can possibly prevent it, you are not going to let your beans ever grow to full size and lose their flavor and natural tenderness. In a home garden you can pick all your string beans when they are one-half to two-thirds grown, and get all the benefit of young sweet beans. The same goes for peas. And these vegetables are much better frozen or canned at this age, too. (See chapter 6 for further suggestions.) In recent years some of the old seed companies have markedly reduced the numbers of varieties offered. To widen your choices, send for more catalogs, especially from specialty houses.

Get catalogs published in your own section of the country, or at least watch for estimated days to maturity which will give you some hint about the appropriateness of various seeds for your section. I watch for seeds appropriate for northern or short-season climates. For example, suitable for these sections are Kentucky Wonder and Kentucky North pole beans; Provider and Tendercrop bush beans; Early Wonder and Ruby Queen beets; Early Jersey and Amsterdam Forcing cabbage; Polar Vee, Earlivee, and Sugar and Gold sweet corn; Burpless, Vesey's Raider, and Sweet Success cucumbers; Black-Seeded Simpson, Oakleaf, and Ruby lettuce; Buffalo, Early Yellow Globe, and Ebenezer onions; Ace and Gypsy peppers; Early Yellow Crookneck and Zucchini Elite squash; and Pixie, Early Cascade Springset, and New Yorker tomatoes. Two early tomatoes for sauce are Heinz and Nova.

The Layout of My Garden

At our semisuburban place we keep the main growing areas to the east and south of the house, not only because that is the area away from the road, but also because that part of the property has the proper southern and southeastern exposure, as well as the right slope toward the southeast.

There are maples in the front yard and across the driveway from the house, and also in back of the garage, but the fruit trees are toward the south and rear, arranged as much for the birds and their comings and goings in the backyard as for us. Trees we chose especially for the birds were Russian olive, elderberry, honeysuckle, highbush cranberry, and mulberry. We have shared the grapes and edible berries, and watched with pleasure the way the house sparrows gobble up the Japanese beetles on the grape leaves in August. The birdbath and birdhouses are placed in strategic spots, and we keep bird feeder tables under the apple and pear trees. The potted flowers and vegetables on the terrace and patio area keep the hummingbirds and bees coming.

Flowers and herbs are conveniently located, with good sunny exposures. Various herbs are sometimes transplanted to the vegetable garden as protection plants, either at the beginning of the season or at times of invasion and trouble. Wormwood, of the *Artemisia* family, is a quick worker to move to a trouble spot because of its powerful root exudate, which goes forth into the soil to fend off marauders. It helps to move garlic around, too.

The rather heavy planting on the northwest edge of the vegetable garden serves both as windbreak during spells of bad weather, and as shade and protection for some plants which like that shade. We used to have a mulberry tree there, though its roots robbed some plants growing near it. It was a great attraction for birds, many of whom ate insects and grubs while they were in the neighborhood. This tree and the honeysuckles nearby served as cover also, for birds like to have some place to hide if they are startled. The garage door was left open in the summertime for the barn swallows who come to nest there. This garden was laid out a good many years ago. If we were doing it today, we'd plan to have raised beds, which save space, stay untrampled, are easy to weed, and can be planted more thickly than rows.

The compost heap is placed conveniently near the vegetable garden, but not too far from the driveway so that heavy things brought in can be wheeled right down. The toolshed part of the garage opens toward the garden and the compost heap, so equipment is handy. Beyond, to the east, are a field (with hay handy twice a summer) and the floor of a pine woods (good source of needles for compost and mulch).

The vegetable garden itself is surrounded by pungent annual flowers, and perennial herbs such as mint, tarragon, and sage. The rows run across the slope, which fortunately makes them run more or less east and west—though for good sun exposure during the summer, north-south rows are perfectly satisfactory. We live so far north that east-west rows suit us; there is a lot of morning east sun and afternoon west sun because the sun up here rises so far north in the summer.

We plant six rows of corn, and move that block around the garden in a three-year rotation; we also move around our four rows of peas, two rows of beans, one row each of carrots, beets, parsnips, and various lettuces. The squashes,

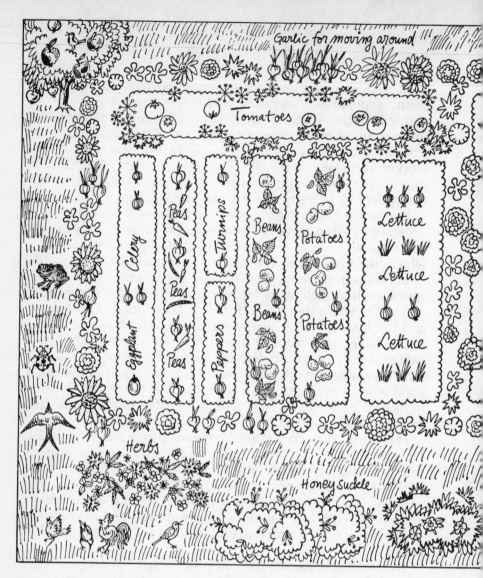

 White geraniums (repel Japanese beetles from corn, asparagus, kohlrabi, soybeans)

 Mexican marigolds (repel nematodes and control club root in brassica vegetables; protect cucumbers)

 Radishes (mark rows and precede long-term crops)

Nasturtiums (rebuff cucumber beetle, Mexican bean beetle)

 Garlic (rebuffs rabbits, many insect pests; protects apples, pears, cucumbers, peas, celery, lettuce, etc.; makes a useful spray)

Onions and Chives (same as garlic but less potent)

 Dill (trap plant for tomato worm)

The garden map shows the following plantings:

Corn (three rows along left side)

Cucumbers

Beets / Broccoli / Beets / Broccoli

Cabbage

Cauliflower / Spinach / Cauliflower / Spinach

Squash

Comfrey

Rosa Rugosa

Rhubarb

Strawberries

Berries

Mulberry Tree

Asparagus

Zinnia (trap plant for Japanese beetle; rebuffs cucumber beetle, tomato worm)

Tomatoes (repel asparagus beetle)

Strong herbs: sage, thyme, catnip, feverfew, hyssop, rue, artemisia, etc. (repel many pests)

Parsley (protects hybrid tea roses)

Ladybugs (devourer of many pests, including many larvae)

Peas and carrots thrive together (as do potatoes and beans, parsnips and peas, beets and broccoli, radishes and cucumbers)

Turnips (repel aphids, spider mites, flies)

planted on the edges near the herbs, are rotated around to different edges; this is not much of a rotation, so we plant protective plants quite thickly in their areas.

Of course your garden will be different. Consult your seed catalogs, read the packets, ask your county extension agent and all your friends for suggestions about the best amounts and varieties to use for your kind of soil and climate.

All estimates, of course, are subject to individual preferences, and the way you do your thinning of plants after they come up. And of course your thinning depends on the way you do your planting. If you eventually want your carrots two or three inches apart so they won't twist around each other and be crowded and stunted, thin them to this kind of spacing, and eat the little ones you pull out. (See chapter 6.) You will have some temptation to plant the seeds at such distances, but not only is this very difficult to do with tiny carrot seeds, but young plants for some wonderful community reason like to be together. It may be that they help each other by the substances they exude from their roots.

Herbs

Herbs are an essential element in the organic gardener's design for growing vegetables, for they serve several purposes, and are excellent additions to many dishes for tasty and subtle results.

In making your selections about what to plant, you might like to plant some "herbs of good influence," as the Bio-Dynamic gardeners call them. They choose borage, to plant at one corner of the bed, lavender in a few clumps at another corner, blue hyssop at another, and sage at the fourth corner. In addition, for "good influence" you can include the equivalent of a row of parsley divided up and spread around, plus chervil, marjoram, French tarragon (the small kind; see page 200), dill (except near carrots), and chives. Two other plants in this category are camomile and lovage. Bio-Dynamic gardeners also stress the value of adding the residues of the "good influence" herbs to the compost heap.

Horsetail plants are brought to the garden and used by these herbalists for brewing a tea to make a spray to control the nonbeneficial fungi. Other gardeners dust with rotenone, but the principle of using the heavy, scratchy silicon content of horsetail plants is well worth remembering. (Slugs hate silicon, too.)

The herbs, flowers, and weeds that I find most valuable are the pest-repellent ones. Some of them turn back insects from their approach to your vegetable plants; others distract them and, as it were, trap them there to consume these weeds or flowers instead of your vegetable plants. The insects are usually quite easy to see on the trap plants and pick off for dousing in kerosene.

For herb teas to use as sprays to protect your other plants from pests, you will want plenty of garlic and some achillea or yarrow, camomile, St. John's Wort, chives, mints, oregano, sage, and horseradish. Two or three of these added to hot pepper make effective sprays.

For attracting bees you can include thyme, catnip, lemon balm, pot marjoram, hyssop, sweet basil, and the mints. Lemon balm is so attractive that old beekeepers used to rub the inside of a new hive with it to entice the bees to stay there. Also plan for some of the following for your hedges: bee balm, *Rosa Rugosa*, elderberry, and privet. These will also please the birds, and for food value you will prize the rose and the elderberry.

Tansy, spearmint, and pennyroyal will ward off ants. Aphids (who are harbored and farmed by ants) stay away from spearmint, stinging nettle, and nasturtiums. Sage, rosemary, hyssop, thyme, and the varieties of artemisia known as wormwood and southernwood will help to keep the cabbageworm butterfly from coming near your broccoli, cauliflower, and cabbages. Tomato leaves, or a spray made from them, also repel the white butterfly, and will turn away the black flea beetle.

Where there are infestations of Japanese beetle, people are glad to learn that white geranium and the poisonous *Datura* called jimson weed or thorn apple are repulsive to that beetle, and that zinnias and knotweed are good trap plants to distract them. Of long-term value is the milky spore disease, which kills the grubs.

Some plants are helpful for the beneficial insects you want in your garden. Members of the carrot family, including the second or blossoming year of parsley, parsnips, carrots, chervil, and angelica are valuable for the predatory tiny wasps such as the valuable trichogramma and also the ichneumon and braconids, as well as the hover fly, tachanid.

Also helpful are such weeds as neetles, pigweed, knotweed, lamb's quarters, black-eyed Susan, and other flowers like yarrow, daisies, and coreopsis. Yarrow and tansy are useful for ladybugs.

Companionate Planting

This is the term used for intermixing plants so that they in some way benefit each other by helping repel pests, or by some principle of association make their neighbors thrive. Mixing herbs, flowers, and vegetables as described above is one way. "Companionate cropping" is the term used for putting certain plants between others in the same row; "intercropping" is used to describe the practice of planting one kind of row between two others of a second kind of plant. It is beneficial to practice companion cropping by planting beets between cabbages, spinach between cauliflowers (or between eggplants or celery plants), and onions or any members of the *Allium* family in the row between beans, lettuce, or young cucumbers, which rabbits or woodchucks like to attack when the plants are young and tender and full of protein.

Other combinations to plan for might include beans and potatoes to control Mexican bean beetles, eggplant, flax, or green beans to control Colorado potato beetle, chives among the roses to chase aphids, and marigolds intercropped with beans. Intercropping to save space can be achieved by planting spinach between rows of beans or peas on wires, lettuce between rows of cabbage or pole beans, early peas between pole lima beans, and spinach or radishes between squash, cucumbers, or pumpkins. The radishes have the extra benefit of fending off the striped cucumber beetles and squash bugs, too. I also use nasturtiums for these purposes, and my neighbor who redeemed her garden from a gravel ledge uses onions. If you select an orange nasturtium and add some orange marigolds, you will perhaps gain added protection, because aphids and other bugs are believed not to like that color and fly right past it.

Vegetables that benefit each other by growing close together are peas with carrots; bush beans with celery; beans or corn next to cucumbers; beets near kohlrabi; corn near potatoes; lettuce on both sides of radishes; celery with leeks. Parsley near tomatoes seems to help them; peas help turnips. These interplantings are space savers, too.

Other Space Savers

Another space saver is the vertical, or double-deck mode of gardening. This can be used on terraces and in small plots and roof gardens. What you do is grow pole beans, wired peas and cucumbers, and staked tomatoes, all of which will climb up and grow aboveground. Then underneath you plant protective herbs, lettuce, radishes, spinach, and squash or carrots. To save more space you can choose any of the dwarf varieties: cherry tomatoes, Tom Thumb corn, little snow peas, and many other bush varieties now available. Also rotate your early, midseason, and late crops and use all the odd corners you can think of. Do succession planting and use tubs, boxes, and pots to expand your planting area. Double-row planting and raised beds are also space savers, of course.

In making all these plans be sure to figure on high-growing vegetables to the north of your low-growing ones, which need a great deal of sun. In fact, most vegetables, except lettuce at certain stages, do need a great deal of sun. Corn or pole beans are likely to be your tallest plants, so put them toward the north. When you have to rotate corn to the south side of the garden, plant lettuce next to it because the lettuce won't mind the shade it will cast. Other tall vegetables include pole peas or wired peas, staked, highly fertilized tomatoes, and in the West, big globe artichokes. Low plants are beets, cabbage, broccoli, cauliflower, celery, chives, cucumber, squash, kohlrabi, kale (unless you let it grow tall), leeks, parsnips, rutabagas, spinach, and turnips.

For the Birds

The planning we enjoy as much as any is that which we do to attract the birds to frequent our garden. We never claim that birds will eradicate insect pests, but we do rely on our phoebes, swallows, and other insect-eating birds to help keep things under control. We also rely on our brown thrashers to eat up some poison ivy berries, and bluebirds, juncos, purple finches, catbirds, starlings, and sparrows to help them out. Ragweed is eaten by redwing blackbirds, starlings, bobolinks, cardinals, all the different sparrows, the tufted titmouse, and the common redpoll. The sparrows also eat crabgrass seeds, and so do the mourning doves and bobwhites.

Birds like tart, wild berries. In fact, they will prefer them to any cultivated berries you have. Therefore plant such bushes and trees as red and black chokecherry, barberry, hackberry, honeysuckle, mulberry, bayberry, staghorn sumac, mountain ash, buckthorn, Virginia creeper, and the various viburnums. They also like the wild blueberries, partridge berry, and huckleberry, as well as Russian olive and evergreens such as cedar, arborvitae, hemlock, and the various pines. Many of these provide nesting sites and the shelter that nervous birds also seek, especially near where they are feeding. Have a bird bath, with a slight movement of water if you can manage it, and provide nice nesting materials like string and hair.

Know When Your
Vegetables Will Mature

Plants that take a long time to mature include Brussels sprouts (100–120 days), celery (110–130), leeks (140–160), onions from seed (100–130), parsnips (100–140), and rutabagas (100–140). Those taking a fairly long time are: onion plants (90–120), pole lima beans (90–115), eggplant (85–100), winter squash (90–125), pumpkins (75–100), tomatoes (80–100), and sweet corn (65–100). The days to maturity may vary from catalog to catalog because different nurseries have different zones for their test sites. Some of the newest varieties of various vegetables are bred for faster maturing, so keep watch, and try out some of them as a supplement to the standard varieties you will choose. Some vegetables can be either early-maturing or late-maturing, depending on the variety. Corn, for example, is purposely bred to mature at different dates. Seed companies offer collections which will do just that.

Planning beans involves many considerations, but a good sequence of supply should be one of the top ones. Include both bush and pole beans, for they mature at 60 days and 70 days, respectively—and last up to 20 days as a crop, if you keep picking them. Also space your plantings, and you'll be able to stretch the season right through until frost. Keep plants far enough apart, especially in dry climates, so they can get nutrients well—2 to 3 feet apart, depending on your climate. The distance between rows depends on your mulching and cultivating program—3 or 4 feet apart if you are going to take a big cultivator down the rows, but nearer if you use a small tiller or are going to mulch and pull weeds (if you have any) by hand.

The especially quick-maturing crops are radishes, spinach, lettuce, and cress, as well as the first returns you take from the little bulbs for onions called onion sets. You can begin to gather young carrots, beet tops and very small beets, young peas, and cabbage leaves after about 40 to 50 days, somewhat depending on which zone you live in. In Vermont we talk about peas for the Fourth of July. Since we often have cold, wet Mays and do not get the garden planted until nearly Memorial Day, this is likely to be a slight exaggeration for some. Even so, peas are ready for nearly everyone in this area by the next week. (Peas grow best when it is cool, so the earlier you can plant them, the better.)

Don't worry if all your seeds do not come up at once. They take different lengths of time to germinate. Radishes are the fastest, so if you want to keep track of where you plant slowly germinating seeds like carrots, or some of the herbs like marjoram or parsley, mix the seeds, and pull the radishes when they're ready to eat. This practice means that when you are making your list for ordering, you should add an extra amount for radishes.

Succession Crops

Since it is sensible to have succession crops—that is, crops you plant several times to stretch the seasons—be sure you know at what date in your zone you must stop planting in order to have the crop mature before it freezes up. Some can bear more cold than others, however. Species that you can plant up to two to four weeks before the first freeze in your area might include such hardy vegetables as beets, carrots, cauliflower, celery, chard, mustard, parsnips, and radishes—even though the carrots, for instance, won't be as good as those planted five to six weeks before. But carrots winter very well, and you should grow plenty.

For succession planting, it is well to know which plants you have to allow for as occupiers of the ground for the whole season, and those which mature fast enough to harvest and make space for another planting. Some of those you can harvest early are peas (especially the early bush peas), lettuce, bush beans, spinach, early mustard,

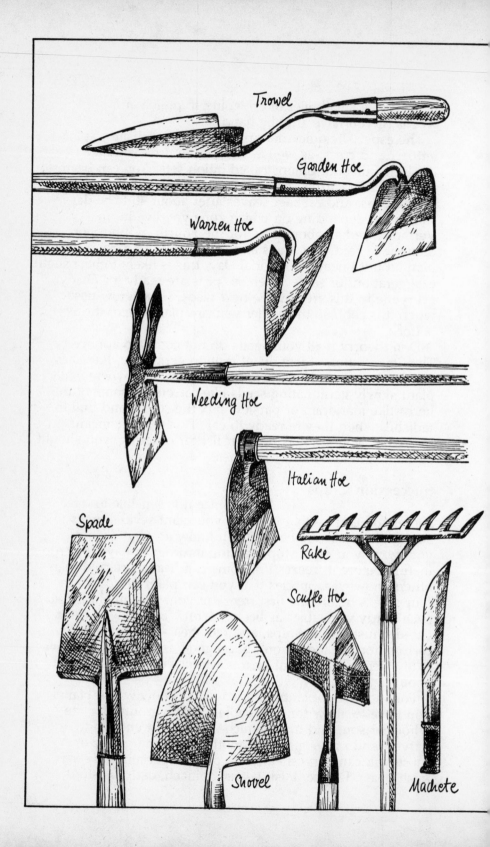

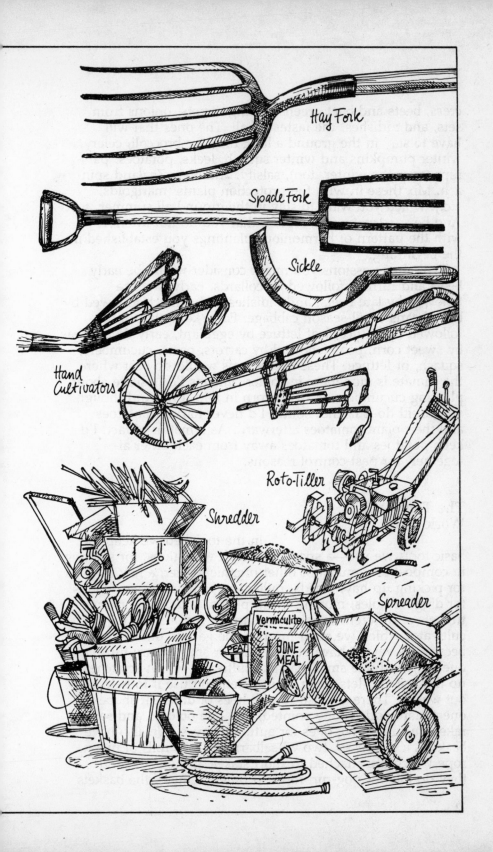

Hay Fork

Spade Fork

Sickle

Hand Cultivators

Roto-Tiller

Shredder

Vermiculite

PEAT

BONE MEAL

Spreader

cress, beets and beet greens, young carrots, onions from
sets, and radishes, the fastest of all. The ones that will
have to stay in the ground a long time are broccoli, celery,
winter pumpkins and winter squash, leeks, potatoes, parsnips (over the winter, too), salsify, and New Zealand spinach. Mix these in with the protection plants (marigolds,
etc.), which you want to stay in the ground all summer, too.
And be sure when you replant that you do not interfere
with the pattern of harmonious plantings you established in
the beginning.

Typical successions you might consider would be early
beets and turnips followed by collards, early cabbage
followed by late beets, and radishes and spinach followed by
bush beans or all-season cabbage. Early kohlrabi can be
followed by lettuce, leaf lettuce by eggplant, early dwarf peas
by sweet corn, peas followed by carrots, beets, cucumbers,
squash, or lettuce. These successions would do best where
the climate is moderate; in colder climates I'd hesitate about
planting cucumbers or sweet corn in mid-July. And though
you could do it farther south, I'd never harvest potatoes
and then plant tomatoes afterward. As a matter of fact, I'd
keep potatoes and tomatoes away from each other altogether, for pest-control reasons.

The Tools You'll Work With

In the toolshed we keep the
basic tools we use—a spade fork with wide tines, for spading
in compost and mulch or other organic matter; a hay fork
for picking up hay, weeds, pulled-up pea vines; two spades
for digging holes, moving earth, plants, sods; two or three
trowels of different weights and handgrips; a small hand
cultivator which we push through the garden ourselves
because as yet we have no Rototiller or small rotary turnplow;
one long and one small clawlike cultivator which scratches
up the soil and lets some air in when you use it to help take
out weeds. There are also several hoes of different shapes—
one square-ended, one pointed, and one oblong, and several
rakes, including big ones for autumn leaves. We also have
baskets, a box or so, two wheelbarrows, two rolls of nylon
rope which are attached to short stakes at the ends (and
they double for dog-run ropes at times). One of the baskets

contains clippers, grass shears, gloves, and at least one trowel, handy to take out for small chores. Bags of bone meal, cocoa shells, peat moss, granite dust, and other such supplies are stored here. One of the best aids is a bucket of oily sand, which will store tools for you—or be handy to slide a tool up and down in to clean and oil it before hanging it on the wall between two nails. Up on the wall also are the scythe, sickle, pruners, and two of the rakes.

Clay pots, peat pots, a basket of dried manure, a bag of vermiculite, a bag of sphagnum moss, and a pail of good topsoil are on the shelf for potting or transplanting. Though we do not have it yet, this area will some day get a Vitalite fluorescent lamp over it for between-season starting of delicate seedlings.

At the far end, beyond the big equipment like the lawn mower, is a root cellar, which is not a cellar but a room, insulated and with sturdy shelves for the storage of squash, potatoes, and heavy root vegetables.

We also have a triple-length hose, several watering cans, and one sprayer, which we use for atomizing garlic spray. There is a fertilizer spreader for bone meal.

Of all these tools, Sam Ogden says the hoe is the one that is most worth having—he cuts his down so it is pointed like a Warren hoe. I think the one my husband likes best is the hand cultivator because he can do so much work with it and get such good results from weeding, aerating, and neatening all at once. For weeding and poking around I like the medium-sized trowel best, though at times, I've noticed that a sharp old kitchen paring knife seems most satisfactory for weeding and aerating.

You will find that you get to have a favorite, too. In addition to those we have, you may want to include a shredder, a rotary turnplow or Rototiller, and if you are still deciding about a lawn mower, you will perhaps choose the rotary lawn mower because it is very good for shredding materials for mulch and the compost heap. Other aids for weeding include a double-disk implement that you push along just under the surface of the soil, and several that slash like a machete or sickle; scuffle hoes that chop and dig; and nursery hoes with sharp points, as well as the square digging blade. If you are going to need irrigation, look into a soaker to put under the mulch from 2 to 12 inches underground. This soaker, called Hydro-grow, has a water pressure regulator and can be adjusted to add fertilizer, too.

Winter is a good time to travel around to various hardware stores and agricultural supply places to inspect and choose what you want. Purchase or construct trellises for your sugar snap peas, and get ready things like the jar you will need for collecting and annihilating Japanese beetles (and the gasoline, kerosene, or paint thinner), and the boards, sections of plastic mulching strips, lengths of plastic hose, or whatever you decide to use for trapping earwigs, slugs, and other night-working insects. If you are going to try out plastic mulching, order black plastic in big pieces. It will serve many purposes, including covering your composting materials. And get enough material for individual and row cloches to extend the growing season. You can also store up tanglefoot or a molasses and fiber mixture to catch bugs going up tree trunks. You can accumulate mulches of various sorts—ground bark, sawdust, and peanut hulls, if you can get them.

The thrifty and canny organic gardener will make, store, and save things for later use.

For example, you can plan to make birdhouses and feeders. (See Appendix.) You can make various new kinds of traps and enticements for bothersome insects. You can find new tools, hoard aluminum foil for reflectors and an insect-fooling mulch, and save your torn nylons or cut-off legs of panty hose for filters and for nice, soft ties for plant support. You can also gather materials for making a frog pond, some beehives, and the poles or supports you may want for tying up such plants like tomatoes and peas, which may need it.

Insect Traps

Some of the insect traps worth considering are:
A screen trap over a pan of sweetened water. This trap is usually made about twenty-four inches high and twelve or fourteen inches square, like a screen box, but with one end open and a screen cone inserted, wide at the entrance, small where the insects would emerge in search of the sweet water. The sweetener might be molasses, sugar and fruit wastes, aromatic oils like oil of sassafras, or some protein like powdered egg or powdered yeast. The amazing variety of

pests attracted to such bait includes cucumber beetles, corn borers, corn earworm moths, and moths of army worms, cutworms, and tomato hornworms. It will also bring in cabbage loopers and wireworms. If you put out such a contraption on a summer's night when these creatures are on the move, you'll be quite gratified with the results.

For hopping insects such as grasshoppers, you can rig up a long trough, with a backboard up to three feet high. It might as well be high enough to knock back the creatures when they jump up to escape. What they are knocked back into is the trough, which you can fill with kerosene, or water with a film of kerosene on top. This trap can be any length that is convenient to pull along a row—probably not more than four feet. It can also be provided with two runners and a rope handle to make it easier to move. If you want, you can coat the backboard and sides with some sticky stuff such as tanglefoot, and plan to pick up some extra pests with that. This sticky stuff should probably not be put on until you get ready to use the device during the summer. When you buy the sticky stuff, get enough so you can smear it on pieces of screen, cardboard, or floppy, heavy plastic, which you can hang in the wind. This too will attract and trap insects. But remember this warning: examine what you catch each morning. If the catch contains your best friends among the insects—ladybugs, lacewings, or trichogramma wasps—stop using that kind of all-night sticky trap and use something else.

The same holds true for the screen box mentioned above, and for the various kinds of black light lamps now coming into popularity.

One effective version of this lamp trap which you can make yourself is a trap devised at the Purdue University agricultural station. It has a fan, put at the top over a screen cone leading to a collecting can. Over or near the opening is an arrangement of one or two ultraviolet or near-ultraviolet tube lights. These can be run by batteries or with a long extension cord.

There is also plain old-fashioned tanglefoot. All you need to have is a supply of this sticky material, or a roofing tar substitute, and all you need to do is paint it in a circle around any trees, such as apple trees or cherries, which might be infected by worms that crawl up the trunk. It traps them all.

Traps

If you can get hold of some bamboo lengths, or old rhubarb stalks, or plastic hose, you can cut one-foot pieces and tie half a dozen together, preparatory to setting out earwig traps. Earwigs like dark, moist places, and will get into your lettuce and broccoli, as well as into your keyholes and behind any loose boards you have around the place. They will also go into a crumpled paper or rag. If you leave these dark lengths among your plants for several nights and days, you'll find that a good number of the earwigs will want to get into them. When they are collected, dump them out in your frog pond, or put them near your toads' holes. One of my neighbors who keeps frogs says that it seems no time at all after his discarded earwigs hit the water before the frogs in his pond have them all gobbled up. In fact, such a little frog pond, with such an insect-disposal system, is a lot more attractive than just a can with kerosene in it.

Winter is a good time to plan that pond, and also if you have room for it, to plan a farm pond for fire protection and fish. Obviously, fish like to be fed insects, too. And I have heard that pound for pound you can get more food value from enriching a farm pond than you can from an equal expenditure of enrichment on the land to grow crops. I believe that this was calculated on the basis of commercial fertilizer, but the principle would be the same whatever you used, I should think.

Organic Sprays

Most of your organic sprays you will make at the time of need, in the summertime. But it is possible to make some in the winter, freeze them, and store them until the time you want to melt and use them.

A very useful spray, suggested by Rose Houskeeper of the Garden Club of the Oranges, can be made by grinding in a blender 1 medium-sized onion, 1 teaspoon of very hot red pepper, 3 cloves of garlic, and a quart of water. She suggests that you strain this juice through a nylon stocking right into your sprayer; but for winter storage, strain it into a large cottage cheese carton, or whatever you are going to freeze it in.

Other sprays to make include one from tomato leaves. Puree a handful of leaves in water. Add enough water to make a quart, and also add 1 tablespoon of soap flakes and 1

77

tablespoon of cornstarch. Chive tea can be made from 5 tablespoons of chopped chives and 1 tablespoon of soap flakes steeped in 10 cups of boiling water. This spray is good for powdery mildew on cucumbers. Nasturtium spray, like tomato leaf spray, is made by mixing a handful of nasturtium leaves with or without pods, well chopped, with 1 tablespoon of soap flakes and 1 tablespoon of cornstarch. Soak in a quart of water and store in glass. Another garlic spray is made from 4 ounces of minced garlic, mixed with 1 teaspoon mineral oil, 1 teaspoon fish emulsion, and 1 pint water. Steep overnight and store in glass. Dilute with a gallon of water. Another hot pepper spray is made from 5 fresh very hot peppers, to which you add 2 chopped onions, a clove of garlic, and mash them all together. Steep with a little water for 24 hours, and then dilute with a gallon of water. This is recommended for beans, and also for roses and chrysanthemums. The tomato spray is also good for blackspot on roses.

Composting For the Cycle's Sake

If there is one thing you, as an efficient gardener, are really devoted to, it is your compost heaps—and especially your participation in the methods of composting. What you do is create an ideal situation for a clean transformation of raw materials by the microorganisms, worms, and insects who work on them to reduce them to a rich, fine black humus or substitute manure. You take part in the most basic cycles of nature, accumulating richness, dispensing it, making life out of leftovers and healthiness out of materials that are going to rot. You remember that all is transformed because there is no throwing away in nature. Ever since Sir Albert Howard urged farmers and gardeners to return to the soil all that they take from it, the organic gardeners who follow him have put faith in the composting methods he devised for doing just that. He made compost himself because he couldn't buy it.

While scavenging, saving, or hoarding things like potato peels or apple skins that are too good to throw out, you know that you are taking part in and aiding the wonderful, recycling processes of nature. All matter is used for one system or another. We talk about things deteriorating, but with every deterioration there is a building up of something new. Any plum or peach that is going to rot is providing food for the wasps that come to it, and the bacteria or molds that thrive on it. And they, in turn, work on the stone to free the seed. The main base for the penicillin so widely used during World War II came from a cantaloupe found rotting in a grocery store. And all modern penicillin comes from penicillin mold. You learn to put every organic material you can onto your heap, except fat, meat, and cheese, and you go on the hunt for new sources to pile up new stores of enrichment. If you are not a scavenger, and take no pleasure in accumulating materials this way, you can buy many of the ingredients you need.

Your scientific knowledge helps you, too. You learn that though tons of nitrates in this country are washed down the rivers and into the sea, the store of nitrogen needed by plants can be kept from erosion and built up to transfer to the soil. Then you get twice the urge to create that store, and promote that transfer. Since good soil health depends on organic matter to keep it rich and loose, you want to provide your garden with a big, rich source of it. You discover that soil gets pale and deteriorates over the long stretch when chemical fertilizers are substituted for the organic fertilizers found in nature, and then you are even more convinced that making compost and spreading it on the garden are absolute essentials for sustained, productive gardening. You also know that you are not overfertilizing and flushing excess nitrates and phosphates into the environment.

Where to Put the Heap

First you find a good position for a heap, or two, or three. According to the thirty-year experience of Samuel R. Ogden, three bins are best. Ogden, who was a canny and successful Vermont organic gardener, came to this conviction not only by way of his master, Ehrenfried Pfeiffer, but also by his own well-thought-out labor-saving habits. But in the suburbs or in a city plot, one heap is enough. In fact, many people settle for one in any location. Heaps have to be aged and turned, and with three you have one coming to perfection every year. To accommodate this three-year cycle, you must pick a site that is long enough for three heaps. That might be 24 feet long, for the usual dimension for each bin is 4–5 feet by 4–5 feet by 8 feet long. The width and height are determined by the stretch of the human arm, the need for insulation, and the need to avoid compaction in the center of the pile.

The site should be flat enough so that the accumulating nutrients will not leach away, and will ripen in a well-moistened condition—up to 50 percent water, but aired and not soggy. To hold moisture you can try to keep the heap somewhat concave on top. It should be far enough away from trees so that their roots will not come up into your piles and help themselves to all the goodness. It should be near enough to the garden and near enough to a driveway or access of some sort so that any heavy materials you bring to add to the pile will be fairly easy to handle. A site within the stretch of your hose is advisable, too.

Since neighbors are what they are, it is a good idea to hide your compost heap. They will have all sorts of myths and misconceptions about what a compost heap will do, and may even look on your carefully constructed, scientifically planned source of soil conditioning as a garbage pile. First they'll ask you whether you will get rats. Then snakes. Then dogs and cats. If you explain that you put dirt over the garbage, and leaves and grass clippings, and if you add that you bury the manure with wood chips, sawdust, or more dirt, they may relax. If you also explain how fast the bacterial action proceeds when the pile has enough oxygen to heat up, and how complete the scraps, excrements, germs, weed seeds, and wood chips are converted to clean, black humus, maybe you can satisfy their questions, or even arouse their admiration and wonder; they may desire to make compost themselves.

You might add that if you do attract dogs and cats, they will obviously control the rats, in case you might have attracted rats. The chances are very slim, however; I've not known anyone who attracted rodents any larger than mice—and those, in fact, moved in under the warm and sufficient haven of a mulch, not the compost. A fast-working heap is too hot for comfort, anyway.

Those lucky enough to have attracted an owl or an opossum have found they will help to control rodents, too. In any case, the neater and more controlled you make your compost heap seem, and the more you disguise it, the easier your life will be. You might even try growing some morning glories or a kudzu vine to bedeck the bin or fence. And many neat, attractive bins are available from seed companies and nurseries now.

Sheet Composting

Some people, if they find that the compost heap continues to bother others, simply move their composting activities to the cellar, the garage, or a closet, and use boxes or plastic bags as described in chapter 2. Others, if the crops are up high enough to disguise what is happening, toss the stuff directly on their garden soil.

Ruth Stout, author of *How to Have a Green Thumb Without an Aching Back*, and other books on organic gardening, recommended a good, deep hay mulch on your garden, so you can just slip your vegetable garbage out of sight underneath it. We use the euphemism "sheet composting" for these methods. Some people make compost in a bottomless barrel sunk right in the soil of the garden.

Constructing the Bin

If you have room in your yard, and you feel like building something, a slatted bin with removable slats along one side is a very good-looking and handy construction to put up. When you want to take out the finished compost, you simply pull out the slats and start filling up your wheelbarrow with the black, fine-grained material. A very easy substitute for this sort of bin is one made of snow fence, with four stakes at the corners. It is even easier to put up a single circular fence form, and then have only one key stake to worry about. We have used this kind, but find that a few extra stakes keep the fence from sagging, especially after it is exposed to heavy snows in the winter. The most rot-resistant woods to use are cedar, cypress, and locust. (A few gardeners still consider redwood but most of the organic gardeners I know wouldn't dream of it, for they are ardent conservationists and belong to the Save-the-Redwoods Federation.) Use an epoxy paint to discourage fungi. Do not use creosote.

Helen and Scott Nearing made a bin with plain thin logs. Both in their Vermont organic farming and in later years on their farm in Maine, they had excellent results from a bin laid-up log cabin style, with four new poles set in place whenever the composting materials reached a height at which more support was needed. Scott Nearing always kept the heaps squared instead of piled, with a dip in the top to catch water.

Not so easy to handle as logs or boards, but very easy to come by are concrete blocks, and many people now use them. If you build up a bin with alternating air spaces, blocks make an airy and durable frame. You can pull out any section you want when you are ready to turn your compost over or take it out for use. Some people don't like the way these blocks look, but they can be disguised with paint or vines if you want to hide them. You can also sink

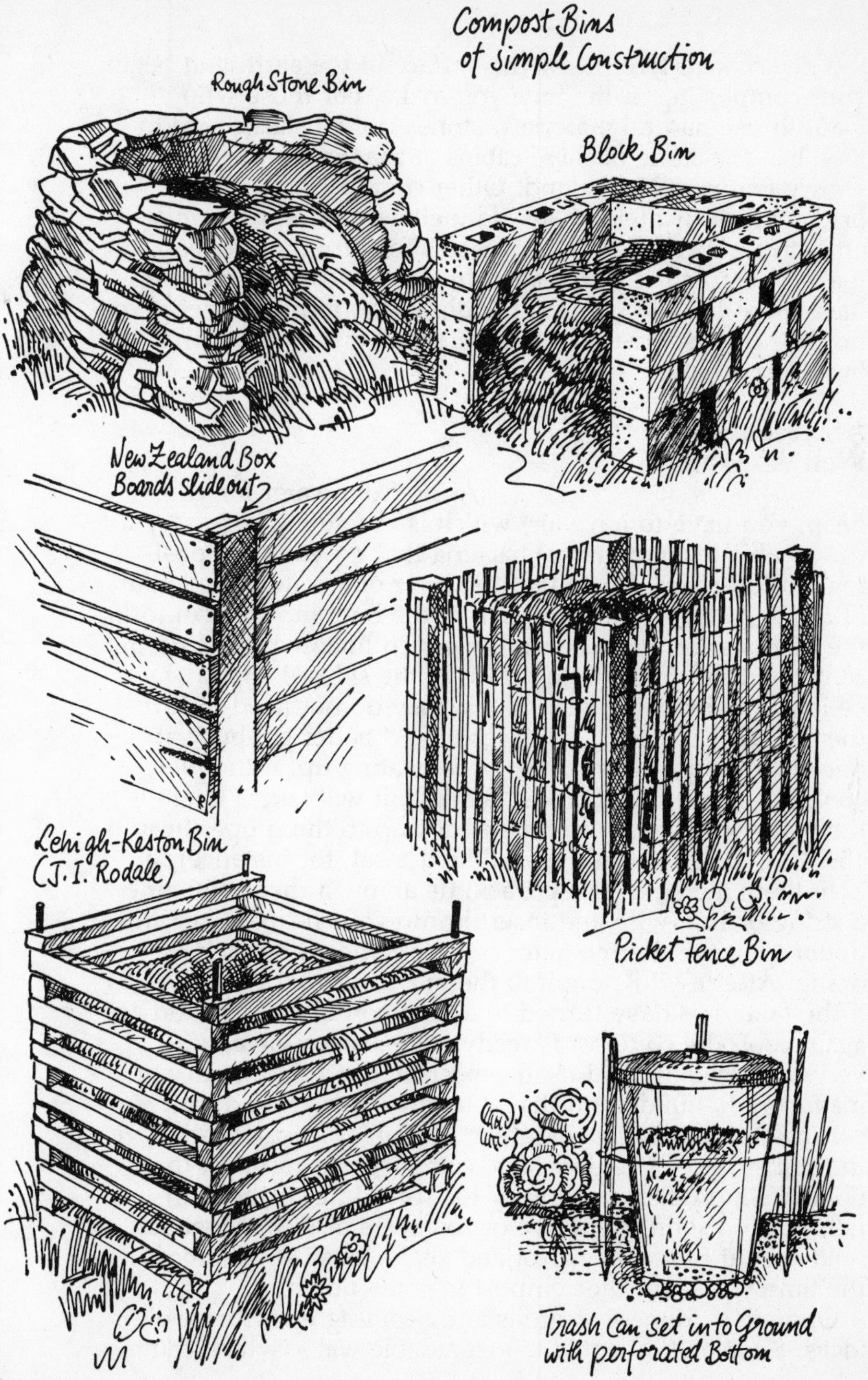

Compost Bins
of Simple Construction

Rough Stone Bin

Block Bin

New Zealand Box
Boards slide out

Lehigh-Keston Bin
(J. I. Rodale)

Picket Fence Bin

Trash Can set into Ground
with perforated Bottom

the first row or two below the surface of the earth and begin
your composting in the hole you make. For those who
want to use natural materials, stones can be stacked up to
look like the stone beehive cabins at the western tip of the
Dingle Peninsula in Ireland. Other compost makers use
bricks which, if they are an old mellow pink, can be very
attractive. Always leave easy access for turning the heap, or
make the structure three-sided in the first place. You'll
have more trouble keeping the dip in the top for water if you
do that, but as most gardeners are well aware, you can't
have everything.

Air Needed As
Well As Water

Aside from water for your
heap, you have to have air, which is absolutely necessary for
the aerobic (oxygen-using) bacteria that do your composting work for you. Make the first layer of a compost pile out
of coarse twigs so air can get in at the bottom. You can fork
the pile over or insert several two-inch hollow pipes into the
center, put in from the top or from the sides. People
believe that by using such pipes, they do not need to turn
the pile. If it cools off, however, you'd better get busy at
once to let more air in. After once heating up, if the pile
cools off before the compost is made, it will take a long
time for the bacteria to bring it back up to the proper heat of
150° F. Quickly add nitrogen (blood meal, for instance) to
help them along. To keep track, tie an oven thermometer on
a string or thin wire and insert it into your heap. When in
doubt, pull the thermometer out to see how your pile is
doing. After a while dig into the pile in several places, and
if the materials have turned to a rich, soft blackness, and are
again cool, the compost is ready to use. If you live in a
very rainy climate and need especially good drainage, you
may have to build a bin that is totally aboveground. But
construct it with a coarse screen bottom at least a foot above
the soil surface. The dark, fine compost that forms at the
bottom simply falls out, ready for spreading. If the stuff
falls out too soon, fit in five or six layers of newspaper to
hold it in at first. They'll rot and shake loose at just about
the time you want the compost to come down.

Organic gardeners are constantly coming up with new
ideas. Someone invented biodegradable walls, which can

be made of many piled-up sods. The rest of us like the idea of this sort of bin with self-destruction built right into it, for the whole thing will eventually break down as compost, and you need not anticipate shabby blocks or a ragged, leftover wooden structure to bother you when the bin gets worn out.

One farmer I know uses bales of spoiled hay for the walls of his compost piles. Some of the bales can be moved easily when it is time to turn the heap. They are biodegradable and are a very handy source of hay mulch if you need to save moisture, or to protect little plants that have just become established.

Most inconspicuous of all are sturdily lined compost pits on a hill, with the side facing downhill used for the opening. They can be put right next to the garden, or, if you want a handy place for weeds, right in the middle of it. Keep them small enough to work with, not deeper than four feet. The proper sizes for pits and heaps were discovered by Sir Albert Howard when he first began composting. Later he had his helpers make very long heaps; but short or long, the intent was to keep the dimensions convenient for turning. The bottom is always bare ground so that earthworms and bacteria can get in. Pits are very appealing to those who like to bury things. And they also save heat. With well-shredded materials and careful management, compost can be made in a pit in quite a short time, and can be insulated for winter warmth.

Earthworms

With a raised or lined bin, or a lined pit, you are not likely to get as many earthworms as you would in your compost heap, where they are readily attracted to the rich organic matter once it has cooled. Many organic gardeners even buy worms to insert in a layer near the bottom when it is cool, not hot. Earthworms condition the materials and help make humus, both in the compost heap and in the garden. Their castings and their tunneling open up the soil to create the kind of structure gardener's want for their land. It is as though earthworms eat their way through the compost pile or the soil. They suck minerals, microorganisms, and other organic matter into their mouths as they move through the earth. In addition to eating decaying organic materials, they eat live plant seeds, larvae, eggs, and parasite cysts. This food is ground up in the pharynx, then neutralized by calcium carbonate secreted from glands in the esophagus before going to the crop and gizzard. In the gizzard the food is thoroughly pulverized by the small stones and mineral particles ingested by the worm; the food then goes to the intestine, where it is digested by enzymes. The castings, therefore, are a good deal nearer the state desirable for plant use.

When you get ready to use compost on the garden, save the worms from your pile by heaping the materials on a tarpaulin or big plastic sheet in the warm sun. In a few hours, when the worms react to the penetrating heat of the sun, the worms will cluster in the middle of the pile where it is coolest, and will be easy to pick up all together and move.

One man I heard of collects his worms that way, puts his compost on the garden in the fall, and moves his worms to a special insulated bin he has built so that he can keep them warm and active in the winter. He adds nutrients to the inside, stacks manure, hay, and other materials up to the top, and wraps two feet of insulation materials around the outside of the bin. (One foot is thick enough in climates less chilly than ours in Vermont.) This way he keeps his worms busy, has new compost ready in the spring, puts it all on a tarp again, and shifts the outside materials to the inside to start once more. A splendid triple-purpose system. The grubs of the insects that go into compost piles also help to grind up the materials.

Winter Methods

Other methods for winter include covering your heap with dirt, sawdust, leaves, a tarp, or hay—all to keep out the wind and prevent the escape of nitrogen. Some very careful composters believe in covers all year round. I find that the most recently added vegetable wastes, or the most recent layer of dirt, serve that purpose. The tarp, of course, will fend off animal visitors. Get oak leaves if you can, because they are highest in nutrient values. If you have none of your own, scavenge from the town park or the road crews who go around gathering up leaves in the fall. Since you will probably be saving them a trip to the landfill, they will be glad enough to let you have their leaves. Sometimes, if you live on a convenient route, they will even deliver them to your yard. If you can't get oak, get maple or ash leaves, but not black walnut or Norway maple, which have a growth inhibitor in their leaves. Avoid the hulls of sunflower seeds for the same reason.

Before adding the cover for winter, test the pH of the heap to see if the materials are too acid (below pH 5.5) and need lime. Sprinkle in enough to raise the pH to about neutral (2 cups of limestone or 5 cups of wood ashes). You can also rototill all your compost into the garden in the fall, and not have any heaps to winter over.

Plastic bags can be used in seasons other than winter. You can make your own, but I prefer the big dark green garbage bags available in markets. Use two or three for extra thickness, and for resistance to splitting when you take it out into the hot sun. Since the bags will be tied up, you can stuff in weeds, grass clippings, all kinds of green stuff, handfuls of earth, manure, bone meal, and whatever else you want. Leave the bags out in the warm weather, and you can expect a rapid and complete composting as they heat up in the sun. Don't leave them too long or the bags will split. When it rains, or at night, they can be hung on hooks in the garage, or down cellar, or wherever you want. A friend of mine uses gerbil cage cleanings, bird cage cleanings, vegetable garbage including some of the old, worn-out lettuce she begs from the chain stores, and hand-fuls of grass she pulls off as she goes by the end of the yard. In the summertime, with four bags going, the first is just about ready to use when she starts filling the fourth bag. This is good speedy composting.

Though there are periods when the smell can be rather awful as you open the bag to add new stuff, the ardent composter will still like this anaerobic method, for there is no worry about keeping the heap well watered, well drained, and well aired, and no need to turn the heap, for the anaerobic bacteria don't need air. There is no worry about leaching—either up to the air because of windiness and drying out, or down into the ground because of rain. All is contained, and working in a small, well-controlled place. In fact, the more you think of it, the more you come to see that except for the smell there is no good reason not to compost by this method. Well, there is one good reason, and it is related to the basic reason gardeners like their occupation so much. That is that they would rather be out of doors, working with things in the open, and enjoying the four elements of earth, water, heat, and air. Everything about the anaerobic method seems tied-in and confined in comparison.

You may have seen ads about adding bacterial activators to compost-making materials. I cannot see that such activators are needed, for the bacteria come naturally from the air, the soil, the plant materials, and especially the manure used, which obviously has bacteria already. Under favorable conditions the bacteria will undergo enormous population growth, and you will have as many as you would if you had bought them. The Bio-Dynamic group of gardeners uses an herb supplement as an activator for nutrients. That's different. I'd suggest you save some compost material to use as your own activator, or "seed compost," on the next compost heap you start, both for nutrients and for bacteria. If you are just starting, borrow some seed compost, rely on the manure, or go ahead and buy an activator.

Use Everything of Organic Origin to Make Your Compost

Most householders first think of grass clippings, autumn leaves, and vegetable garbage as the materials to use in their compost heaps. All can be used, and at least two out of the three can be used for mulch materials first. In fact, a basic source of composting materials is last year's mulch. Green grasses, especially young blades, are high in nitrogen, so are good for both mulching and compost. You'll find yourself wishing you had three times as many lawn clippings as you do, for they do the lawn a lot of good when left where they fall. They are excellent as mulch to spread directly on the garden, and they do well on the compost heap, especially if you add blood meal along with them, or fresh manure. Spread them around in all three places, or mete them out according to the weather and the current needs. But I think best of all is to use spring grass clippings as thinly spread mulch on the garden when the first vegetable seedlings are coming up. The nutrients are good, and the fine grass will not choke the tiny plants as some bigger, coarser mulch might. Do not spread thickly. The clippings will get hot and slimy if you do, because they have a lot of water in them.

The leaves from a big shade tree will provide your garden with a lot of nutrients—up to twice as many as you'd get from an equal weight of manure. In fact, plant scientists have estimated that you can get back from a plant just about the amount in nutrients that went to make it. Perfect cycling would take place if humans never entered the cycle to take off crops of plants, and meat or milk from animals that eat the plants. In dollar terms, considering the cost of fertilizers, peat moss, and mulching materials, the leaves from a big tree might add up to the equivalent of nearly twenty dollars. For best results they should be run over with a rotary lawn mower (or by cars on the driveway), or put through a shredder before composting them. The more surfaces there are for the microorganisms to work on, the faster and more complete will be the composting. If leaves are spread right on the garden and allowed to rest there over the winter, whether or not shredded, they can be rototilled or plowed in the spring. Rototilling or digging-in is better. By midsummer most will have disappeared except, perhaps, in a few places where there has been a heavy bunching up of unshredded leaves. Don't let that happen. Your plants will get nitrogen starvation and be sickly and stunted.

Vegetable garbage is an indispensable compost pile ingredient for several reasons (and be sure to include coffee grounds and tea leaves). It is full of a wide variety of nutrients and growth factors, which supply the bacteria, fungi, actinomycetes, earthworms, and later the plants with both their major needs and the trace elements. In addition, you get the satisfaction of putting them to good use in the composting process that transforms these wastes into something clean and wholesome. To take part in cleaning up and enhancing the life of the world around us is exactly what the organic gardener aims for.

Residues from the kitchen can be shredded before being added to the compost pile. I put a lot of my vegetable garbage through the blender or food processor before adding it to the pail. I also grind up eggshells and all such things as melon rinds or orange and grapefruit peels that take months to degrade if left in large pieces. The water you use for blending is needed for the compost heap anyway, and the many small surfaces suspended in it are good for the bacteria to work on. The earthworms are not fussy, but some gardeners think they like a finer-textured pile to work in, too. Earthworms particularly like sawdust, ground bark, and wood chips, which are excellent for composting; so do fungi. Any acidity in the heap is only temporary. Don't worry about it.

Black-and-white newspapers are all right for composting, especially if shredded or crumpled—never flat. You can compost second-class mail, too; but do not use the colored pages of mail, magazines, or newspapers.

All weeds can be added, as well as plants culled when you thin the rows, and those left over after a crop has been harvested. This certainly applies to cucumbers, carrots, cabbages, and lettuces, and the plants of all their families, unless you have cabbage club root (see pages 154–55) on the cabbage family plants. (Burn them and use only the ash.)

The legumes that have finished bearing in your garden, such as peas and beans, can be added to the heap or pulled up and heeled in right there on the spot. You can improve them by running them over with a small Rototiller to chop them up. This makes their plentiful nitrogen quickly available for your compost heap or garden, with as little loss as possible.

Incinerator and wood ashes are very fine to use, but they leach easily, so it is better to put them right on the garden. They are also useful to put on the cabbage worm if it decides to come in. It won't if you have used *Bacillus thüringiensis*. And remember to collect hair for its valuable nitrogen content.

Do not worry about disease germs and weed seeds if your heap heats up properly. The heat generated by the bacterial action during composting kills off all but a few fungus spores. The only seed to come through alive, in fact, is the tomato seed. I have friends who never buy tomato seeds or plants, they just wait to see what will come up. If cherry tomatoes get started they will pop up all over your garden for several years. Whenever compost is completed, spread it on your gardens, lawns, around trees and shrubs as needed. In the fall, half-completed compost can be put out to weather over the winter—under the snow if you live in the right climate.

Getting the Major
Nutrients
Nitrogen

Convenient and reliable sources of nitrogen for your compost pile include: blood meal, or dried blood, which has a nitrogen content of 12 to 15 percent; cottonseed meal, with 7 percent; feathers, more than 15 percent; hair, about 14 percent; slaughterhouse refuse, called tankage, with 6 percent; bone meal, 5 percent; and activated sludge, 5 percent. If you can get hold of some of the following, the nitrogen content is very favorable: ground leather, 11 percent; dried shrimp heads, nearly 8 percent; hoof and horn meal or dust, 12 percent; waste from wool or felt hats, 3 to 4 percent; ground-up lobster shells, nearly 5 percent; fish scraps (as we learned in school when studying the American Indians) yield 6 to 8 percent, and the very special king crab, 10 percent. Fish products can often be found in garden stores as fish meal or as fish emulsion, but percentages of these are lower. I have been pestered by little animals who come to dig up the fish products, however.

Of the manures there is quite a difference between the wet and dried nitrogen percentages. Dried manures provide 3 to 4 percent more nitrogen. Here is an estimate for wet manures. I've seen others even lower.

Cattle manure	.29%
Duck	1.12%
Hen	1.63%
Horse	.44%
Pigeon	4.19%
Dog	1.97%

Nitrogen is needed in every cell, for good greenness and for rapid new growth.

Phosphorus

Higher yields of the essential element phosphorus can be had by using some of the following on your compost heap. Government reports say that residues from a sugar factory, if you live near one, will give 8.33 percent; ash of lemon skins, if you incinerate such a thing, 6.3 percent; ash of cucumber skins, 11.28 percent; and dog manure, 9.95 percent. Other good sources for phosphorus are ground cocoa shell, 1.49 percent; common crab, 3.6 percent; Milorganite, the sludge from a Milwaukee sewage treatment plant, 3 percent; basic slag from a steel mill, 8 percent; cottonseed meal, 2.5 percent; cottonseed-hull ash, 8.7 percent; castor-bean pomace, 2.25 percent; apple skins (ash), 3.08 percent; and bone meal, way up to 21 percent, or steamed bone meal at 27 percent. Burned, ground bone gives up to 34.70 percent phosphoric acid, and that's about the highest compost element you can find—unless it's waste from a paint mill at 39.50 percent. Fish scraps from red snapper can yield 13 percent; ash of raw potato skins gives 5.18 percent; sardine scrap, 7.11 percent; and siftings from oyster shell mounds, if you live on the Chesapeake Bay or certain coastal areas of the Gulf of Mexico, 10.38 percent. What you are aiming for with a good supply of phosphorus is good root growth, sturdy growth of stems, good flowering and fruiting, and—so it is reported—an increased vitamin content in your plants. Bone meal can be found at all garden supply stores.

Potassium

Potassium, or potash, is the third major nutrient need you want for your garden. It strengthens plants, makes them disease resistant, is needed in cell development and cell division, and helps plants use and control the nitrogen they receive. Though it is difficult for plants to use potassium in all forms, incinerator or fly ash is helpful, as well as powders and dusts which contain potassium, such as greensand and granite dust, which have 7 percent and 5 percent, and also various vegetable residues. If you can get it, fly ash has 12 percent. A whopping 49.4 percent of the ash of banana stalks is potash; and 41.76 percent of the ash of the skins of bananas is potash, also. Ash quantities of others include apple skins, 11.74 percent; cantaloupe rind, 12.21 percent; corncob, 50 percent; cottonseed hull, 23.93 percent; and fire-pit ashes from smokehouses, 4.96 percent. Milk will yield .18 percent; oak leaves, .15 percent; the ash of pea pods, 9 percent; and wood ashes, 7 percent as determined in government tests. (You don't have to burn these things. The figures are to give you an idea of the inherent nutrient values.)

Wood ashes are the old-time gardeners' standby for potash. They guessed something about the corncob, too, but were quite ignorant of the beneficial potash value of the ashes of apple skin, citrus-fruit skin, and potato skins, let alone of pea pods and bananas. Nevertheless, an age-old ingrained knowledge or intuition about the soil and its needs has dictated to many farmers that it was better to put wood ashes back on the land than it was to remove them from the cycles of plant nutrition. Country people also understood the value of sea products. Fields in old-time cultures like those on the Channel Islands off the coasts of Britain and Brittany indicate an age-old knowledge of sea-product fertilizers. On the island of Jersey I have walked beside plowed fields festooned in January and February with the maroon and cream colors of kelp spread along their furrows for fertilizer. As the season for planting approaches, these decorative fertilizers will be plowed under and the rest of their nutrients released for the plantings of the Jersey people's crops. Seaweeds are good sources of trace minerals, too.

Obviously all those exotic sources of nutrients for your compost heap are not going to be available without a great deal of effort, and probably expense. But the figures suggest that you should save and scavenge all such things as banana skins or crab shells when you can. If it is nitrogen and phosphoric acid your soil test indicates you need, you can even send away for bat guano, which has 6 percent nitrogen and 9 percent phosphoric acid. That's a pretty good proportion, considering that common sources like alfalfa have only 2.45 percent nitrogen, .5 percent phosphoric acid, and 2.1 percent potash, and cowpeas have only 3.1 percent nitrogen, 1 percent phosphoric acid, and 1.2 percent potash.

When they find their soil is low in phosphorus, organic gardeners apply phosphate rock—preferably pulverized and interspersed with pulverized limestone. For potassium they often get greensand and granite dust. Go to your garden center, grain or hardware store, or organic food shop as possible sources for these materials. If you find you have to send away, see the list of addresses in the Appendix. If possible, contact a buying cooperative, and get in touch with your local organic gardening club to see whether arrangements have been made to buy in bulk in your area.

A useful multipurpose supply to have on hand might be a pile of sludge—free—which you can put in the compost for nitrogen and phosphorus; manure—free—for nitrogen and potassium; bone meal—to buy—good for phosphorus, especially; greensand and granite dust—to buy—good for both phosphorus and potassium; and the following good for all three major nutrients: cottonseed meal, seaweed, fish meal, cocoa shells—expensive—and wood ashes and incinerator ashes—free, and especially good for potassium.

If you want to spend a lot of money for ground volcanic ash (known as perlite) or expanded mica (known as vermiculite), you can create a wonderful loose, water-absorbant texture by adding such materials to your compost piles or directly to your soil. Chopped-up corncobs would be cheaper, as would tobacco stalks or sugar cane. But remember that mice like these materials—especially the sugarcane. Do not merely dump. Mix the additions in thoroughly.

Trace Minerals

In general, trace minerals for organic gardeners are derived from organic matter itself, or from rock phosphate, lime, granite dust, or sludge. The leaves of big, deep-rooted trees, for instance, are a fine source of minerals because of the way the roots burrow way down into the parent rock zone and bring up a rich supply.

Boron is needed, and is deficient in the soils of many parts of the country. Good sources for composting are vetch, sweet clover, and muskmelon leaves, as well as granite dust. Copper, deficient in some eastern states, can be derived from spinach, tobacco, dandelions, wood shavings, sawdust, and bromegrass. Iron, available from many weeds and vegetable residues, is deficient only in most eastern states and the north central states; it is necessary for animal metabolism and can be derived from several of the basic rocks, vetch, most legumes, and peach stones.

Manganese can be gotten from carrot tops, red clover, leaf mold—especially if from white oak or hickory—and alfalfa. Zinc, which is deficient both in the South and on the West Coast, and is needed by both plants and animals, can be found in ragweed, hickory, poplar, vetch, cornstalks, horsetail, and peach tree clippings. Vetch, alfalfa, and rock phosphate are sources of molybdenum, which is deficient in many soils.

Calcium, which comes in the form of lime, is very slow to break down to the particle-size usable by plants. It is best when finely ground, preferably small enough to sift through a very fine 100-mesh screen. It is not exactly a fertilizer, but it is valuable for adjusting the alkalinity and loosening soil structure. The best source, since it is mixed with other nutrients, is dolomitic limestone. For the compost pile, it is enough to sprinkle a little on every fourth or fifth layer, since it does leach. You can rely on the leaves you add to the pile for a certain amount. Maple leaves have between 1 and 2 percent, oak leaves nearly 1.5 percent, beech nearly 1 percent, and white ash, which is plentiful in the temperate zone in many places, has nearly 2.5 percent. If you keep piles of leaves near your compost pile, reach down and pull out the wet lower layers when you plan to add some. Not only are these leaves already partly decomposed, they are also less likely to blow when the wind comes up. One more good source of lime is glass. The ground glass frit now becoming available to gardeners contains calcium, sodium, iron, potassium, and sometimes boron. Several companies are preparing glass materials that will be soluble enough to make them practicable for farmers and gardeners.

Humus and the Soil Chemistry

One of the best reasons for compost gardening instead of chemical gardening is that both the major and the trace elements are conserved and protected by organic fertilizers, whereas chemical fertilizers might release elements so quickly that they leach away. Since such tiny amounts are required by plants, it is difficult not to be excessive in applying the trace elements chemically. Your potato crop, for instance, if given too much boron, would be ruined.

Humus, the end product of your composting, has other unusual properties in its fine-grained, dark-to-black organic material. According to Nobel prize winner Selman Waksman, it can probably solubilize nutrients from the insoluble state to make them available to plants. It has dozens of organic compounds in it, with fifteen or so different acids, aldehydes, carbohydrates (carbon-oxygen-hydrogen compounds), and proteins (carbon-oxygen-hydrogen plus either sulfur or nitrogen or phosphorus). One analysis of humus showed:

carbon, 44.12 percent; hydrogen, 6 percent; oxygen, 35.16 percent; nitrogen, 8.12 percent; ash, 6.6 percent. The ash contained calcium, phosphorus, boron, zinc, magnesium, manganese, and the other trace elements. Though, it is commonly known that humus aids storage of nutrients, and promotes the right tempo of release of these nutrients into the soil solution, it also has a rather mysterious power to control the action of the organic compounds. Sometimes organic compounds stretch out or move around in a swimming motion until they reach the mineral particle, to which they will cling with a claw-like grip. This is the chelating power. Then the mineral comes out in the open where plants can use it. Plant scientists now believe that the mobility of plant nutrients may be largely due to this curious grabbing (or chelating) ability of organic matter. In many scientific reports on the action of organic materials in the cycles of plant life, there comes this point of maybe. It seems to me that every report I've seen has two or three maybes, pointing to powers and actions going on which scientists have not yet discovered. Even a 1-percent possibility of error in chemical manipulation still makes humus and compost 99 percent safer to use on your soil.

Yet there is a host of already discovered life processes which go into the making of compost or humus, in which the biological and chemical changes are made cohorts of microorganisms with the help of enzymes to do the errands.

Why We Want Compost and Organic Matter

Organic matter exerts some other important influences: it turns the brown or gray soil to black; it encourages granulation; it reduces lumping and cohesion; it holds six times its own weight in water; it improves the supply and availability of nutrients. There will be good exchanges and easily replaceable cations; there will be nitrogen, phosphorus, and potassium held in organic forms; and there will be continual, slow extractions of elements from minerals by the more or less acid humus.

The decline of 30 to 40 percent of the organic matter in American soils, experts say, is serious, and should go no further if we can afford to prevent it. Some progress has been made, but unfortunately, unless we catch on pretty soon to what's needed to shift our sense of economy from wastage to salvage, we may find that the ideas of what we can or can't afford have snowballed so farcically that we will be saying, "Well, no, we can't afford to grow plants or even breathe anymore. It is much too expensive to clean up the air."

Scavenging

When you are out on a pickup trip for composting materials, swing around for free manures, free old vegetables, cannery, winery, or dairy wastes, or beauty shop sweepings. Go to an employee and see whether you can't get the lumberman to give you some free sawdust and some free ground bark. If the employee demurs, or wants to charge you something, ask what is causing all that smoke coming from the incinerator. Nine chances out of ten it is from burning sawdust, or bark. You might better have it, for you will recycle it, whereas the lumberyard incinerator is simply polluting the air.

All such materials that you can save or scavenge are good both for composting, which takes months, or for quick composting, which can be done in a few weeks with some special tricks. Some gardeners still think a compost must be several years old and fine-grained before it is ready for use; others, who claim equal success with their gardens and equally sizable vegetables and flowers, say that a perfectly adequate compost can be whizzed into shape in fourteen days.

Composting in a Hurry

To use fast methods you hasten the ripening process by physical, biological, and biochemical means. Since the idea is to get the pile to heat up very rapidly, there must be lots of bacteria at work, lots of oxygen to keep them going, and, of course, all the organic nitrogenous matter that they can use. You make the whole heap at once, layered carefully with alternating materials such as shredded dry leaves, manure, and high-nitrogen green stuff and vegetable garbage, and add some loam or old compost here and there. Cottonseed meal, sludge, blood meal, or fish meal will do as well as manure. (When you are adding to a compost of autumn leaves, use twice as much manure, because dry leaves in the fall are low in nitrogen.) Also see

97

that the organic matter is physically multiplied by giving it many, many surfaces for the bacteria to work on.

Water for fast composting must be kept at half the weight of the pile. Hose it well when you first make the pile, and let it go for a week or more unless the weather is very hot and dry. In moist, warm, autumn weather—one of the best times to make a fast compost, for then you have lots of leaves—one watering may be enough. The next day take the temperature—it should be 150° F. The third day the pile will have shrunk. Turn it all to get more oxygen in, and see whether it has dried out. At this time, to speed up biochemical change, add enrichments such as rock phosphate, colloidal phosphate, granite dust, greensand, and small amounts of limestone. Use from a shovelful to fifty pounds of each compost material. Turn often for the next ten days.

For shredding compost material, a rotary mower is the preferred machine. Some of the commercial shredders on the market get all gubbed up when you feed green stuff or gooey stuff into them. Dry twigs, cones, and bark are needed to unstick them, but if your aim is for the fastest composting, the lignins in this dry material will delay the action, and you'll want to avoid them. For shredding vegetable wastes in the house, use a blender or food processor. A large-sized blender called a Hydramill can be used outdoors. It produces a slurry you can put on the heap for nutriments and for water benefits all at once.

Hints from Municipal Composting and Sludge Production

A few of the practices used in municipal composting give some good hints to home gardeners who want to do high-speed composting themselves. For example, it's been found that it does pay to start with a seed compost of 5 to 10 percent old materials. The moisture in the heap should be around 50 to 58 percent, and 50 percent oxygen should be introduced by frequent stirring.

Moisture content above 70 percent is bad because the pore space for entry of oxygen decreases. Then the pile cools, gets soggy and putrefying, with anaerobic bacteria taking over. The best pH is in the range of 5.5 to 8 to prevent undue loss of nitrogen. The heap will be acid at first (pH 5.5), and when it goes up to pH 8, you can consider that the processing is just about complete.

Fresh municipal garbage fed into big layered bins can be completely converted within 70 hours when all conditions are right. That will usually mean continuous stirring by machine.

Sludge for Your Garden

Many towns now have sewage-treatment plants where the end product is activated sludge, which is germless, dry, and smells like the floor of the forest. It is a good source of nitrogen and minerals. A decade or more ago it was reported that 50 percent of the sludge in the state of Connecticut was being returned to the soil. This is half as good as the Hunzas and the Chinese recyclers, who omit the treatment plant and put their garbage, manures, and night soil directly on the land. Using human excreta is hazardous because of intestinal bacteria and parasites, unless there is enough heat in the compost for enough days to cook them to death. The heat needed for killing off typhoid, paratyphoid, and dysentery is 150° F for a week or so. Without that heat, these coliform bacteria could survive all winter. Ice, in fact, preserves them. Salmonella bacteria can survive a month, unless cooked, and the hepatitis virus much longer. In this country sewage is given a 200°F heat treatment before it is sold for fertilizers such as Milorganite. Any use of night soil buried in a compost heap is therefore extremely precarious, for the borderline of safety is too thin for an amateur to be able to control. Today the main hazards in municipal composts are heavy metals. Our town no longer gives away sludge for that very reason.

By the time the organic gardener gets heated and bubbled activated sludge, the nitrogen content is up to about what it would be in cottonseed meal—that is, 5 to 6 percent—and its phosphorus up to 3 to 6 percent.

Sludge has other nutrients, such as calcium oxide, magnesium oxide, sulfur, iron oxide, and ash. Its pH runs somewhere between 4.5 and 7.2, but higher when certain industrial wastes are in it. Trace elements come from copper sulfate, zinc, sulfate, borax, manganese sulfate, or sodium molybdate. In addition there are celluloses, lignins, and crude proteins, and sludge is 25 to 36 percent carbon.

With this knowledge, almost any organic gardener will be

willing to use certified sludge, especially when it has been heat-dried. Another advantage is that it is slow to be nitrified. It is good for a new lawn, for instance, at the rate of one part sludge to two parts soil, mixed down to a depth of six inches. For an established lawn, put it on in the winter, one-half inch deep, and let it freeze and thaw. For gardens and farmland, season it outdoors in all weather for six months and then put it on before rain, preferably in the autumn. Sludge will not only provide the major nutrients, it will also improve the physical properties of your soil and increase productivity of some if not all plants. Therefore, if you can acquire safe sludge, it can truly help your lawn or garden.

Sludge has been recommended by the Connecticut experiment station for lawns, melons, squash, and other vine crops. (But a warning is given to add lime after a while if sludge is continually used.) Connecticut sludges have been heat-treated, thus destroying any dangerous bacteria. This is normal treatment of all sludge, such as Milorganite, which is offered on the market. Many untreated sludges have been pronounced all right for all uses except vegetables. If in doubt, cure the sludge you get by letting it sit on the ground in the open for at least three months. Also if in doubt, use it only for vegetables to be cooked, or for those whose edible parts are totally aboveground. If still in doubt, apply composted sludge only in the fall, and let it cure again on the soil over the winter. I'd recommend this for beets and turnips.

To compost sludge, put it with materials such as grass clippings, sawdust, wood chips, leaves, weeds, and vegetable residues. Unfortunately, sludge may contain undesirable runoffs or discards that are not biodegradable; then even the usual purification in the compost heap won't help. If you handle it with bare hands (which you are advised not to do), wash afterward with warm water and laundry soap. Ditto for blood meal, by the way, because of possible infectious fungi not killed by the heat treatment.

Composting in Africa and the Orient

Composting in African and Eastern countries is often introduced for the sake of disposing of all domestic refuse—not only garbage but also animal excreta and street sweepings. Many towns and villages now adapt the Indore method of Sir Albert Howard, with results as successful as Sir Albert's, if not more so, especially where the weather is good and hot. The refuse used to be burned, or buried in pits, and the nutritive values were mostly lost to the community's farms and gardens. Sometimes the cow, horse, sheep, and goat manure was heaped up in smelly piles, which leached away, or the cowpats, as in India, were used for stove fuel or plaster.

Now the people in many villages are taught a new practice of mixing their night soil, vegetable wastes, and animal manures to compost all together in their pits. In their hot climate, with three turnings, they can achieve compost in about a month. The villagers are taught to keep the mass well moistened, use plenty of fresh green materials, insert ashes from domestic fires, and keep the pits well aired, lightly packed, and protected from becoming waterlogged. They then see that the mass can heat up on the second day, and shrink and be free of smell by the fourth. If made so this happens, the pile should attract no flies or other vermin, and will harbor the helpful bacteria and fungi as needed.

The costs, of course, are much less than they would be for municipal incinerators or sewage-treatment plants. The adjustment from dumping is not hard for citizens to make, especially when they find that the results are so very beneficial. In five years, according to one report, compost production in a Nigerian village totaled 43,800 tons. That's a lot of fertilizer.

Where the night soil is too wet, the villagers dry it by mixing it with dust, wood chips, sand, and sprinklings of dry dirt and lime before putting it with the other materials.

I have read that at one time in Hungary everyone was ordered to take their refuse to the city composting center. Night soil, garbage, refuse, the lot. Hungarian rules for composting were rigid and suggestive. Night soil was mixed with peat, composted for at least 21 days, covered with a layer of previously aged materials, and then mixed with other wastes and further composted, or sold. The final mixture had to come out, according to rule, with specific carbon-nitrogen and other ratios, and proper density and ash content. The Hungarian compost centers, as in all big municipal composting processes, removed all the iron, aluminum, and glass. Presumably any heavy metals were removed, too. As for the pathogens, temperatures of 140° F for the period of heat in the pile—maybe three or four days—would be hot enough to kill many, and 150° F for the rest. In fact, 30 minutes or an hour is long enough at those temperatures to kill several strains of salmonella germs.

Such activities around the world show that composting really is believed in by many peoples, and is studied in great scientific detail. As organic gardeners we get ideas from them for what to do for ourselves, and what to use as arguments for nonbelievers—especially about the rapid conversion and purification possible, and the superior nutritive value of this potentially plentiful fertilizer. If we had compost centers in this country, too, many a solid waste problem might be solved. The habit of sorting household wastes can be easily acquired once a person makes up his or her mind to do the sorting.

The Soil In Your Backyard Lives

Everything I've learned about what happens in the soil I've found exciting. As soon as I began to see that soil is not just that flat brown stuff good for building houses on or burying things in, the whole earth suddenly became alive and full of wondrous events. I suppose our wrong notion of the soil comes from looking down at compacted, barren paths outside schools and across vacant lots, or from seeing the bared profile of a gravel pit as we pass by. We see the lowest layer of rock, followed by layers of different-sized pebbles, gravels, and sands in the subsoil, and the finer silt and loam in the topsoil. The soil is not just that compound of minerals and nitrogen, phosphorus, and potassium we were once taught it was. Far from it. It is teeming with many forms of life, millions of underground organisms that are continuously making physical and chemical changes in the soil, and in all the plants and animals springing from it. Scientists can now tell us about various kinds of bacteria, ray fungi, true fungi, molds and mushrooms, green algae, blue-green algae, and other plants; about yeasts, many different kinds of protozoa, earthworms, nematodes, centipedes, ants, other insects and their larvae as well as the moles, shrews, and all the small animals that live in the soil. They can also describe many (though not yet all) interconnections between the organic and inorganic events going on in the soil all the time, and can tell us that there is streptomycin in cow manure and penicillin in mold, and that vitamins do come from bacteria. They now use the term *biochemical* (or more ponderously, *colloidobiological*) for what's happening—even for the weathering of the bedrock into small particles (now known to be caused in part by acids generated by bacteria).

I like these terms, for they do away with false separations

of the so-called living and nonliving, and they show a good advance from the NPK mentality which seems to have viewed the soil as essentially dead. Plants and animals cannot eat lifeless minerals. But a miracle of plant life is its ability—not only aboveground in the green leaf, but also below ground in the mystery of the dark—to transmute soil materials, both organic and inorganic, into living sources of energy and food.

Learning About Soil

Before going on to say what I liked learning about the soil and its millions of beneficial

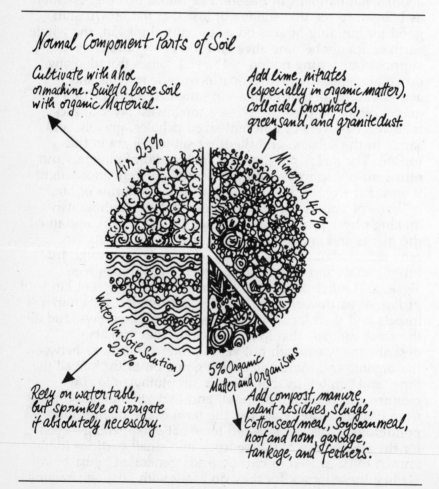

Normal Component Parts of Soil

Cultivate with a hoe or machine. Build a loose soil with organic Material.

Add lime, nitrates (especially in organic matter), colloidal phosphates, green sand, and granite dust.

Air 25%

Minerals 45%

Water (in Soil Solution) 25%

Rely on water table, but sprinkle or irrigate if absolutely necessary.

5% Organic Matter and Organisms

Add compost, manure, plant residues, sludge, cottonseed meal, soybean meal, hoof and horn, garbage, tankage, and feathers.

bacteria and fungi, and the chemical reactions they promote in the cycles of soil life, I am going to stall a minute for
a few words about the two ways there are of learning, and
the two kinds of enjoyment you get out of it.

The first is learning how to do something that will work. It
is somewhat superficial, but very satisfying to the gardener
when it brings results. The second kind of learning involves
analysis and probing, takes a lot longer, and brings understanding and feelings of clarity and wonder that are pleasur-
able and reassuring. You learn why it works.

The first kind is ancient, persistent, perennial, and quite
satisfactory for many gardening situations. For instance,
when it is a question of how deep certain bulbs should be
planted, you can consult a chart with diagrammatic sketches

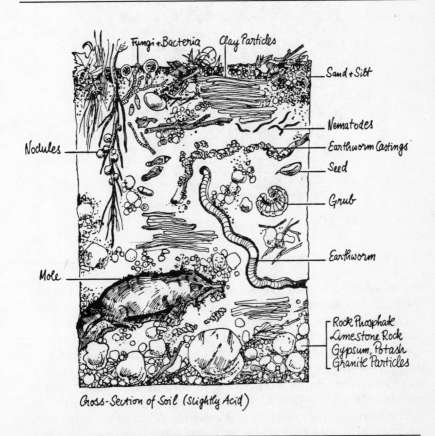

Cross-Section of Soil (Slightly Acid)

of the bulbs of crocus, narcissus, tulip, and so on, with marks showing whether they should be planted at 3, 5, 7, or 9 inches. As a novice gardener you go ahead and do what you are told, and chances are it will turn out well. You simply put your trust in the chart and have no temptation to do otherwise. You rarely stop to ask yourself or anyone

Wire Cage around Bulb

else why. You instinctively know, of course, that the size of the bulb has something to do with it.

When it comes to questions of preparing the soil and of controlling pests that come to attack these bulbs once they are in the ground, however, you seek the kind of learning that gives you explanations. This learning may even change your attitudes. Bulbs are inviting to certain little pests. Some people rely on the first kind of learning and do what an advertiser tells them to do: Use poison. As organic gardeners we have attitudes that make us resist advice to use fast-working, hard chemicals because we want our own foods clean, and a clean world for all living things from birds to bacteria (and humans who might be affected by the poisons). We are glad to learn that wire cages fastened around the bulbs before planting will deter mice and perhaps gophers, for they turn out to be the pests.

As a novice you may not yet have had experience with a wire cage or its good results, but you can see the reason for it because a mechanical barrier of fine enough mesh will of course repel any little animal. You have already heard about the need for air in the soil, seen people scratch it open to let air in, and you can understand that alleyways made by mice, gophers, shrews, moles, and earthworms are good things to have—so why kill these animals with poisons? And why chance killing any of the beneficial microorganisms?

More complicated are the reasons you learn for having organic matter in the soil. When you hear it said that you should put a lot of it into your garden soil, and accept the statement that it is good for the soil and the plants, a few first reasons are obvious—that bulky, airy stems and straw make the soil lighter, the drainage better, and create room for roots and worms to get through. A hard-packed, clayey soil clearly does not make room. You can see that spongy leaves, manure, and buried peanut shells will take up and hold water a lot better than a hard soil where gullies form instead. And you probably respond to the ethical appeal and the large reason that humans should return to the soil whatever they have taken from it, so it can cycle again and not be lost to the sea. If you are gardening where sprays and chemical fertilizers have been heavily used, it will help the vitality of the soil to add some of the inoculant powder sold to put in the soil when you plant legumes. It will contain many of the rhizobial bacteria which can fix nitrogen and prepare it for use by plants.

There are many other good reasons for having organic material in the soil, and the explanations are rather long, complicated, and biochemical. If all that follows is more than you ever wanted to know about what goes on, skip the rest of this chapter and go to the next chapter, which will invite you to do what you are told about planting, growing, harvesting, and cooking vegetables, herbs, weeds, and berries. For those who want to look into some of the whys and wherefores, read on.

The Beneficial
Microorganisms

We have known for more than
a hundred years that armies of beneficial bacteria and other
microorganisms are essential contributors to the life cycles
that keep plants alive and thriving. Soil must support them
and take part in the symbiotic relationships among plants
and bacteria, fungi, larvae, molds and their antibiotics,
worms and robins, moles, wasps, and many other creatures. Soil harbors hydrogen, hydroxyl, calcium, many other
ions, nitrates, phosphates, and many other chemicals, as
well as proteins, enzymes, and numerous other organic
materials. As a gardener you influence and try to enhance
all these interrelations and the conditions of air, water, and
warmth that favor both microorganisms and plant growth.

If your soil feels smooth, soft, and slightly oily, and if its
pH is not too acid or too alkaline, you know you already
have a good start. Unfortunately, soil tests are often gov-
erned by a chemical attitude to the soil that concentrates on
the mineral content. Tests don't tell you what bacteria you
need to convert nitrogen to usable nitrates, or whether you
need fungi for the healthy plant-fungus relation (called
mycorrhizal association) that provides a remarkable exchange of nutrients—the plant gives carbohydrates to the
fungus and the fungus gives proteins to the plant. The
fungus grows up between the cells of the root to bring this
about. It does not kill the plant or parasitize it either.
Blueberries, for example, depend on mycorrhizal association,
not root hairs.

Most good soil-test reports do tell you whether you need
to add lime or organic matter to lighten your soil structure.
Where there is plenty of manure and vegetable matter
subject to decay, there will be organisms multiplying to
take care of it. There will be both the bacteria that don't need
oxygen and those that do, including the indispensable
nitrogen-fixing ones whose activities provide much of the
nitrogen that plants use. This kind of beneficial bacteria
you can buy if you want to, though I don't know whether
anyone's soil-test report ever advised it. They are called
activators, or inoculants, and are sold sometimes by seed
companies along with the legumes that have nodules in
which these bacteria work. (See page 135.) In a good soil
there might be billions of bacteria in a pound of dirt, and

108

they have the capacity to multiply rapidly.

These billions of bacteria and other soil organisms feed on dead materials. Under the ground they prey mostly on dead plant materials, but also on dead animal organisms, most of them microscopic. Occasionally other species of bacteria, fungi, and some of the little nematode worms attack the living higher plants, but they are minor compared to the many others who act on soil materials, converting them to plant nutrients. Other predatory nematodes are now available to buy as pest controls for the attacking nematodes. Organic gardeners say you also need earthworms and the protective ladybugs, lacewings, and praying mantises, all available from many seed companies. Anyone will tell you that you need bees and birds to keep the cycles going that provide for the needs of the soil and the plants.

Scientists now know that the bacteria need roots, for they also use the organic foods that ooze out of the roots during their processes of metabolism. These interdependencies between higher and lower plants, among trees, flowers, and vegetables and bacteria or fungi, are the main reasons why Sir Albert Howard and his followers have all been so reluctant to hazard putting nonorganic substances into the soil without understanding their full effect. It is not a simple matter of putting in one shot to hit one target. If you touch off one reaction in the soil, it may lead to a hundred (or eventually even a hundred thousand) others.

The Soil Air and Soil Water

Soil scientists have not yet shown conclusively what nonorganic substances do to the soil air and soil water, or what acid rain is actually doing to them. But they do know that the oxygen content of the soil atmosphere is essential for the metabolism of almost all soil life, for the exchange of carbon dioxide and nitrogen in the respiration of the roots of plants, and for nearly all the chemical reactions that go on in the soil water that films all soil particles and flows through the soil, touching all the minerals, all the organisms, and carrying everything into solution that will dissolve. Soil oxygen is necessary for the conversion of minerals into the salts that plants can use. Soil air also brings in some of the atmospheric nitrogen that is essential for bacterial conversion to ammonia, then nitrites, then to the nitrates which are available to plants. It circulates the sulfur dioxide, carbon dioxide, and some of the hydrogen that take part in other reactions, and opens pathways for roots to find their way to nutrients, and to aerate the soil solution. Rain enters, and when the soil solution dries up or leaches out, the air comes in again to fill the spaces. The soil solution is of course essential to transport nutrients. It is usually slightly acid compared to plain water, and this helps make it capable of aiding many chemical exchanges, including eating away rock minerals in the soil.

The minerals are the silicates, phosphates, potassium and calcium compounds, magnesium salts, and dozens of others. To the chemically minded these soil components are of prime importance. To organic gardeners they come second, because no chemical reactions occur at all without the aid sooner or later of living biological agents.

The Liebig Analysis

Actually such distinctions are merely academic, for the events of the soil are cyclic, or rather in a network, and all parts are needed for a plant to thrive or grow at all. When the chemical events in the soil were first discovered in the early nineteenth century, people jumped to the conclusion that the mineral content and the chemical reactions were the whole story. They threw over the long-honored theory that it was humus which made plants grow, and rushed to adopt the new notions. When German chemist Baron Justus von Liebig came forth with the theory that soil is chemicals, this had a potent effect on agricultural circles, especially in England, where converts to the theory formed hundreds of farmers' clubs to study soil chemistry.

What appealed to everyone was the clarity and simplicity of Liebig's notion that what plants needed was simply nitrogen, phosphorus, and potassium—N, P, and K. He demonstrated this by burning a plant, analyzing the ash, and stating his findings as mainly phosphorus and potassium. He said the third component, the nitrogen, had gone off into the air. Large deposits of phosphates and muriate of potash were opened up in Germany at about the same time, and the new owners vigorously supported this new idea. If farmers and gardeners would buy these salts and nitrates, all the needs of their plants would be filled, Liebig and the sales personnel claimed. These, not manure or humus, were what plants essentially needed, he said. Scientists had not yet discovered bacteria, or that there were bacteria in manure and humus as essential as the nitrogen in it.

Soon a demonstration station was founded at Rothamsted in England, and it conducted experiments for many years to support these claims of the chemical nature of the soil. From that day to this, many English and many Americans have believed that plant life, which farmers and scientists for centuries had thought of as a mysterious complex process, was really a neat, simple, chemical process, easy to understand and control by applications of N, P, and K.

But old-time, conventional horticulturists and estate gardeners, as well as various plant scientists, began to object. Out of their objections has arisen the organic gardening movement, especially out of the objections of Sir Alfred Howard at the time of his very practical findings about soil in India. Sir Albert and the leaders of the organic gardening movements in England and this country have attacked the logic of Liebig's thinking that since N, P, and K were the main constituents of the plant, all it would need as food to make it grow would be nitrogen, phosphorus, and potash. "Now, if the human body is burned up, its ash will be found to be similarly rich in these chemicals," wrote the late J. I. Rodale, founder of the organic gardening press, "but does that mean that we should take it in chemical form? Of course not. We get our N, P, and K in ham and eggs and in vegetable soup. In the same manner, the soil should secure its NPK from living, organic foods, not from dead chemicals." Liebig's way of approaching plant physiology has seemed to many of us to be dead, lifeless, and wrong. We feel that analyzing after the plant is killed and burned is neglectful of practically all the living factors. Macabre as it may seem to us, many forces in England's rapidly industrializing society in the 1840s made the public of that day all too eager to adopt a view of a plant's requirements in terms of inert and simplistic chemistry. It made a plant seem like one of their new machines, and it spurred them on to invest more and more machines to plow, drill, harvest, and spread the new chemical fertilizers to manage the plant "machine."

It also changed agriculture and horticulture from an art to a commercial enterprise, and shifted the emphasis from quality to quantity. Once the machinery was there, it had to be used, and the spiral began. Machinery led to monoculture; monoculture led to feasts for pests; pests led to pesticides. Pesticides soon led to resistant pests, and then the hybridizing of plants that must have pesticides. Pests learn to go for new hybrids, and trouble results again. Rodale commented, more than twenty years ago, "It is exceedingly dangerous to operate with only 99.99 percent of a formula." Today the effects of residues of many hard pesticides and of mercury on living tissues are known by nearly everybody, and people are aware now, as never before, of the importance of one part per million, or even one one-hundredth of a part per million when it comes to the cause of illness or poison, or to the cause of health and well-being of living things. The tiniest trace of cobalt deficiency in the soil can cause plant trouble; minute soil deficiencies of iodine in a community can cause goiter in humans. It is only in recent years that "sustainable" (or organic) agriculture has been adopted by the government as a desirable goal.

Calcium

All trace elements in the soil are essential, as are the more plentiful elements such as calcium, which leaches out and has to be replaced in many soils by liming when people disturb the soil.

Calcitic and dolomitic limestone are used; they both derive from sea salts, or the ancient shells and bones of prehistoric creatures deposited on ocean bottoms before the continents were formed. The calcium in your bones, in your garden, and in the lettuce or broccoli you ate yesterday has been cycling in and out of the water, soil, plants, and animals in nature's ecosystem since those presedimentary eras. To bring back a leached-out calcium content, organic gardeners prefer dolomitic limestone because it dissolves slowly and also has a valuable magnesium salt (needed for chlorophyll), as well as the calcium salts. Your plants need calcium for the cellulose in their cell walls, and the soil needs it for texture and for the ion exchange that is the basis of all biochemical events in the soil. And we know that humans and other animals need it all their lives.

112

Test your soil for calcium, for if your composting and fertilizing programs involve high-nitrogen materials such as lots of green grass clippings, pea or bean plants, or leaves, you may need to add lime to help slow down excessive releases of nitric acid. This acid would inhibit the nitrogen-fixing bacteria, and the garden would suffer. The soil becomes acid when the calcium ions are replaced by hydrogen ions, or rather when too many are replaced. The calcium ions leach out, leaving the acid hydrogen ions to dominate. Then you have acid soil. In humid, temperate climates like the Northeast's, this happens a great deal, so we must be wary and put on lime when it's needed. There can also be an increase of toxic aluminum ions. Acid rain probably has the same effect. And aluminum that gets into our food is dangerous. Its poisonous effect has been thought to be a probable cause of Alzheimer's disease.

You are lucky if you have limestone deposits on your land, or a cave with stalagmites. Both are fine sources of calcium.

Phosphorus

The soil must have phosphorus, which is also a building block in all organisms. Unfortunately, many soils are low in this nutrient, and we consume and flush away tons of it that were in grain, milk, and meat. Rock phosphates in pulverized form are the fertilizers organic gardeners use to return phosphorus to the soil. They prefer it in this form to superphosphate, which has had sulfuric acid added to it. Superphosphate makes the phosphorus rapidly available for plant use, but it may leave a residue of calcium sulfate.

In addition to rock phosphates you can get colloidal phosphates, but if you decide on these you have to use half again as much to get the same amount of phosphoric acid into your soil. (Mix it with manure, and apply 10 to 15 pounds per 100 square feet in both spring and fall.) Before the present sources of phosphates were found in Florida, Tennessee, Nevada, and the German mines, bones were used to satisfy the demand for calcium and phosphate fertilizers. Old Liebig complained in his day that England with her craving for fertilizers was robbing the graves of battlefields, in Sicily, the Crimea, even Waterloo, to use up, flush out, and "squander down her sewers to the sea."

Potassium

A good potassium or potash (K_2O) supply is necessary for fine strong plant growth, for the transformation and transport of materials that are made into sugars, and to aid maturation and seed production. Potash deficiency means weak cell walls, weak stems, and slow photosynthesis. (One example you might see in your garden is the cucumber that stays narrow at the stem end, but bulgy at the flower end. If you see this, add a good mixed compost. Also spread some extra wood ashes, and mulch with buckwheat straw, dried cow manure, or alfalfa hay. Or spread greensand and granite dust.) Greensand, an iron-potassium silicate from under the sea, contains many nutrients, including 6 to 7 percent potassium. The related green glauconite, like kitty litter, has clay particles that absorb and store quantities of water. Granite dust, from quarries and stonecutters (or in a product from Georgia called Hybrotite), can provide from 3 percent to a whopping 11 percent of potassium. These dusts also contain feldspar and mica. They are cheap, long-lasting, and without bothersome residues. Apply at the rate of 20 pounds per 100 square feet, preferably in the spring. Though potassium is already plentiful in the soil, without aid, plants can get only 1 percent of it.

Summary of Mineral Supplements

The four sources of natural mineral fertilizers that appeal to organic gardeners, then, are rock phosphates, colloidal phosphates, greensand, and granite dust. Add them as I have said to manure and compost, keep air in your soil, give it good drainage, and protect it from drought. Then you are well on your way to excellent loam soil—if it has enough nitrogen.

Nitrogen

Nitrogen, the third major nutrient (which is usually listed first), is derived almost exclusively from organic matter, dead or alive. You have a good start or a bad start with nitrogen depending on where you live: If you are in a prairie state, the soil is still rich and high in organic content, with an average of 4 tons per acre down to a depth of 3 feet or more. If you live in the

114

Southeast, however, you may have only 1 ton per acre, and in the Northeast little more than that where the leaching and erosion have been considerable. The air over every acre of land contains tons of unusable nitrogen, maybe 80 percent of the air.

Almost every cycle in the soil-nutrient process depends on the nitrogen cycle, which depends on two kinds of bacteria that change the nitrogen compounds into forms that plants can take up and use. The sequence is N to NH to NO_2 to NO_3, the usable nitrate.

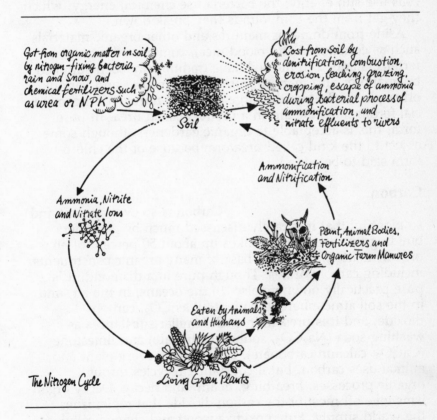

Got from organic matter in soil by nitrogen-fixing bacteria, rain and snow, and chemical fertilizers such as urea or NPK

Lost from soil by denitrification, combustion, erosion, leaching, grazing, cropping, escape of ammonia during bacterial process of ammonification, and nitrate effluents to rivers

Soil

Ammonification and Nitrification

Ammonia, Nitrite and Nitrate Ions

Plant, Animal Bodies, Fertilizers and Organic Farm Manures

Eaten by Animals and Humans

The Nitrogen Cycle

Living Green Plants

The bacteria living in the nodules on the roots of legumes, such as clover, peas, or beans, are capable of combining nitrogen with the carbohydrates they get from the legume plant to form proteins with the energy they use coming from the carbohydrates. This produces enough nitrogen compounds for both bacterial and plant use, probably as amino acids. This happens only when two such organisms as higher plants and bacteria are involved.

Aside from these symbiotic bacteria, there are free-living ones (both aerobic and anaerobic) which transform up to 40 pounds per acre of the carbohydrates from organic materials to proteins. And some bacteria break down proteins, form ammonia, and then the nitrites. Others then form nitrates, which are used by plants. When they manufacture food from raw materials, these bacteria are mysterious and potent as the cells in the green leaf which make food there. Those cells use sun energy; the bacteria use chemical energy, which they get from the compounds they break down.

Aside from domestic manures and other organic materials such as cottonseed and blood meal, commercial nitrate fertilizers added to the soil have traditionally been supplied by guano or bird manure from South America and various other places. Today, the large source of nitrogen for commercial fertilizers is the air, in a product called urea. In pure form, this is acceptable to organic gardeners, though some object to the kind called ureaform because of the chloroform said to be added.

Carbon

Carbon is so ever-present and so plentiful that it is rarely discussed much by gardeners building up their soil. It makes up about 50 percent of all organic matter, and is the base of many organic constituents, including carbohydrates. Though pure in a diamond, it is pure practically nowhere else. In the oceans, in the air, and in the soil atmosphere it is plentiful as CO_2, carbon dioxide, and it is present in such familiar substances as washing soda (Na_2CO_3, sodium carbonate) and limestone ($CaCO_3$, calcium carbonate). Every cell of every plant and animal uses carbon, but it constantly recycles through organic processes, breathing, death, and decay. Decay organisms give off most of the carbon dioxide that replenishes the world supply. Fungi oxidize wood and change cellulose to sugar, and then use up the sugar for their own respiration. So gradually wood turns to carbon dioxide and water. And, of course, the leaves of plants as they respire are another major source of carbon dioxide.

Sulfur and magnesium are the other two more or less major elements in the soil. They are needed for plant

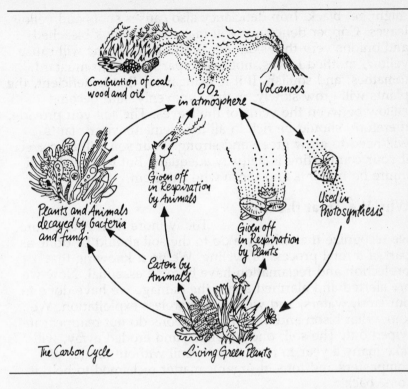

Combustion of coal, wood and oil

CO_2 in atmosphere

Volcanoes

Given off in Respiration by Animals

Used in Photosynthesis

Plants and Animals decayed by Bacteria and fungi

Given off in Respiration by Plants

Eaten by Animals

The Carbon Cycle

Living Green Plants

structure, both as an element in the plant cell (magnesium) and as a process aid (sulfur). Magnesium, in fact, is the central atom of each chlorophyll molecule.

Trace Elements

The trace elements in salts of manganese, zinc, copper, iron, boron, molybdenum, and sometimes cobalt, iodine, and fluorine, as needed by plants in very small amounts, are found in nature in manures, humus, and all sorts of organic wastes. They are one good reason these materials are used by organic gardeners for recycling soil components from one organic form to another.

In the lab or on your windowsill, deficiencies of trace elements in your plants are easy to spot, but outdoors in the average composted garden you are likely to miss them. Celery deficient in boron will have brownish spots, beets will get mushy or corky, cauliflower will be stunted and hollow-stemmed. The tip of the growing stem of tomatoes

117

might get black. Iron deficiency also causes spots and yellow leaves. Copper deficiency will make lettuce look bleached and onions very thin-skinned. A shortage of zinc will cause yellow, mottled leaves, noticeable particularly in mustard, tomatoes, and squash. If it is manganese that is deficient, the plants will grow slowly, mature unevenly, and become yellow between the veins of the leaves. The soil you provide, therefore, should be rich in all the elements your plants will need to grow green and strong. Your soil will be correct if your composting is halfway adequate. But too much will injure both plants and those who eat them.

Why We Treat the Soil

Today more than ever before we recognize that what we do to the soil should be done as part of a total process of cycling. We do it knowing that protection and reclamation have become essential. Now we are alerted and alarmed about the damage we have done to our land, waters, and wildlife by careless exploitation. We know that bison and passenger pigeons do not reappear if wiped out. The soil, once depleted and eroded away, will take many a year to regain its topsoil without armies of composters and tons of organic matter reclaimed to help it come back.

I think all this enters into the desire of gardeners and the new conservationists to do something more sensible and more moral with the land. A busy and conscientious gardener or farmer can aid in the reclamation of topsoil and, aside from the benefits of better food for the family, can feel that he or she is entering the process and contributing to narrowing the downward path of planetary degradation. The Food Security Act of 1985 includes a new emphasis on reclamation of erodable lands, with prohibitions and inducements for farmers to comply with.

We are also aware that one of the terrible outcomes of depleting the soil are the impoverished and ill-nourished farmers and their families who have had to remain on worn-out land. The rundown conditions resulting from thoughtless, ignorant, or avaricious practices rarely if ever have been followed in America by efforts to restore what was lost, let alone to prevent its happening again. People just moved on; and as you can see when you cross the country, there are many places where the subsoil has actually come to the surface. The rich virgin topsoil disappears, its nitrogen content gone down to about zero, the mineral nutrients nearly exhausted, and the microbial life quite vanished. We know that people trying to subsist on such soils are appallingly malnourished. Their plants achieve no proper size, and are very deficient in proteins, vitamins, and other essential sources of nourishment.

What a Plant Gives to the Soil

A good healthy plant will keep on making and providing organic nutrients for itself and for the soil from its roots. It makes sugars, carbohydrates, and starches. The simple sugar made in the leaf builds to oils, and when nitrogen is added it builds to amino acids and then proteins. Not sent out into the soil from the roots are the cellulose and woody lignin fibers. All of these and some of the other products such as vitamins, enzymes, gums, even alkaloids, are necessary for plant, animal, and soil life. The enzymes, vitamins, and antibiotics come and go, back and forth. In the patterns of interdependence, for instance, soil bacteria evidently supply vitamins as well as proteins to plants, and such molds as the penicilliums provide the antibiotics. In our climates these thousands of soil processes all transpire in the short range of temperatures between 40° and 100° F.

The New Analysis

Today when scientists dry out plants and reduce them by a dehydrating process different from old Liebig's simple burning, they find that 95 percent of the dry weight of a plant is material that has been organically synthesized. Half of that is carbon. They also analyze sap as it comes up the stem from the soil solution and find that its mineral content is only .03 percent to .13 percent of the total. Many now believe that the actual role of these minerals is to be catalyzers in the organic processes. The sap also contains organic compounds that it takes up from the soil, about as many again as the minerals.

Long before all these discoveries were made about the living elements in the soil, and long before antibiotics or enzymes were thought of, the battle was raging rather bitterly between the NPK advocates and the organic gardening advocates. One side said that chemical fertilization—and the pesticide poisons it and other agricultural practices necessitate—is bad for the cycles of life in the soil. The other side said that soil exhaustion by cropping, leaching, erosion, and so on makes it obligatory to replenish the losses with quick-acting supplies so farmers can feed livestock and people. Farmers know that, unless they're paid not to use their soil to raise crops, up to a point they can make bigger, faster profits from using nitrogen fertilizers (or the so-called complete NPK fertilizers). Published for these farmers in books such as the United States Department of Agriculture yearbooks are charts indicating the exact points of diminishing return—when it is no longer economically feasible to add another ounce of nitrogen on the corn crop, for instance. The contention you also can hear is that a world food supply would never be possible without pesticides. (See chapter 7.)

The agonies that organic farmers and gardeners began to have in the early part of this century when they saw the disappearance of earthworms, for instance, from artificially fertilized plots are now agonies ten times worse since the introduction and use of millions of tons of pesticide poisons. They deplore monoculture and the spiral of chemically grown crops needing sprays, needing new varieties, and so on. The southern field-corn blight in the Midwest in the 1970s showed exactly what can happen. We can only wish that these unfortunate farmers had used organic methods such as composting, mulching, rotating, and organic sprays where needed. But corn is a fast-money crop, and even the wisdom of rotating has all too often been neglected. The farmers say that their county extension agents, schooled only for corn in those areas, did suggest leaving stubble for organic matter. This was more of a bane than boon when the infestation came from the South and began to spread.

Perhaps, also, the period of distress led to further reconsideration of the methods of rotating, fertilizing, and health protection to be used by the farmers and gardeners who want good crops and a healthy environment for them, as well as safeguards for their economic security.

One Ray of Hope

In recent years the experts at most agricultural schools in this country are again stressing

120

that organic matter in the soil is good for several reasons. They remind farmers that it granulates the soil particles, making a loose and friable structure; that it is a major source of nitrogen; that it increases the soil's capacity to hold water and helps to regulate the plant's waterholding capacity and the flow of the soil solution. They also teach that organic matter in the soil is the main energy source for the soil organisms, and that without it biochemical action in the soil would stop. They point out that the humus particles hold both water and nutrient ions (and can do it better than the clay particles, which also promote ion-exchange), noting the fact that humus, or organic matter, in the soil contributes in essential ways to the soil chemistry. In addition, it produces, through the action of the bacteria that live in it and work it, that odd gelatinous substance which makes the lumping of soil aggregates possible. "Indeed it can even be said that practically all natural soil reactions are directly or indirectly biochemical in nature," is the cautious word of the experts. The focus will be on the reduction of residues to humus by soil microorganisms, and the consequent colloidal particles as major controllers of both chemical and physical properties of the soil. This has led to what the experts call the "colloidobiological viewpoint."

Let us rejoice that the agricultural schools will take this stand, and that a leading textbook used at many universities now expresses it.

CHAPTER 6

Vegetables, Herbs, and Wild Plants

So far my message has been: Know your yard and what's in it, how all things cycle, and what they need. Also make compost, understand it, and use it and other organic materials for the sake of a good soil, good nutrient cycles, and a well-protected and healthy garden.

This chapter will now get down to details about your vegetable garden. I will also recommend in my alphabetical list some useful flowers, weeds, beneficial insects, herbs, and recipes, because I think all those things go together to make you and your garden organically interdependent. Here and there I'll recommend biological controls, dusts, sprays, birds, and pest traps to use so your life as a gardener will be happier.

I do not want to entice you into any belief that gardening is foolproof. With luck and good mulch, it can be fairly easy, as Ruth Stout was fond of preaching; but gardeners can never get the idea that they have mastered the tricks, or that they absolutely know what they are doing. With ingenuity and care, you can grow a fine garden and probably achieve the second best; but who ever grew the absolute best? I am reminded of the sentence used by the humble and pious Dr. Ambroise Paré, the surgeon who traveled with the sixteenth-century French army caring for the wounded. After each episode he narrated, he added: "I dressed him and God cured him." Gardeners can but hope for equal success in the dressing of their gardens.

You know you want to grow good vegetables and that the freshest, young vegetables are not only the most delicious you can have, but also the most healthful, especially if picked just before sundown at the end of a sunny day.

Studies of vitamin C and other nutrients in leaf vegetables

and in mulberry leaves picked for silkworms have revealed that picking leaves in the late afternoon or at dusk is indeed the scientifically correct time for harvest. Nutrition values are highest then. Vitamin C can be 20 percent higher in the leaves of plants in the evening than it is early in the day. Proteins and sugars are also in larger supply after a whole day of sun, and especially at the end of a sunny spell of weather.

The younger the plant when harvested for food, the higher the protein proportion as compared to the carbohydrate. And the lower is the cellulose roughage. You have to grow your own plants to get young ones. And besides, a vigorous young plant, not yet at the age of being senescent, is a disease-resistant, pest-resistant plant. It does not need to be sprayed. Usually it is only the weaklings that get pests.

Actually, aging of plants in the sense of their getting to the stage of becoming pest-susceptible is not just a matter of a number of days. Vegetable plants allowed to stay unthinned and crowded will get old and sick in a very short time if there is a rainy or moist, cloudy spell. When it's wet the fungi get in, and the earwigs and slugs, and you can have a fine mess on your hands in a few days.

It will be a gooey mess at first, and then when the rain stops and the sun comes out, you will have brown, dead, no-good lettuce, for example, wherever there was crowding and decay. Another cause for susceptibility can be excessive dryness, then starvation.

Along with this kind of aging goes stunting, and it, too, can come from neglect of thinning. Improperly thinned carrots or radishes, for example, will be skinny, stunted little plants with no root development to speak of, or with crooked and distorted roots. In either condition they, too, are subject to attack by pests that come to bite into any warped or abnormal spot they find. Once pests find a welcoming environment, they can multiply and then really cause trouble.

A clean garden, properly thinned and aired—if the soil is well composted and rich with plenty of organic matter in it—is really and truly more likely to be a healthy garden. Organic gardeners are repeatedly testifying to this. The microorganisms in rich soil prefer dead organic matter first in their diet when they can get it, and so they clean out those materials and leave your live plants alone. Slugs and snails also prefer to live on dead plant matter, attacking only the living parts of plants after dead materials have become scarce. (Pick off dead leaves and toss them aside for traps.) Earthworms eat as much organic matter in the soil as they can get, and there are many more scavengers who stay in their place as long as there is the food they require. Good mulching also helps.

This is why we use biological aids and controls so as not to harm such useful creatures.

You can grow nearly the best vegetables in the world and then ruin them by the way you cook them, or the way you maltreat them before cooking. If you want to preserve the high quality you have attained by your good growing methods in the garden, study what happens to the original food values in vegetables from heat, light, pressure, seasonings, and milk or water.

We have all heard that freshly picked vegetables, rushed to the oil, boiling water, or milk, and cooked a very short time, are the best vegetables. We judge this to be so because we know they taste better that way.

Now scientists have studied all the changes and have assured us that the vitamin content, as well as the proteins, sugars, and minerals, are all protected by methods that also favor a better-tasting vegetable. For instance, if vegetables, after picking, are left in the light and warmth, they lose half their vitamin C content and much of their folic acid and vitamin B in a few hours. It is only sensible, therefore, to go to the garden with a paper bag or other dark container and pop the vegetables right in it. And only sensible to put the bag in the refrigerator as soon as you get back to the kitchen. Never soak. If you do, you may lose 75 to 100 percent of the sugars, minerals, and water-soluble vitamins. If you have chopped or peeled the vegetables, you stand a chance to lose all three, whether you cook the vegetables or not. So go easy on peeling and chopping. The aromatic oils are lost too, as you remember from the taste of the gray, overcooked peeled vegetables that you have eaten in the past. Even letting vegetables sit for a few minutes drenched in the water you washed them in will leach out good flavors and good nutrients. Always wipe or whirl vegetables in the air immediately after washing them. If you don't whirl, the water that clings to them will dissolve out the sugars, iron, much of the vitamin C, and other nutrients. Then chill, unless you are putting them right into the oil in the pot, or the oil of your salad dressing.

Do not salt. Salt draws out the moisture and more of the dissolved vitamins and minerals. Salted spinach will lose nearly 50 percent of its iron, something which Popeye never told us. Braise vegetables in as little water as possible, and save every bit of cooking juice from vegetables to use in sauces, soups, and drinks.

A good method (taken from old Japanese and Chinese practices) is to sauté vegetables in a little soy oil, corn oil, peanut oil, or stock, simmer them slowly in the oil and their own juice, and add only enough water or more stock to keep them from burning. Since oxygen depletes the vitamin C content, before you put the vegetables into the oiled, preheated pot, you can add a few tablespoons of hot or cold water to replace the oxygen inside the pot by steam. Contact with oxygen will then be cut by both the oil and the steam, so loss of vitamin C is reduced. If you have hard water, add a drop or two of vinegar or lemon juice to reduce the alkali. Better still, cook your vegetables in milk, at about 200° F, for proteins combine with both acids and alkalis. Or use soybean cooking liquid, for that is protein, too. The vegetables will taste very mild and pleasant, and you will have more of an urge to keep the cooking liquid for soup. Keep a lid on the steaming vegetables while cooking, and keep the heat low.

All this shows how you can save in the healthfulness, taste, and eventually cost of your food, for this method of cooking vegetables takes very little heat. (Savers of electricity, take note.) A pressure cooker, which is what I use, will give the same results. Put the vegetables into ¼ cup or less of hot water. Peas take about a half a minute after 15 pounds of pressure is reached; asparagus takes a minute; beans perhaps two minutes; and even hard things like soy grits or soaked wheat berries take only twenty or thirty minutes.

The top of a double boiler is probably even better. Have the water hot in the bottom part. Put a few tablespoons of oil and water, or oil, milk, and water in the top, add vegetables, and bring them to a boil over direct heat. Let them cook a few minutes so that the enzymes that change the nutriments are destroyed, and then return the top to the base of the double boiler and simmer until done.

Remember that after being heated through, vegetables do not need to go above 206° or 210° F to cook.

If you bake vegetables, presteam them for a few minutes to stop enzyme action and thus the loss of vitamin C. Leave on the peels and oil them if possible. When adding vegetables to stews, always have the stew juice hot first. Keep the lid on to prevent loss of steam and contact with oxygen.

If you do wish to cook shredded or cubed vegetables, chill them, then put them into hot oil, and sauté them quickly. Even people who do not like root vegetables find carrots, beets, and turnips very palatable if cooked this way. You can add milk or water, if you wish, or dip them in batter first.

For further flavoring, add a little more oil just before serving. The oil is better for you than butter or margarine. Corn, safflower, soy, olive oil, or a bit of homemade mayonnaise will do well. To cream vegetables, cook them in milk, and ten minutes before serving add a thin paste of flour rubbed into the milk in the proportion of 2 tablespoons to 1 cup. Do not let it boil. Vegetables recommended for slow cooking in milk include Jerusalem artichokes, asparagus, beets, carrots, celery, celeriac, spinach, snow peas, shredded string beans, kohlrabi, mushrooms, peas, cubed summer squash, and all greens, for their acid or bitter flavor always disappears if cooked in a protein food such as milk. Or make a cream sauce, and then simmer the greens in that for about eight minutes. In addition to those you are familiar with, try watercress, parsley, radish tops, endive or escarole, celery leaves, cauliflower leaves when young, broccoli leaves, kale, and the outer leaves of cabbage. Sorrel, Swiss chard, beets and beet tops, and turnip tops also do well in milk or cream sauce for gentling them. Or cook first in ¼ cup of milk and then add a little sour cream.

If you cook your food any old way, and throw half the nutriments down the drain, what is the use of going to all that trouble to grow high-quality vegetables in the first place? The least you can do if you think these methods are too fussy is to eat most of your fruits and vegetables raw.

Edible Weeds

Grow whatever herbs, berries, and edible flowers your land will permit, and leave room to cultivate some of the edible weeds which can make a nourishing, savory addition to your menus. Try winter cress, wild violets or garden violets, ostrich fern, twice-rinsed milkweed, mints, and Juneberry. Such classes of plants are grouped together in the following list for the reader's convenience, though an occasional outstanding culinary treat such as the daylily can be found in the main alphabetical list under its own letter. The dandelion, which is either wild or cultivated, can be found there in the main list, too, and the rose that is richest in vitamin C, *Rosa rugosa*. The standard vegetables that appeal to most gardeners as essentials for their larders are given fullest treatment; others get only a few lines for special interest or entertainment. The cross references here and there will help you find the things you are looking for. So will the index.

Ants

You will have ants in your garden, and you can value them for the hundreds of fruit fly and housefly larva that they eat, as well as caterpillars in orchards and some of the insects pests of the forests. Chinese orchardists like ants so much that they provide little bamboo highways for them from tree to tree. If you don't want these creatures to walk into your kitchen, plant mint and tansy by the door to drive them away.

Apples
Malus pyrus

Buy two- or three-year-old trees, standard, dwarf, or semidwarf. Do not plant on hardpan or gravelly subsoils, or near a night light, which prevents the tree's preparation for winter. Mulch for winter if the soil temperature is likely to go below 15° F.

The topsoil should be very fertile, dressed with lime, compost, and fish emulsion, and given plenty of earthworms. A legume cover crop around the trees helps, as does a year-round mulch. The planting location must be well drained, protected from harsh winds, and up from cold valley areas where the blossoms might be nipped in the spring. Also avoid any barriers that block the downhill flow of air. For cross-pollination you should plant two or more varieties. Jonathan, Delicious, and the cold-tolerant Lodi are especially good pollinators. Suitable varieties for colder

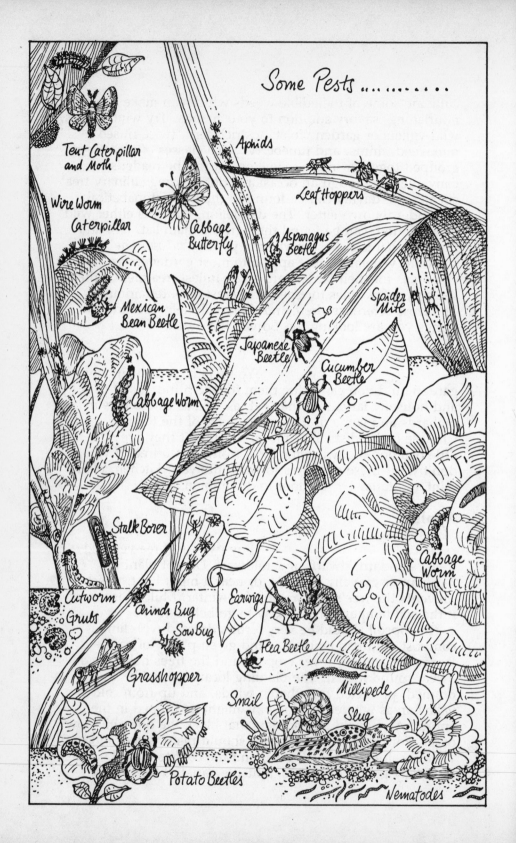

Some Pests ....

zones include Canadian McIntosh and others of the McIntosh type, Redwell, Imperial, and the very hardy Reid. For zones 3 and 4, Northern Spy, Cortland, Pound Sweet, Duchess Red, Honeygold, and the old Baldwin are possibilities. Farther south, good zones 5 to 7 choices would be Jonathan, Red and Golden Delicious, and the Winesap family, and on down to zone 8, Granny Smith. Stayman Winesap, however, is not a good pollinator. Lodi is good for early apples, Empire for mid-season, Cortland and Delicious for mid-to-late, and Delicious, Granny Smith, and Rome Beauty for late.

All these varieties come in standard, dwarf, and semidwarf sizes. There is also a new development (available from Miller Nurseries for certain varieties) called Compspur, a more compact version of semidwarf. You will be able to get both Red and Golden Delicious, Granny Smith, and the Winesaps, and probably more varieties of Compspur trees in the future. In this more compact version the apples grow on many of the short branches called spurs, and the yield is good and heavy. They are said to bear the second year after planting. People usually count on dwarf trees to bear in three to five years, and in general know that standard trees take eight to twelve years to bear.

Some gardeners prefer to plant in the fall after a summer's cover crop, in ground that has been prepared very thoroughly beforehand. Later, fertilize each tree once a year at the drip line (just under the ends of the branches all the way around the tree). Blood meal is recommended at the rate of 2-½ pounds per tree.

Since many apples tend to bear only in alternate years, it pays to thin the cluster of fruit after the June drop. Reduce the cluster to one per spur, being very careful not to injure the spur, and when you are picking pollinators be sure to select trees that will blossom at the same time, as suggested above.

If you spray, use only dormant oil spray of miscible oil and water, early in the spring before the buds come out. Catch the apple maggot fly with traps made of jars filled with one part blackstrap molasses to nine parts water, plus a yeast cake. Let this ripen 48 hours. Hang from a branch. Will catch 100 flies. One ounce of ryania in 2 gallons of water will sicken codling moths. Flush out borers with boiling water, or prick them with a wire. At all times practice stringent sanitation, and clear up absolutely all debris that might harbor disease or insects.

Test your soil once in a while, and if it's acid, apply 1 pound of lime and ½ pound of rock phosphate per tree. Avoid simple sod around your trees. Use alfalfa, first as a cover crop, then as a mulch. Try to keep the trees trimmed and well ventilated. Cut out suckers.

Make apple pan dowdy at least once a season, cider and apple wine if possible, and make apple butter. To make your own apple pectin for all jellies and jams, wash a pound or more of unripe apples, cut them into thin slices, and add a pint of water per pound. Boil slowly for about 15 minutes and then drain through cheesecloth or nylons and keep the juice. Reheat the pulp with another pint of water and boil 15 minutes. Let stand for at least 10 minutes, then drain. Mix the two juices. Now you have pectin, which can be used immediately with strawberries, pears, cherries, mulberries, blueberries, and elderberries—whatever you are preserving—or it can be cooled and saved for another day. It is especially useful for berries and fruits that do not jell well with their own pectin.

Apricots
Prunus Armeniaca

This is the fruit tree that kept the Hunzas healthy for sixteen centuries. Grow it if you can in your growing zone (zone 6 and warmer), or be bold in cooler zones and try it in a warmish microclimate at your place where there is a protected area. Try a place south of a white wall, which will warm that area to at least a zone or so warmer than zone 4 or 3. There are several nurseries that now offer much more cold-resistant varieties than have been previously available. Early Golden has been recommended for New York State, and Sweetpit from Gurney's is supposedly hardy to zone 3. Moor Park is the old standard variety dependable in the warmer zones. In California, Dwarf Early Golden is often planted. Since apricots are usually self-fertile, you only need one tree. Where it's cold, plant two. If the trees are dwarfs, plant two. Whatever the zone, plant young trees in deep, rich soil in a spot that will delay budding until after any danger of frost. The vitamin A and potassium contents of apricots are quite remarkable, especially in the fruit's dried and more concentrated state. In unsulphured dried apricots you'll get 14,000 I.U. of potassium and 1,830 mg of vitamin A per 100 grams.

Artemisia
Artemisia absinthium

This is wormwood; use it for a deterrent. Plant it along with camomile and spurge to fend off mice and moles; mix a spray in the blender of one part artemisia to ten parts water for weevils, and add half a clove of garlic for a spray for other pests. Remember that it's poisonous.

Artichoke, Globe
Cynara scolymus

Be faithful to it, in some fashion; it is a thistle-like but wonderful plant, needing lots and lots of room, usually on the West Coast. It should be tried on the Gulf Coast, too, and the Atlantic up to Massachusetts, but not inland. Perennial. Grows up to 5 feet given good soil well composted. In winter cover the crown with a bushel basket filled with leaves and manure. Start by buying two-year-old shoots or suckers. Clip off any dead leaves or roots before planting, and plant 6 inches deep. After two or three years of good heading, it may retreat. Propagate new shoots, or send away for more. Make rows 8 feet apart, and set plants 6 feet apart. Cut 1-½ inches below lowest bracts, just before flowers open, and don't expect during the first year or so that any besides the terminal bud will amount to much. Cook promptly after cutting, though this is one vegetable, being pretty tough, that does not lose very much nutritional value by standing. Clean a little under running water and pop into boiling water seasoned with juice of a lemon and cardamom seeds. Cook until a leaf pulls out easily (perhaps 25 minutes) and serve hot or cold with hollandaise, spiced mayonnaise, or French dressing. In early spring, for hors d'oeuvres, boil very small artichokes with a clove of garlic, a tablespoon of peppercorns, and ¼ cup of vinegar. Chill, then remove outer leaves and the choke. Fill with chopped egg mixed with mayonnaise and parsley, lightly salted or chopped shrimp, or crab with chive.

132

Artichoke, Jerusalem
Helianthus tuberosus

A great favorite with organic gardeners, the Jerusalem artichoke does best in a cold climate, but will grow almost anywhere. It is related to the common sunflower. One eats the roots, or rather the tubers, which have a nutty flavor. It is starchless, for it stores its carbohydrates as inulin and its sugar as levulose, not as starches and sugars. Provides good vitamins—thiamin and pantothenic acid—and potassium. Plant 2 feet apart in April or May and cultivate as you would potatoes. Harvest any time in the fall and right through the winter. Mulch well for both easy digging and protection in winter. Keep moist in a crisper or cool cellar after harvesting until you eat the tubers. Replant what is left over. You can grow 15 tons an acre, if you or your organic food store wants that many Jerusalem artichokes. (A good potato yield is 3 or 4 tons an acre.) They are free from disease and very prolific, will spread anywhere and could fill up your garden.

To cook: Boil and serve with herb butter made by mincing 1 teaspoon sweet basil, 1 teaspoon parsley, ⅓ teaspoon thyme, 1 shallot, 1 small clove garlic, ½ teaspoon grated lemon peel, a dash of cayenne pepper mixed with softened butter and rehardened. As usual, the best advice is to eat the vegetable raw and lose no vitamins. Scrub, peel off the dark spots if they bother you (or learn not to let them bother you), and serve with lemony mayonnaise.

Arugula
See Rockette, page 231.

Asparagus
Asparagus officinalis

There is nothing like the first sprouts of asparagus during the first days of spring, cooked within six minutes of picking, before the nutrients begin to depart. There is no sense cutting below the ground as commercial growers do. I feel the stalk, and break it just where the stem turns from hard to tender. If you do get some hard cuticle, you can slice it off just before cooking, but for maximum food benefit, do not peel and do not cut up. What tender tops, cut like this, you don't eat and freeze, send to your organic food store. Customers will be glad to get such a pure food produce with no waste.

Steam it standing up in a little water, or give it a few seconds in the pressure cooker. Have water boiling to save vitamin C. Pour asparagus cooking liquid over toast (save vitamins, proteins), add hollandaise or melted butter. Very rich in vitamin A: six stalks give 500 I.U., plus as much thiamin as an equal amount of rye bread or lean beef, and half as much B_{12} as spinach, but twice as much as whole wheat bread or Swiss chard. Vitamin C is 15 milligrams in six stalks, compared to 25 in a tablespoon of lemon juice. You need 70 (female) or 75 (male) milligrams a day, so asparagus is a good start for the day if you eat it for breakfast, as I do in the spring. Six stalks of asparagus also provide a goodly 160 milligrams of potassium. If you get totally bored with all other ways of serving asparagus, try the kind Alice B. Toklas once recommended. Tie the asparagus in a bundle, plunge it in boiling water for a few minutes, then leave it to steam for 6 to 8 minutes more. For a pound of asparagus, melt 4 tablespoons butter very slowly, add the cooked asparagus, still tied, and 4 tablespoons heavy cream. Turn so the asparagus gets coated. Do not stir. Put it on a plate, cut the string, add ½ cup of whipped cream with ½ teaspoon salt mixed in. Whiz to the table before the whipped cream melts. How does that sound? You are lucky if you have an old asparagus bed that is well limed and well weeded (which you can harvest for four or five weeks). A new bed shouldn't be harvested until the plants are three years old. For a new bed, if you start with seed, select a variety that is rust resistant, such as Martha Washington, an old favorite. Others available include Mary Washington, Roberts, Waltham, and Brock Imperial. Most gardeners start with two-year-old roots because growing from seed is difficult and takes three years before transplanting to a permanent bed. Set roots in trenches 12 inches deep and 12 inches wide, dug early in the spring, filled 4 inches with a very rich soil of well-rotted manure and compost dug into the bottom of the trench, and rained on at least once. Set roots in holes scooped out of this, about 18 inches apart. At first, sift 2 inches of soil over them and water them. As stalks grow, keep adding more rich, sifted loam, and water, about every week. Do not plant near trees and big shrubs. Weed, and lime yearly. Also manure well. For extra protection, use a winter cover crop of soybeans or cowpeas. Or plant these between the rows. Plant parsley, tomatoes, and rue over the bed for repellents. Be glad to have moles and skunks that eat Japanese beetle grubs. Plant white geraniums if those pests get in. Even the USDA now recommends no chemical pesticides because they kill off the normal parasites on the asparagus beetle. Permit the parasite to grow. If you keep hens, ducks, or guinea fowl, turn some onto the plot, and keep the house sparrows coming with chick feed and bread crumbs. Pick off spotted cucumber beetles, and dust plants with bone meal and rock phosphate (both good fertilizers, anyhow). If you see a diseased top (crooked, stunted), cut it off and burn it. It might have rust. To fend off the cucumber beetle, try planting zinnias, asters, and especially nasturtiums, all of which can be started indoors in early spring. Nasturtiums resent transplanting, so start them in peat pots, which you can move right into the asparagus bed. Grapes and white roses can be used to attract Japanese beetles away from your asparagus. These pests are easy to see on asparagus, so pick them off and drop them into a jar of water with a little kerosene or gasoline added.

Basil
See Herbs, pages 180–202.

Beans
Phaseolus, vicia and
Dolichos genera

Bush beans, green beans, string beans, snap beans, or whatever you call them are such favorites, and are so easily grown, that some people plant them six or seven times a summer—from late April to late July for a last fall crop. You need 2 pounds of bean seed for each 200 feet of row. The seeds are viable for three years, so save what you don't use. Most nurseries offer an inoculant of extra beneficial rhizobia bacteria, and I think you should order and add these bacteria, especially for the first year. A dollar package will treat 5 pounds of bean seeds. Many beans will boost the nitrogen you have in your soil, for they are legumes, and harbor beneficial bacteria in nodules on their roots. Sow in wide rows of 18 inches, or in single rows 18 to 30 inches apart and 1 to 2 inches deep, with a hill of garlic every 4 or 5 feet, at alternate spots from the garlic in the row opposite. If that's too much garlic for you, vary it with onions, shallots, leeks, or scallions, but garlic has the most antibiotics. These onion-family plants not only repel insects, they ward off woodchucks and rabbits, too, especially if planted around the edge of the garden.

For prettiness, and ease in picking, plant some wax beans and purple beans. In food value they are no different. Remember to cook them whole as soon as you pick them, to save nutrient values. Beans provide vitamins A, B, C, and riboflavin. We serve the purple ones raw as hors d'oeuvres, and get no complaints. As with other vegetables, there are more nutrients if eaten raw and if picked at the end of a sunny day. It is imperative to pick string beans before they are mature, when the seed is one-third grown or about one-fourth inch in diameter. If you get too many and there is not an organic food store that will take the extras, freeze them in late afternoon, preferably whole and as soon as picked. In warm weather, pick every day; when cooler, every few days. By frequent picking you make the season for each plant last longer. If all the beans on a plant mature at once, the bush gives up and dies.

This is why you get only one picking of the French Horticultural variety, those nice pinkish ones we call shell beans, which do mature all at once. I usually let the last picking of string beans go to full maturity, and save them for dried beans to make soup or to sprout, though soy or mung beans are really better for sprouts. The pods will get brittle right on the vine, and also, sometimes, get mildew. So pick them before they are fully dry, and spread them out on papers in the sun. Never let them get damp. A steam bath of three minutes will help to control weevils. Dry them quickly afterward.

Various pests and diseases might bother your beans, especially if you are not growing in soil that has been brought up to high fertility by humus and manure. One is bean rust, which will respond to a dusting of garlic powder or a spray of water and garlic juice. (See page 77.) This is also good for bean anthracnose and bacterial bean blight. The force of the garlic antibiotic is such that the University of California scientists use 1 part garlic to 20 of water, though this is much stronger than necessary, they say.

Try never to touch beans when they're wet; they bruise very easily, and diseases move right in on the wounded spots. Organic material to put on or in the soil to help prevent fungus attacks includes oat straw, mature soybean hay, and corn stover. Scientists at Beltsville, Maryland, have discovered that the streptomycetes that exude the antibiotics are especially attracted to the afflicted area by these particular organic materials. Such discoveries make the organic gardener who grows beans (and whatever else he or she wants to mulch with those straws) very happy, for they offer still another clear scientific reason for relying on the processes of nature instead of hard chemicals.

An old-fashioned cure for unwanted fungi, well understood before the days when scientists discovered antibiotics, is wood ashes. If mixed with lime and applied the minute a pest attack begins, they help.

Aphids can bother you, especially in dry weather. Get out the hose and turn it on the plants—or the undersides of the leaves if you can manage. Then use an onion-garlic spray on them. Plant nasturtiums among beans to control aphids. Strips of shiny aluminum foil on the ground beside the rows also befuddle aphids, and the strips do an extra job of reflecting and thus add to the light the beans get. Insecticidal soap helps control aphids, as do the predator insects ladybugs and lacewings.

If you get white flies and the brown curly leaves they cause, tear up the attacked bean bush immediately. Clean out all weeds such as mustard that might harbor them, and keep feeding compost. Garlic sprays help, as do pungent plants such as tansy, mint, and wild marjoram. Use yarrow, or the flower garden version, achillea, if you have no tansy.

Mexican bean beetles (brown, one-third inch, sixteen spots) can be annoying if they go for your bean buds and young pods. One thing to look forward to is that they won't attack your late beans, anyway. Go after these beetles every morning and pick them off by hand. Also pick off their egg clusters on the undersides of leaves. If the beetles get ahead of you, pull the plants up and bury them in your compost heap. Plant summer savory or nasturtiums, or move in some nasturtiums from a growing bed. Keep praying mantises, whose egg cases you can send for in the spring. Some have reported that planting potatoes nearby has a magical effect of repelling bean beetles. Easiest of all is to go back to the old standby garlic, and add a clove in each hill.

If you live in the South, you may have trouble from nematodes. For beans and all other garden plants, nematode enemies are controlled by marigolds—not only in the current year, but also for one or two years afterward. This means that you'll want to plant marigolds both for this year, where your sensitive plants will be, and also for the following year, where they will be in the future. Plow or dig them under.

Some of the recently favored varieties of green beans have been Provider, Contender, and Tenderette, as well as Blue Lake and Tendercrop. Burgundy and Royal Burgundy, or Royalty, are favorites for purple beans. For wax beans try Burpee's Brittlewax and the long-season Pencil Pod Wax. There is a bush Kentucky Wonder (57 days) that is only 18 inches tall. One gardener reported that his best beans were planted right in straw mulch, spaced three feet apart. He happened to plant cucumbers between, and that is a good suggestion for anyone. You not only get their antibiotic effects to go along with that of the marigolds, you also get shading and sun at the right periods, and provide ideal conditions for both plants through this arranged symbiosis. This gardener used no nitrogen fertilizer but nevertheless produced 200 bushels per acre of beans, with five pickings.

If you find you need a new recipe for string beans, heat 3 tablespoons of soy or olive oil in a frying pan and add ¼ cup capers, 1 crushed clove of garlic, and 4 cups of previously boiled or steamed string beans, with ½ teaspoon salt and ¼ teaspoon pepper. Toss them around until they are well mixed and warm. Top all with chopped parsley and chopped spring onion.

Or try putting already-cooked string beans in a casserole, sprinkling them with grated Swiss cheese, covering all with 1 to 1-¼ cups béchamel sauce, and sprinkling the top with more grated Swiss cheese. Dot with butter, or soy sauce, and bake in a preheated 400° to 450° F oven for 10 to 15 minutes. This makes a good vegetarian entrée. These two recipes disguise the flavor of string beans. If you like the taste of beans, add sliced mushrooms and butter, slivered almonds and butter, or the juice of a half lemon and butter. All of these can be served with or without mixing in ¼ cup of sour cream. Not bad. And not bad, either, as an addition to a green salad or a cold brown rice and pimiento salad.

Grow also pole beans, beans for drying, and lima beans

(and see *Soybeans*). For heavy crops, and for saving space, grow pole beans. The plants are big and need space. Up on the pole or along the fence, where they are aired, they are less subject to ills. The old favorite variety, Kentucky Wonder, is still widely grown, and still notable for its deliciously beany flavor. If you let it go by and develop brown seeds, they are a good substitute for shell beans. The pods sometimes grow to 8 or 9 inches long. There is a rust-resistant Kentucky Wonder, and Scarlet Runner to grow on fences. Thin the beans to three plants per pole. All these mature in about 60 to 65 days. For a large wide Italian bean, try Romano, which matures in 70 days. These beans are stringless and tender. You can also grow pole lima beans, such as Prizetaker or King of the Garden, which take about 85 days to mature. They are quite vigorous, and very good for space-saving. Try some at the side of a sunny patio, or along the front fence. Why not?

Beans like a warm soil to get started, between 75° and 80° F, and even warmer for lima beans—about 85° to 90° F. The preferred pH is almost neutral, 6.8. After they get started cut down on nitrogen fertilizer so they won't go all to leaf.

The French beans called *haricots verts*, or sometimes *filet* beans, can be ordered from three Vermont seed companies: Le Jardin du Gourmet, The Cook's Garden, and Vermont Bean Seed Company. (See Appendix for addresses.) Triumph de Farcy, an heirloom variety, is ready to pick in about 48 days. Vernandon takes 55, and Fin des Bagnols, 50. The yellow one, Roc d'Or, takes 52. They must be eaten very young. Another French bean, Flaveol, is a *flageolet*, used when the seeds are plump but still green for that fine dish, *cassoulet*. Other possible varieties are Flageolet Rouge and Maberl.

When the ground is warm (70° F for a spell of five days), plant Fordhook bush lima beans or Burpee's Improved bush limas, maturing in 70 to 75 days. For quicker maturing and for patio pots or window boxes, use Baby Henderson limas or Baby Fordhook bush lima beans. A packet will sow 15 feet, or five pots. They are somewhat fussy plants in cold climates, so it is best to start these beans indoors if you live where it is cold and damp. Set the seeds with the eye down, and see that they get moisture during their five-day germination period. Plant them in very good, well-drained, sodless soil (go easy on the liming and the nitrogen supply).

Do not put any fresh fertilizer near the seeds when you plant them.

Easier to grow in cold areas, and substituted by many gardeners for lima beans, are fava beans, also called English broad beans. Long Pod will mature in 85 days and is not fussy about the soil it germinates in. Other varieties are Windsor (75 days) and Ipro (75). Plant early, for they do not like summer heat. The 7-inch pods are glossy green but not edible. Use as a shell bean.

Some people use an inoculant powder for beans. It costs little and will provide nitrogen-fixing bacteria. If you are gardening where sprays and chemical fertilizers have been heavily used, you may find this a useful aid to bringing back the organic liveliness of your soil. A small package treats 5 pounds of legume seed.

Beans for drying include navy beans, white kidney, and red kidney beans. They are rich in protein, vitamins, and minerals, and should be part of any garden. Black beans (Midnight, for instance) will grow in the North. California red kidney beans take 100 days to mature; one pound of seed will plant 150 feet of row. An amusing novelty to grow is the asparagus, or yard-long, bean. Eat it very young, when actually only about 10 inches long.

Try the following recipe for vegetarian chili. Soak 2 cups red kidney beans for one hour, then simmer for one hour. Sauté 2 chopped onions, 2 chopped cloves of garlic, and half a green pepper in 3 tablespoons oil until soft. Add half a hot pepper, 3 tablespoons very fresh chili powder, and 4 finely chopped ripe tomatoes. Simmer for 20 minutes. If you have 1 or 2 cups of water from vegetables, add at this time, and ⅓ cup honey, with ½ teaspoon oregano, and 1-½ teaspoons cumin seeds. If no vegetable water is handy, make 1 to 2 cups in a juicer, out of greens or carrots. Simmer for an hour and serve with corn bread.

Beets
Beta vulgaris

If you like beets at all, plant them. They are an easy, satisfactory, and nourishing crop to grow. Varieties favored by experienced gardeners include Early Wonder (55 days), especially for beet greens; Early Red Ball (48 days); Baby Beet Spinal (60 days), very small; and for the cylindrical beets, Cylindra and Forminova (60). For later beets, try Late Detroit Dark Red and Winter Keeper. A novel golden beet, called Golden, is quite sweet and will mature in 55 days. It won't bleed into your green salads. There is also an off-white beet, Albino White, which takes 50 days. A tiny beet is Little Mini Ball (54 days). A variety that holds well in the garden for a long harvest is Chioggia.

Beets grown in raised beds have fewer troubles with slugs, and whether you grow them in raised beds or in rows in the garden, it is good to plant twice, early and late, because beets like cool weather. Put some in the flower garden for the benefit of their very attractive foliage, especially a variety like Ruby Queen or MacGregor's Favorite.

When you manage to get the seeds to germinate, to keep the early seedlings, and to transplant your thinnings instead of eating them, a 100-foot row of beets could yield you two bushels. This should be enough for a family of four with some to can and some to store in moist sand.

Plant 1 ounce for each 100 feet of row—or a packet for each 25 feet—and plant them early, for beets do not mind some early frost. Keep planting, at intervals of five to ten days, until early July, so that you will always have young greens and small beets ready for harvest. See that the soil is in good soft condition.

Beets like a pH of 6.5, and enough nutrient matter and mulch for fast, vigorous growth. If the soil is slightly sandy, that is fine, for the roots like to have the earth fairly loose around them. Make the rows 12 to 20 inches apart if you are going to use a cultivator, but nearer together for a mulch such as salt hay, cocoa shells, or ground bark. Warning: Do not plant the seeds too close together, because several plants come from one cluster of seeds. A good precaution is to soften and loosen these clusters after soaking the seeds for 24 hours before planting. Don't throw out leftover seeds; they are viable for four years and can be used another year.

The flea beetle may turn up to bite the leaves of the young seedlings. Thin them if this happens, and spray with onion water mixture (one medium onion to a not quite full blender of water), and trust your vigorous plants to send out fresh, unbitten leaves. When the tomatoes and cauliflower come along, the flea beetle will probably move over to them, anyhow.

Keep the young plants weeded. When they reach about 5

inches, the tender greens are ready to thin and eat. In a week or so some of the roots, as you will see, will have widened enough to be small beets.

Beets provide vitamin A, riboflavin, folic acid, and vitamin C. The greens are rich in this vitamin. Protect these nutrients by putting the greens in a dark bag as soon as you pick them, and into the pot within five minutes after picking, to preserve vitamin C.

In the fall, the rest of the crop can be dug and stored in a cold place (just above freezing). Though some people object to leaving beets in the ground until after the first frost, it really does them no harm. Select beets you plan to keep during the winter from rows planted later. In this way they will not be too heavy and course. In case your storage place tends to dry out, beets, like other root vegetables, can be stored in moist (but not wet) sand. Do not allow them to freeze. In the long run, canning may be the best mode of preservation because it's least risky.

For those who think they do not like beets, the first recipe to try is cream cheese balls with finely chopped beets rolled into them. The beets should be washed but not peeled, and put through a meat grinder or blender just before mixing. Add finely chopped chervil, parsley, or tarragon for extra flavor. Rosemary and marjoram also go well with beets, but not the strong herbs such as thyme or oregano.

Another good variation for beets is a puree made by baking whole, unpeeled beets, then putting them through the potato masher. Add one-third their volume of thick cream sauce. Warm this mixture over low heat and add a tablespoon of butter or soy oil. Do not boil and do not stir. This can be sprinkled with a finely chopped mild herb and served in a mound or as a border around a pile of rice.

Another way to cook beets is to mince the tops and grate the beets. Then put these with a bayleaf and ¼ teaspoon basil into a pressure cooker with enough stock to moisten the bottom of the pan—about ¼ cup (a steamer can also be used). After quick cooking, add 1 teaspoon of honey and ¼ to ½ cup yogurt. Odd, but good. What is left over can be put in a blender and then added to ½ cup milk powder, 3 tablespoons flour, and 4 eggs, separated and beaten to make a beet soufflé. Put in an oiled casserole and bake for 30 minutes at 375° F.

In late July when the beets in our garden begin to plump

up, we like to sliver some to add to the salad, and also to braise. The slivers of four beets in hot vegetable oil to cover the bottom of the pan will cook very quickly. Then add 1 tablespoon of mixed water and lemon juice, and cook over moderate heat for 5 minutes. Put on the cover to keep the steam in. Make a mixed platter, sometimes, with carrots, peppers, and daylilies cooked the same way. You can use butter, but with delicate vegetables we like the milder oils such as soy, peanut, or safflower.

Some year, just for variety, grow white or golden beets. They are said to mature in 55 or 60 days, and to be exceptionally sweet.

Belgian Endive
See Chicory, pages 164–65.

Berries
If you have plenty of space for perennials, grow some berries. Try blackberries, boysenberries, dewberries, currants, gooseberries, raspberries (red or black, but not both), or strawberries. If you decide to attempt currants or gooseberries, be sure to see that there are no white pines in your neighborhood to be pestered by the fly that likes to spend part of its cycle in currants or gooseberries. Ask the county extension agent, for in many places there are state laws prohibiting growth of these berries. (Instead, think of elderberry, barberry, mountain ash, whortleberry, or Juneberry, also called shadberry or serviceberry—a delicious little fruit like an apple, wonderful after stewing to add to muffins, or make into jelly.)

Blackberries, Raspberries, Dewberries
The brambles of blackberries, raspberries, and dewberries grow on canes that sprout up, bear fruit, and die back; therefore clear out old second-year canes as soon as the crop is picked. If you don't, you'll have a big messy bramble patch. New growth should be helped along by the gardener. Black and purple raspberries, dewberries, loganberries, and trailing blackberries all should have several of their tips turned under in 3 or 4 inches of earth in early fall. Keep the soil loose and moist, with plenty of organic nutrients, until the new roots form. Choose

one-year-old plants for tip layering, and aim for four or five layerings from each plant. Be sure that you stick them in vertically, never horizontally. When you move the new plants, put them in deep, friable soil, 3 or 4 feet apart in rows 6 feet apart.

Avoid planting red and black raspberries in the same garden, and clear out wild berries that might happen to grow nearby, because they might pass a virus to your new plants. These berries need a cold winter, so expect them to do poorly in the South. They do best in zones 5 and 6, and also on Puget Sound and in the Willamette Valley. New-burgh is a variety good for both the North and West; Latham is an old favorite in the East, a midseason berry that is large and pleasantly tart. Another good, especially large and vigorous berry is Hilton. One of the sweeter ones is Summer. Amber is the favorite among yellow raspberries. Southland is grown in the South. For a purple berry, try Clyde, and for the familiar old blackcap, try Allen or Black Hawk. Farther south try Bristol or Logan, often just called loganberry. Among the everbearing raspberries, Durham or Fallgold are best for the North. You might also try Indian Summer. Farther south, but not in coastal regions, again try Southland. The thornless raspberry, Mammoth Thornless, is early, but it fruits for a long season. It also produces lots of suckers.

Remember to plant these varieties several feet apart, and at a depth 2 inches deeper than they grew in the nursery. Rows should be 6 feet apart.

Red raspberries are suckered; that is, new shoots from the roots (or underground stems) are permitted to grow up to plants. After they get good roots, they are separated and replanted.

One of the pests on raspberries is a mosaic that makes the leaves look spotty. Leafhoppers and plant lice bring in this difficulty, so try to get plants that are resistant to mosaic. These include Viking, St. Regis (in the South), Latham, Chief, and Van Fleet (in the West). If you do get mosaic, dig out and burn all infected plants. Never plant cultivated berries anywhere near wild ones. Of course, if you already have enough wild ones, you won't need to, anyhow.

Latham may be subject to gall, too, a disease that makes knobs on the roots and canes. Destroy plants if you get it. Rust is another possibility and may turn up in anyone's

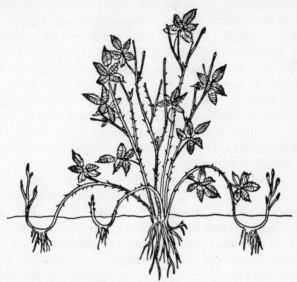

Layering Blackberries

Suckered Red Raspberries

garden. You know it by the red spots with white centers, on leaves or stems, and you can expect them to arrive after rain. Of all the brambles, red raspberry is least likely to get rust, but as sure as I say that and get someone's hopes up, that very person will probably have it turn up on her canes. The fungus causing this disease hibernates in infected canes, so try to see that everything you winter over is clean of it. Look for any cracks in the canes, or other signs that it is there, such as berries that never ripened. Destroy all such canes. When you have to plant again, get only stock that is certified disease-free, and move the field to an entirely different position.

Once in a while you may see borers. The same treatment of ruthlessly cutting out all infected canes is recommended.

The descriptions of these diseases make it sound as though the growing of berries is a terrible chore and a terrible hazard. It is true that they are not exactly easy. But plenty of good sturdy mulch, patient attention, and a real enthusiasm for the excellent results you can get make the chore and hazard a lot less for organic gardeners than for some others. Thick layers of leaves and manure, or thick ground bark and manure would make a good mulch. A layer of folded newspapers at the bottom will add protection from weeds coming up from below to mess up your brambles.

One dish of berries for breakfast is a good start for the day, recommended in natural foods and yoga routines. Or you can make homemade berry juice in a blender or juicer, and this can be frozen and used later for sherbets, sauces, and jellies.

Make berry jam, with honey, adding 1-½ cup of honey to 1 cup of pulp and letting it stand in sterilized jars for two weeks. (Honey has a powerful bactericidal property.) Use it with homemade cottage cheese made from skim milk and buttermilk added lukewarm to a rennet tablet soaked in water. Heat this slowly and keep it at 110° F for half an hour. Then let it stand for a day. Strain and wash out the whey, then condition with ½ cup of cream or skim milk powder. For a gallon of skim milk you need only ¼ cup of buttermilk to get started.

If you prefer homemade jam with homemade yogurt instead of homemade cottage cheese, that is easily made by adding 3 tablespoons of commercial yogurt to a quart of milk. Heat the milk to lukewarm, add yogurt, stir, and

cover with a warmed blanket. Let stand overnight. A quart
of yogurt dripped overnight through a double cheesecloth
bag (or nylon stocking) makes cheese for breakfast.

Blueberries

In locations with good sun and
a soil which you can keep quite acid, grow blueberries. With
the proper varieties (and two at least), you can grow
blueberries from Florida to Maine, and in the Pacific Northwest, but they do best where they can get a winter chill.
The planting location should be where there is very good
drainage, plenty of organic matter in the soil, and a
capacity to maintain plenty of moisture. The cold-zone
blueberries grow from North Carolina and on north; in the
South you can only grow rabbiteye blueberries such as
Bluebelle, Briteblue, Florablue, and Southland.

For early berries in the North, try Earliblue, Blueray,
Bluecrop, and Berkeley. These are good for New England
gardens. Choose at least two. Midseason to late varieties for
that area include Coville, Darrow, Jersey, and Herbert. For
southern Connecticut, New York, New Jersey, and Pennsylvania, appropriate choices are Blueray, Earliblue, Collins,
and Bluecrop; and for later ones, Darrow, Herbert, and
Jersey. Farther south, those that will do better include, for
early, Angola, and Morrow; for midseason, Croatan, Scammell,
and Wolcott; and for late, Jersey and Murphy. In the
Northwest the old varieties are no longer used. Try Dixi and
Stanley. For the very hardiest blueberries, select Northsky,
Northblue, or Northland.

Do not feed blueberries the first year after you plant them,
but prepare the soil well, treating it with peat and aluminum sulphate to reach a pH of about 5. Never use manure,
for that is alkaline. Cottonseed meal can be used after the
first year. Make a big generous hole for the bush, especially
if you get highbush blueberries. Where there is lime in the
soil, it is best to arrange some sort of containment so the soil
around the roots will remain acid. Plastic, or two or three
big tires in the hole might help, but be sure to be careful
about watering because moisture is very important. It is
best to mulch rather then cultivate blueberries. The roots are
very tender and depend on a symbiotic relation with
beneficial soil fungi in mycorrhizal association.

147

Currants and
Gooseberries

I repeat: Do not plant until you
find out from your county extension agent, your state
Department of Agriculture, or an experiment station whether
or not there is a quarantine in your district against these
berries. If you are permitted to grow them you are lucky.

Currants seem marvelously simple to cope with after the
complications of the brambles. Almost any land will do,
but they like cool, well-drained areas best. Add plenty of
organic matter, such as leaf mold, manure, and hay mulch.
Keep the plants pruned, and watch for the best fruits on the
two-, three-, and four-year-old canes. Keep only the sturdy
ones, and of course get rid of all that look diseased, cracked,
or galled.

Send away for new cuttings, or you can take hardwood
cuttings for new plants yourself, and tie up 8-inch lengths
to store in moist sand. By spring the ends will have
hardened; plant them 4 to 6 inches deep and 8 to 12 inches
apart, to grow roots. In the second year, move them to 4 feet
apart. By the third year they will be ready to bear. Do not
cultivate—mulch. The delicate roots are too near the surface
to hazard any instrument used for weeding.

If the foliage is curling and warping, you may have leaf
lice. Look for their eggs in the bark of the plant's new
growth. They hatch in early spring, so get to them early. Or
late October and thereafter. Wash off what you can't pick
off. Also pick off worms and scale bugs.

The rust disease is what gets into the white pine, where it
is called blister rust. On the pines you'll see reddish spots
on the trunk; on the currants the lower surface of the leaves
get spots with curving tines coming out of them. Keep
currants and white pine at least a mile apart.

All this applies also to gooseberries. But if you can have
them, what marvelous tarts, jam, and gooseberry fool they
make. For jam: Take 3 pounds of gooseberries and add 2-½
pounds of sugar boiled 5 minutes in 2 cups of apricot juice.
Add gooseberries and simmer for 35 minutes. Let stand for
24 hours before draining and putting berries in sterilized
jars. Reduce liquid to thick syrup and cover berries. In a cup
of gooseberries the food values include: 59 calories, 440 I.U.
of vitamin A, and 49 mg of vitamin C. Compared to these
values you get from a cup of blackberries: 280 I.U. of

vitamin A and 30 mg of vitamin C.

Varieties to choose include, for red currants: Cherry, Perfection, Red Gross, Red Lake, or Stephens No. 9; and for white currants, the very fine White Imperial. Red or pink gooseberries include Pixwell, Clark, Poorman, and Welcome. Green or yellow are Downing and Green Mountain.

Strawberries

Of all the berries, the one with the most vitamin C is the strawberry. In one cup there are 54 calories, 90 I.U. of vitamin A, and of vitamin C, a high 89 mg. (In comparison: raw cabbage has 50; fresh cooked peas have 20; cooked spinach 50; thoroughly cooked turnip tops have 260 in one cup.)

To cultivate strawberries almost all soils in the United States are possible, but different treatments and varieties are required. The only soil not suitable is one that is very alkaline, though any dry soil will need watering, and a wet soil will need drainage. The best pH is between 5 and 6, a bit more acid than the soil of an average garden. Where it is cold try Cunlap, Earlibelle, Sparkle, and the hardy Trumpeter, especially for the upper Midwest. For farther south recommended varieties are Blakemore, Catskill, and the old favorite Howard 17. Surecrop is good for most zones, and it is disease resistant. Headliner and Guardian are recommended for the South; also Missionary, especially for Georgia. Guardian is the most disease resistant of these. Everbearing varieties to consider are Gem, Geneva, Streamliner, Ozark Beauty, and Superfection. Recommended for California are Salinas, Sequoia, and the handsome, large Shasta. Tioga is an early, firm strawberry for the West.

The Alpine strawberries, grown from seed and used frequently in flower gardens for an edging, are available as Mignonette, and for a yellowish one, Pineapple Crush. Strawberries are long-day plants, but one variety, Tristar, has been bred to be day-neutral. It is advertised to bear three times.

You can extend strawberries to produce for up to ten years if you will mow the plants about a week or so after bearing has stopped, with the lawnmower, set high. Then till or turn under strips to create a narrow row. Hoe up soil around the crowns and mulch well. Let new roots grow runners, but don't let them get crowded. Weed and water well, and feed cottonseed meal. This extra care is well worth it.

Before planting strawberries, use your soil for something else for two years, cultivating carefully. Then set aside a portion of it for strawberries. The purpose of avoiding newly plowed land is to get rid of grubs, which are always left over in soil just converted from grass. It will probably also get rid of wire worms, especially if you have planted marigolds during those two years.

A slope that has winter drainage is imperative, preferably facing south and protected from late frost. In the fall preceding planting add a good lot of manure (at the rate of 500 pounds per 1,000 square feet). Also dig in compost and/or leaf mold. Fifty or 60 bushels per 1,000 square feet would be a good dosage.

Buy plants and spread out the roots in deep holes half-filled with loose, soft soil. Tamp this down a bit, add water, and fill the holes. While planting, avoid exposing the roots to air or sun. Cover with wet peat moss if necessary. Keep the soil moist several days after planting. We used to plant in one spring for harvest the following spring, pinching off all buds the first year to encourage green growth. We let the runners grow, and developed walkways between every other row. You have to keep strawberries well watered, and well mulched especially in winter, with pine needles if you can get them. Fork the mulch over in the spring, and remove it for a while to help the ground warm up. Straw is a good mulch, too.

I haven't gotten around to trying a strawberry barrel for everbearing French berries, but the idea appeals to me because you fill the barrel with earth and grow the plants out the holes that are made in the sides for that purpose. Watering is easy if you run a hose down the center of the barrel. Of course if you run in liquid manure instead of straight water, all the better. Good loam and nicely spread-out roots are essential. Put the barrel on a turntable so that all the plants get sun. Great for a terrace or patio.

Elderberry
Sambucus canadensis

This is a splendid bush to place around your lawn or in your hedge. It likes good soil and a sunny location, and will serve you well with blossoms in early summer to make a delectable tempura, and berries a month later for juice, jelly, and wine. In many parts of the country you will find it growing wild; it is hardy in the northern states. If you bring in cuttings and plant them, first in wet sand, then in soil, you can get them to grow into bushes. Pest-free. Arabs used dried elderberry leaves for a repellent. You can also use the berries for lilac and deep purple dyes. The hybrid varieties of this berry are Adams and New York 21. A later bearing one is York.

Juneberry, Serviceberry or Shadberry
Amelanchier

The beautiful white shad flower of early spring, the Juneberry has small, dark red fruits. It belongs to the rose family. The trees need some moisture and shade, and some species will grow 30 or more feet tall. Feed, water, and mulch well if you decide to get a few for yourselves or for the birds. Makes fine jelly, and is rich in vitamin C—as a cousin of rose hips should be.

Broccoli
Brassica oleracea italica

One year we had wonderful broccoli, which we gathered right through the time of the early frosts, though at the end the heads were only the small-sized ones. But they were good. I hadn't yet learned the trick of cooking in milk and caraway to suppress the smell of *Brassica* family vegetables, so the next year all were "forbidden" by my husband because the whole last half of the summer became associated in his mind with that smell. It is nothing but a sulfur compound anyhow, and broccoli ought to be worth it with or without milk or caraway for the excellent supply of vitamins A, B, and C, as well as the calcium, potassium, and iron this vegetable provides. Pick while the head is still in bud and firm. After blooming, it gets flabby.

Plant your broccoli in the spring when the weather is still cool and moist, and keep it well watered until it is established. If you live in a warm climate, you can also plant broccoli outdoors in the fall. Farther north the seed can be sown indoors or outdoors, but not later than the end of May. An indoor March planting, if set out in May, might mature in late June. Give it some compost, but not too much.

151

Broccoli does not need rich soil. Seeds are viable for three years.

A packet will produce about 200 plants, if all come to maturity. That would take 200 feet of row. Green Comet is the best variety, or for a longer-growing follow-up, Waltham 29 is excellent, too. This variety has low plants, and fine, broad heads. Other favorites are the hybrid Emperor (58 days), Green Valiant (70), and a new blue-green variety called Cruiser (60 days). The kind called Calabrese is a sprouting broccoli—it doesn't form a head. Cut the shoots when they are 4 inches long. Another one, Raab, sends out shoots, too. It is actually a form of turnip, with very small heads. Among the violet broccolis you have your choice of Violet Queen (70 days) and Hybrid Packman. Romanesco is a beautifully shaped pale green variety that can be set out in early spring or late summer. It has a mild flavor. All these are excellent for fiber, vitamins, and potassium.

Sauté 2 tablespoons minced onion in a small amount of butter, soy, or safflower oil. Remove from the heat, stirring in 1-½ cups of sour cream or homemade yogurt (see page 146). Add to this 2 teaspoons sugar, 1 teaspoon vinegar, ½ teaspoon poppy seed, ¼ teaspoon paprika, ¼ teaspoon salt, and a dash of cayenne pepper. Cook two heads of broccoli and arrange them on a heated platter. Pour the sour cream mixture over the broccoli and sprinkle with ⅓ cup chopped cashews.

Brussels Sprouts
Brassica oleracea gemmifera

Plants started in late spring in a cold frame may be planted out in early summer, spaced about 2-½ feet apart in rows 2-½ feet apart, in well-composted ground. It is best to till in the compost two weeks before setting. Jade Cross is a vigorous hybrid variety which matures in 90 days. A newer variety, Oliver, also 90 days to maturity, has somewhat larger sprouts. Two hybrids, Prince Marvel (98) and Long Island Improved (108), as well as the earlier one, Dolmic, are fairly sweet, especially after a frost. A red one, Rubine, is a late-season variety, taking 110 days to mature. Most Brussels sprouts improve after the first frost.

Start picking from the bottom, then remove the big lower leaves and keep right on picking until the snow flies. If you produce too many to eat, or to sell to your organic food store, remember that Brussels sprouts are very easy to freeze for later use. They are also easy to transplant to a greenhouse or cold frame for late crops. They have to be kept moist. Boiled or steamed Brussels sprouts can get boring, so dress them up once in a while with a sauce such as hollandaise or spiced mayonnaise.

Cabbage
Brassica oleracea capitata

There is a tremendous advantage to growing your own cabbage, because you can select and produce varieties that you never see in a market. Commercial growers choose to produce harder, more durable kinds, which unfortunately do not have the taste of varieties like Early Jersey Wakefield (70 days to maturity), Market Topper (62 days), or Copenhagen Market (56 days). Also early is Derby Day, as well as Perfect Action, a small cabbage with a short core. Midseason cabbages include some of the Chinese cabbage such as Jade Pagoda. Late cabbages are the most suitable for storage, including Surehead (93 days), Premium Flat Dutch (100), Erdeno (80), and the very late Superior Danish (98). An especially good one for storage is Lariat (125).

The nutritional values of cabbage are excellent. In a half cup of raw cabbage there are 80 I.U. of vitamin A (as compared to 20 in a baked potato) and 52 mg of vitamin C (about the same as a medium-sized orange). There are about 3.2 mg of vitamin K in cabbage, not quite as much as in spinach, but of minerals you will get 46 mg of calcium, 31 of phosphorus, .5 of iron, and 7 to 24 mcg of cobalt (40 in beet tops).

Since cabbage is a cool-weather plant, it is hardy and will tolerate a spread of temperatures. Give it plenty of compost, and some extra cottonseed meal or hoof and horn fertilizer for nitrogen. Get the soil into good loose tilth before planting, and try for a pH of 6 to 6.5. The early cabbages, such as the first two named, do well if started indoors or in a cold frame, and set out after the danger of frost is gone. Indoors six to eight seeds to the inch may be planted in a flat or peat pot and lightly covered. The rows are best placed 2 inches apart. Harden the plants off by moving them to 3 inches apart when they are 2 or 3 inches tall, and expose them to open air on good days. The seeds are viable for four years.

Late cabbages, which can be kept for winter storage, are best planted outdoors in light but not in too rich soil, on a date that will just about bring them to picking on the first day of frost and before they show any tendencies to burst.

When spaced for final growth to maturity, they should be set 12 inches apart for early cabbage, and 18 inches for larger ones. Protect the newly set-out plants with a basket, a brown paper shield, or even a shingle. Don't plant any specimens that are not strong and vigorously healthy. Keep the weeds down until you mulch, because cabbages have horizontal roots near the surface that need all the nutrients they can get. If you use a hoe, do it very gently so as not to injure the delicate rootlets.

At the first sign of a cutworm, get a piece of tarpaper or other heavy collar to put around each stem, and watch every morning for intruders; also poke up any that lurk in the soil near the stem. A disk of tarpaper laid on the soil around the stem will defeat the white maggot also, by preventing it from laying eggs near the stem just under the surface of the soil. If the leaves turn yellow and the veins black, you have something called black rot, and if your broccoli, Brussels sprouts, or cabbage leaves get black pimply spots, you have black leg. These diseases come in with the seed, but if you use the best heat-treated seed, or if you buy plants from someone who will grow them to your specifications from pest-free seeds, you ought not to be bothered by such troubles. Good ventilation and a rich, well-composted soil will also help. Destroy all infected plants either by burning or by burying.

If cabbage worms turn up, spread wood ashes between the rows when the worms' white moths appear—the cabbage butterflies. But best of all, get out there with the tennis racket when they appear, and whack them. Broccoli and cauliflower are less likely to attract these pests than cabbages.

For all these cole plants subject to worms, gardeners now apply a bacillus which paralyzes the gut of the worms: *Bacillus thüringiensis*, known as Bt, and available commercially as Dipel, Biotrel, or Thuricide. Use it as dust or spray, and repeat the application after rain. This is a surefire cure for that wormy pest, the cabbage worm.

In order to avoid club root, which is caused by nematodes,

grow marigolds nearby—Mexican ones if you can get them. Also grow marigolds in the area of the garden where you plan to have cabbages the following year, and till them into the soil so they will exude their antibiotic substance that nematodes cannot endure. Burn up any infected plants. Do not bury.

When the cabbage head is large and hard, twist the stem in the ground to break some of the roots, and thus stop further development of the head and avoid danger of cracking. On a dry, cool day a little later, harvest the cabbage and store it in a cold, dry place with a temperature of 33° to 40° F.

The best way to get healthy cabbage plants is to have good tilth, an airy location, proper spacing, good companionate planting, wood ashes, Bt, and habits of watchfulness. Harvest directly into a dark bag, and keep the heads in a cool, dark place. Do not wash until ready to use.

Red Cabbage

Red cabbage is a delicious, sturdy variation of green cabbage. Grow both early and late varieties. The recommended early one is Red Acre (76 days), and for the late crop either Red Danish, Mammoth Red Rock (97 and 100 days respectively), and the new variety called Ruby Perfection.

Savoy Cabbage

A favorite with a few people. In some places it can be sown in the fall. The heads are big and heavy, and one 90-day variety, Savoy King Hybrid, is likely to be heat resistant. An especially attractive Savoy cabbage is Blue Nun. People enjoy Savoy cabbage for its mild, slightly sweet flavor, its big handsome curly leaves, and the fact that it usually stays a nice green when properly cooked (no soda).

Chinese Cabbage
Brassica pekinensis

An excellent cabbage for salads, and it can be used for braising, also. The Chihli or Michihli variety is considered a good one, or Wong Bok, which is shorter and stockier. Pak Choi has been gaining favor in recent years. One packet will sow 40 feet, enough for a family of four. The seed is viable for four years.

Since this vegetable will bolt, plant it in very rich soil around July 1, right where you want it to grow, for it does not like being moved. The root system is very sensitive and needs a friable soil to stretch out in. Thin very carefully to 18 inches. Control leafhoppers with wood ashes or possibly rotenone. Keep well watered.

The entire plant is edible, though you may want to break off the outside leaves for tempura or boiling. Salad made from the inside leaves, if doctored with ginger as the Chinese do, can be crisp and tasty. It is good for freezing.

Carrots
Daucus carota sativas

First of all, it is better not to slice carrots, and anyone can see why after reading what J. I. Rodale says is lost through our usual maltreatment of carrots when we prepare and cook them.

If carrots are not fresh, 5 percent of their vitamin K and magnesium is already lost (especially if they were kept in the light). When the skin is taken off, there goes another 10 percent of the nutrients. If they are sliced before boiling, all the vitamin C is lost, as well as the niacin and 20 percent of the thiamin. If you soak them along the way, all the B vitamins and some of the natural sugar, plus all the minerals except calcium go out. (This would indicate that you should not soak carrot sticks in cold water to make them curl.) When the cooking water is drained off, down the sink goes all the rest of the vitamin K and more of the minerals. If sugar has been added to the cooking water, there is another 5-percent loss of nutrient, namely of calcium.

Last advice: Eat your carrots raw. And by the way, eat the tops, too.

Shredding carrots just before eating them raw does increase the amount of carotene available to the body, by 5 to 35 percent. The tough cellulose walls of the cells are broken down, and the carotene released. But do so immediately before eating, as the loss in vitamin C will otherwise be great. In half a cup of carrots, the vitamin A supply is 10,000 to 12,000 I.U. (twice the daily requirements), so yes, they are indeed good for the eyes.

Carrots are best for you raw, but they taste so good in so

many other ways, too, that you may also want to try carrot chiffon pie, carrot-rhubarb jam, carrot stuffing, baked carrot ring, soufflé, and a half-dozen other goodies. In her *Natural Foods Cook Book*, Beatrice Trum Hunter gives recipes for all of these. A vegetarian neighbor of mine makes a mixture of grated carrot, potato, an egg, and chopped chives, which she fries quickly in small patties in safflower oil. Delicious.

In the early days of this country the settler Francis Higginson wrote home to say: "Our turnips, Parsnips and Carrots are here both bigger and sweeter than is ordinarily to be found in England." This was written in 1630 and reflects the fact that carrots grown in deep, rich, humusy soil, as the new soil then was in the Northeast, will be large and sweet and full of good nutrients.

In today's soil this may mean you need big doses of compost, fall and spring, and a seedbed very well prepared. The soil should be broken up and the particles fine, for the seeds of carrots are tiny. In fact, they are so tiny that it is a good idea to mix them with the larger seeds of radishes and sow both together. Radishes come up very quickly, so you'll know where the row is and be able to watch for the very small seedlings of carrots when their lacy leaves first appear. They will need some weeding. Also, planted this way the carrots will be farther apart and the thinning will be easier. Thin carefully to avoid disturbing the roots. In fact, you may have to cut instead of pull, unless the soil is very loose.

Other aids for planting carrots are pelleted seeds and seed tapes. The seeds remain viable for three years. It also helps to plant them in raised beds where the soil can be kept soft and pliable. Here is one warning. Your temptation will be to pull out the larger plants, which may look just about ready to eat as tiny fingerlings. Resist this. You may pull one or two, just because they are so marvelously tender and sweet to eat raw then and there at this early stage. But remember that the very small, weak plants are more than likely to be plants that won't ever amount to much. Pull these weak ones out and eliminate them from the contest for nutrients. They will be recycled anyhow when you put them on the compost heap. Plant carrots several times to keep these crops of young ones coming. Small whole carrots, quickly washed, blanched, and frozen, are a treasure to have in your freezer.

The spacing for carrots left in the ground to mature in the late summer should be no nearer than 1-½ inches apart, or they'll curl around each other. Your harvesting should be with the forethought that big strong carrots (Chantenay, especially) keep well in the ground not only until after frost, but throughout the whole winter under deep mulch.

To keep carrots in the ground over the winter, pile up autumn leaves over the row. If there is not a rain soon after you do this, weigh them down so the leaves won't blow. Considering how hard it is to find plants under the snow, it is also a good idea to put some bushel baskets along on top, and more leaves over them to help keep out the cold. Then, when you want to go to the garden to dig carrots in the winter, you'll know where they are. The leaves will have prevented them from freezing.

Carrots kept this way are very crisp and sweet. In spring, if the frost gets in again after a warm spell, the carrots will get mushy very easily. Some people lose their carrots during the winter from a period of alternating warm and cold that spoils the vegetable. Guard against this by adding leaves or sawdust to make the mulch airtight, and manure to keep it warm.

If you don't think you'd have luck with this method, dig your carrots up and pack them in boxes of moist sand. The boxes can then either be stored in a cool place or be buried and covered with earth and then leaves, with some sort of marker for the spot. Do not use plastic—the carrots will rot like anything—and do not let them remain in the light.

With all these points in mind, select your varieties to suit your need. For earlier carrots to eat in summer, select Pioneer, the midget Short 'n' Sweet, and Scarlet Nantes, which are rather short and stumpy. The best later ones for storing are Royal or Red Cored Chantenay, and Commander, all very satisfactory, we find. The ones we winter in the ground are Chantenay. The very long, tapered carrots called Discovery are ready to eat in 62 days. Most of the others take around 70 days, but the truly tiny carrots, such as Baby Sweet Hybrid and Minicor, will mature in around 50 days. One to plant in midsummer is Fincor. The seeds do best when the soil temperature is around 75° F.

Do not be fooled by this early and late distinction. They all mature within a few days of each other if all are planted at the same time. These terms imply, rather, which carrots are

Winter Protection for Carrots (Bushel Baskets and Autumn Leaves)

considered appropriate for early or later plantings. The very earliest and latest plantings, however, are never as good as the middle ones, say between May 15 and June 15 in moderate zones. If you have heavy, clayey soil, plant Commander; if you live where you have droughts, choose a long variety with a long root—Danvers, for example. Do not be surprised if you need a long spade to dig them out to eat; drought conditions make the root go way down into the earth.

Avoid using much manure, but do use compost. And mulch.

One cool evening try carrot tempura. Have ready a batter; at the very last minute cut the carrots diagonally and very thin, and after coating the slivers in batter, drop into 350° F corn oil, sesame seed oil, or safflower oil, two or three inches deep, and allow the carrots to come to the top. Turn and brown the other side. Batter: 1 cup pastry flour, 1 to 1-¼ cups water, ¼ teaspoon salt. Mix lightly. Lumps don't matter. Variation: 1 cup whole wheat flour (freshly ground), 1 teaspoon cornstarch, 1-¼ cups water, ½ teaspoon salt. An egg can be added, if desired. Decorate tempura with watercress, onion, thinly sliced burdock root, lotus root, whole radish leaves, or elderberry blossoms.

Cauliflower
Brassica oleracea botrytis

Go easy ordering seeds for this vegetable, because a packet will yield 150 plants, and for best nutrition and taste the head should be eaten as soon as picked; or frozen for use a little later. For varieties, choose Snowball or Snow King (53 days) for white; and Purple CapHybrid or Purple Head (80–85) for the dark ones (which do not cook purple, but green). Quick growers include

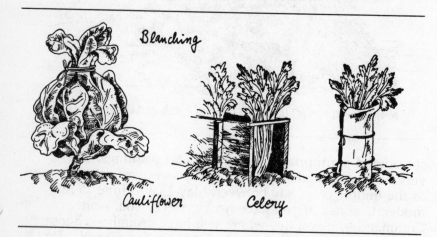

Blanching

Cauliflower   Celery

Snow King Hybrid, Early Snowball, and Snowball Imperial. For minicauliflowers try Garant (82) and the late Predominant (90). The self-blanching Snowball takes 70 days, and a quicker one, Alert, takes 55. All these are figured from the date of setting out transplants.

Be sure not to plant cauliflower in the same ground twice. Rotate, for example, by planting where carrots were the previous year. Start seeds in the cold frame and plant in succession so they won't all mature at once.

Cauliflower is a delicate vegetable, or rather flower, and you need to keep watch for cutworms, cabbage loopers, maggots, and club root. Dust freely with wood ashes or Bt and some of your troubles are under control. Build a very good soil, rich and loose, with plenty of nitrogenous materials such as blood meal or cottonseed meal. These plants can endure cold, so you can put them out in the garden quite early. Many people buy plants to be put out when the soil is ready. Others buy seeds and start them indoors, or in a cold frame, four weeks before the time to set them out. Germination is best at 70° F, and for early growth 60° F is best. Keep watered, for any setback either indoors or later after transplanting is injurious to the plants. If you prefer seeds not treated with fungicide, tell your seed supplier that's what you want. Seeds stay viable for three years.

Place the plants 2 feet apart, or 15 inches if small, but discard all that have stunted leaves, for you need the leaves later to tie over the head as soon as it appears. Cut early, or when the head is about 6 inches wide and the florets are still compact and tight.

A good steamed cauliflower under a slightly cheesy sauce is a very fine vegetable. Served in this way, it is usually left whole. Undercooked florets chilled with a sauce are second best. For the sauce, melt one tablespoon of butter and add 1 tablespoon of flour and 1 tablespoon of homemade mustard. (See page 210.) Mix this roux and add ⅔ cup boiling water and stir. When melded, add the yolks of two eggs and 1 tablespoon cream. Beat well and cool before adding to the cauliflower florets. A very delicate hors d'oeuvre. Uncooked florets with a green dip of mayonnaise, chopped greens, and cream cheese is less delicate, but even better.

Celeriac
Apium graveolens rapaceum
Celeriac is also called celery root, turnip-rooted celery, or knob celery.

Why this is not popular in the United States is hard to understand. It is quite easy to grow, and it produces nice large roots which are eaten any time after they reach a size of two inches. No blanching is needed, and the roots last into the fall and winter. What's more, it is easy to store them, and to enjoy their rich, nutty flavor cubed, steamed, boiled with or without a sauce, in a stew, or cooled for salads throughout the year. Varieties available include Globus (110 days), Large Smooth Prague (110), Marble Ball (110), and Jose (110), a new variety in 1987 which is less likely to get pithy than some others. It takes a long time for celeriac to grow, so choose the variety Alabaster and get started planting early. This is a thick, firm-rooted variety which takes 120 days to reach maturity, and then may be stored for the winter in a cold cellar.

One recipe for celeriac which you may not have thought of is a puree of celery root and potatoes. Take about a pound of roots, wash, and remove any tough skin or fibers. Then boil until tender, and boil ¾ pound of potatoes. Mash together the potatoes, the celery root, and one hard-boiled egg with 3 tablespoons butter, ½ teaspoon salt, and a pinch of pepper. Reheat until hot again. Do **not** let it burn. You can also let this cool and mound it under mayonnaise for a salad. Either cold or hot, it is a welcome variation from the same old mashed potatoes, potato salad, or plain boiled celeriac.

Celery
Apium graveolens

Quite finicky to grow, and we never have grown it, but those who have give good advice after their experiences. The pests are few, they say, but you have to have just the right kind of soil, moisture, and guards for the celery stalks so that they do not get too tough.

Compost and rich topsoil are obligatory, but the organic gardener will already have such soil for all his or her vegetables. Start them indoors or in a greenhouse, rather early, or buy the plants from a nursery. This means an eight-week preparatory period before the plants are ready to put in the ground. But they will withstand cold, and can be put out when it is still rather chilly. If the young plants, when you first set them out, need to be protected from hot sun to make them sturdy, provide shade. Two thicknesses of material are best, with one removed after the young plant gets used to the outdoor environment. Do not plant where there has been lettuce or cabbage in recent years. Remove all diseased plants if spots appear on them, or if nematodes get at the roots and cause galls.

When stalks are nearing the size you want, to make them tender and to keep the hearts growing, you can blanch or bank them with boards held up by stakes. (See illustration, page 160.)

Pascal varieties do not demand blanching. Anyone concerned with nutrition prefers pascal because of the added benefit of the green cells. Giant Pascal and Burpee's Fordhook are recommended. For caterpillars, use *Bacillus thüringiensis*, described above in the passage about cabbages. Not everything is understood about how it works, but it is known to invade the larvae of insects at a stage when they are geared to eat continuously. This bacillus paralyzes the gut, and the insects cannot eat. Yellows is also controlled by planting clean seed in clean soil, and seed suppliers now offer clean seed. The old favorite variety is Utah 52–70, and some of the new improved Utah-type seeds available include Tendercrisp (100), Ventura (100), and Tall Utah Improved (105). These can be trenched for blanching or not, as you choose. Other good new varieties include Golden Self-Blanching (105), and a good dark green Deacon (120). For Southern gardens, Florida 683 and its improved Surepak (100) are recommended. If you have nematodes, keep planting and plowing in marigolds. Browning rootlets may indicate these pests, and chlorosis, or whitening of the leaves, can mean that the infection is bad. Leave the area fallow for two or three years, and always keep a celery bed absolutely free of weeds and trash.

The seeds of celery are very tiny and rather hard to germinate. Soak them overnight before planting, and expect around ten days for germination. Sow them in good rich soil and keep it watered. Use pelleted seeds if possible, or plant about eight to the inch. Ten weeks after planting you can set them out. Fertilize at that time and keep watering. Celery is a biennial, and if you will let a plant or so winter over, and you wait until seeds come, you will have a huge supply for future plantings. The seeds are viable for 3 years.

Celery can be stored in moist sand in a root cellar in the winter. It keeps well for several months.

Sweet Cherry
Prunus avium

These fruits are hardy in zones 5 through 7, and you need to plant two varieties for cross-pollination. The variety Windsor is a good hardy one to choose, along with Bing, the hardy Montmorency, and the early Black Tartarian (which is also a good pollinator, like Yellow Glass, one of the hardiest). Yellow Glass, Montomorency, and Windsor might survive in zone 4, too. Some of the other varieties newly bred for cold zones include Northstar, Meteor, and Gold. Nanking hedge cherry is very hardy.

Prepare a rich, big hole for the trees, and expect newly planted dwarfs to bear in three to four years. Standards take longer. Black Tartarianan is an early ripener; a month later comes Yellow Glass. Bing is also a midseason cherry. When the crop comes in, you may need to put nets over your trees to fend off the birds and save for yourself a good basketful to make cherry pies.

Chicory
Cichorium intybus

Called Belgian or French endive, but also (in many seed catalogs) witloof (white leaf) chicory. It is a delicious tidbit to have in the cellar or dark closet during the late winter, to cut when practically nothing else freshly grown is available. Its cousin, Magdeburg chicory, is used to flavor coffee, and has gone wild along our roadsides—the sturdy weed with fragile, round blue flowers.

Sow the seed thinly in good soil in May or June, cover lightly, and firm down. When plants come up, thin to 6 inches apart; if you wait until they are 3 or 4 inches high, you can use some for greens in the summer. Let the rest grow. One packet of seeds should give you a final crop of about 25 feet. You will have no pests on it. Get seeds, which are viable for five years, for the variety called Witloof (110 days), or a new variety for 1987 called Toner (130), an F1 hybrid to harvest in the fall for forcing. For the endive called escarole, see *Lettuce*.

In the late fall, cut off the tops within an inch of the crown, lift the roots with a fork, and store in a cool place. Bring eight or ten into your cellar or a dark closet, and plant them upright in damp sand or soil, covered with inverted boxes or something to keep out all light. You can also plant them in a box turned sideways between layers of sand, soil, or peat moss, with the box open on the side away from the wall. Then when they grow, and turn upward on reaching the air, they are openleaved instead of in a tight thin head.

Like carrots and parsnips, chicory can be left in the ground, if well protected by leaves, hay, and manure covered with a ridge of soil. Manure as the last layer will help to keep the pile unfrozen until the snow provides the final mantle.

Cut when ready, wash gently, toss in the finest French dressing you can make, or stuff with mashed avocado and a few drops of garlic juice. I think that the best cooked chicory is braised: Melt ¼ cup butter in a pan that has a tight cover. Put in 6 heads of chicory, ½ teaspoon sugar, and the juice of half a lemon. Heat very slowly over a low flame. Push down a piece of well-buttered waxed paper over the chicory, and quickly put on the lid. Reduce the heat to very low for 5 minutes, then raise it a little for 15 to 20 minutes longer. Shake the pan once in a while to prevent sticking, but do not raise the lid. Add salt at the last minute and serve on hot toast.

Collards
Brassica oleracea acephala

This member of the cabbage family is an old favorite, eaten by Europeans ever since the days of Pliny, who named it *caulis*, or stalk plants. Our modern words cole, kale, kohl (rabi), and cauliflower (and the French *chou*) all come from that name.

The stalks and leaves of all members of the *Brassica* family, when young, make good greens, though Americans make use of few of them except collard leaves and, of course, cabbage. Collards are often grown in the South, because the plant withstands heat very well. Easy to grow, especially if you plant the varieties called Georgia (60 days), Vates (75), Morris Heading (60), Louisiana Sweet, or Champion, a Vates type. In the South they can be sown both spring and fall, and left after thinning about 2 feet apart. In the North people plant collards in the summer, and let them mature for late greens. They improve in flavor after a frost. In fact, they can stand 10 degrees of frost. Unlike kale, they can also withstand heat. You can pick and pick the outside leaves as the plant grows. Take them while still young and not yet tough. As the plants are stripped of their lower leaves, it is best to stake them. If you see cabbage worms or other cabbage pests, treat them as you would if they were on cabbage. Collards are wonderfully nutritious, providing lots of vitamins A and C as well as good supplies of calcium and potassium.

Corn
Zea mays saccharata

That Latin name shows why Europeans call it *maize*, and since this plant, for us and for the American Indians before us, was a staple grain, we use the English word for grain, which is corn. It seems to express the early settlers' first surprise that the native plant they found was good enough to be a reliable crop in the

165

virgin soil of those days.

Actually, what we call sweet corn was developed by hybridizers during the past 150 years. Maybe that's why it is subject to so many pests. With a small garden you may have to experiment to see which variety of this now temperamental and susceptible vegetable is best suited to your control program, climate, slope of land, and soil conditions. The hope of the plant breeders has been, of course, to bring out varieties that are high yielding, vigorous, and more or less resistant to disease. When they happen to taste good, all the better. Long inbreeding and crossbreeding are now at such a high point of scientific exactitude that you can send away for prepackaged collections of standard varieties which will give a crop lasting over weeks instead of days, and will even provide many varieties of taste, color, and texture.

The latest breeding experiments have produced gene-altered corns which do not change sugar to starch after harvesting, but convert it to other sugars so the corn remains sweet, or "Super-sweet," or "Extra-sweet," as these new varieties are called (or E.H. for Everlasting Heritage). Another kind of corn that stays sweet is referred to as Sugar Extended, S.E. The E.H. corns must be isolated from other corns; the S.E. need not.

In general corn is white or yellow, but you can also get corn with kernels both yellow and white, such as Butter and Sugar, or Honey and Cream as standard varieties, and among the super sweets, Kiss 'n' Tell and Honey 'n' Pearl. The standard bicolors have a fairly good taste and tender kernels, but I think the excellent Seneca Chief and Illini Chief are still superior. Other Extrasweets (E.H.) to try are How Sweet It Is (87 days), a white corn, and the golden Earliglow, Kandy Korn, and Mainliner. Other whites to try are Snow Queen, White Kandy Korn, Polar Vee F1, and Early Arctic (60) for northern zones. All those need isolation. Among the Sugar Extended (S.E.), which need not be isolated, try Bodacious, an early yellow; D'Artagnon, an early bicolor; Sweet Silver; and the midseason, yellow Summer Flame. Country Gentleman and Golden Bantam, the old-time favorites, are still carried by several seed suppliers.

If you are short on space, grow midget varieties such as White Midget or Golden Midget, which yield ears less than 6 inches long in a crop that matures in 65 days. Stokes has a short-season standard corn called Polar Vee (50 days). These little corns are good for boxes and patio pots if they're kept very well nourished and well watered.

There are dozens of varieties of corn available. Look over various catalogs and see what appeals to you. Since the corn earworm can be such a pest, it might pay to order varieties with an especially tight husk, which foils that worm. They include Spring Gold (67 days), often used in the South and West; Golden Security, also good in the South; and one favorite, good in both South and North, Seneca Chief. Iochief, Silver Queen, and Golden Beauty are said to be resistant to bacterial wilt. Anyone with a yen to grow a freak giant can order Giant from Gurney and see whether it really will grow to 20 feet high.

Wait to plant until all danger of frost has passed, though you can start a few seeds indoors, or plant some in a big, permanent cold-frame whose top you remove when it gets warm, or even under a series of curved plastic guards or cloches that you can remove later. Warm up the soil before planting, and keep it warm. Have very rich soil, especially rich in nitrogen, of which corn needs a great deal. Fertilize again when the plants are two-thirds grown. We sow in hills, four seeds to a group, one inch deep, and with the groups 2 feet apart. Separate the seeds in each hill about 2 to 3 inches. Plant in blocks of at least four rows, not in one long single row, so that pollination will be adequate. If the silk doesn't receive enough pollen, the ears will not develop full kernels. A big packet of seed will usually plant about four 25-foot rows and yield sixty to seventy-five ears.

Make successive plantings to stretch the season, saving for last, one of the early-maturing varieties such as Royal Crest, EarliKing, Spring Gold, or Early Sunglow. Some seed houses send bright pink seeds, dipped in an organic compound that is a fungus repellent. They look awful, but aren't, though there may be some mercury in the dip.

Watch the young plants coming up, and if you see weaklings, thin them out. Cultivate often and carefully until the plants are well established and you can put on mulch. Do not cultivate deeply or you will hurt the shallow roots and prop roots. Corn takes gallons of water and needs all the big strong roots it can get.

There are special directions for growing the new Extra-sweet (E.H.) corns. You should wait until the soil is good and warm (75° F) and plan to give these corns twice as much moisture as you give standard corn. Be sure you attain good isolation; that is, at least 100 feet from other corn. Plant at 1 inch or 1-½ inches for proper germination. Keep moist. Watch for half-silk, the point at which half the silk has emerged, and plan to pick the ears eighteen to twenty-two days later. Rush them to a cool place as soon as picked, as you do standard corn, but of course these E.H. varieties stay sweet for days instead of minutes.

The corn earworm (greenish and striped) is also the tomato fruitworm, so do not plant the two crops near each other—that just encourages the pest. Predators that will control this worm include the polistes wasp; the ichneumon fly, which feeds on and lays eggs in the worm; and the trichogramma wasp (see Appendix), which destroys eggs—a good thing because corn earworms emerge three from each egg. Best of all, this wasp attacks early, before the plant begins to succumb to attack. And remember that worm larvae will succumb to Bt.

You can also use a quarter of a teaspoon of mineral oil with or without a dab of pyrethrum, applied to the tip of the ear of corn when the silk begins to brown at the end. Ryania or sabadilla as a dust can also be applied at the tip, and you can set blacklight traps to catch the moths before they lay eggs at the tips of the ears. The larvae of earworms feed downwards, so if you can get them at the top of the ear before they begin their damage, you will have control. See seed catalogs for mention of varieties with a very tight husk (Burpee's Honeycross, for example), which means a strain that would be fairly resistant to the corn earworm. One more control is the woodpecker. Use suet to keep it coming to your garden all year-round.

The European corn borer, a common pest, is the larva of a night-flying moth, so during egg-laying time in May, when the moths are moving in on the leaves of all kinds of plants, trap them with blacklight lanterns. Seven weeks later they start a new cycle, and this time they lay on corn. If the larva survives to emerge, it will bore into the plant anywhere, into the stalks, the ears, the stems. The best defense is a thorough cleaning-up every fall, preferably by plowing under the infected stalks so that they are buried, or by tilling them into the earth deeply enough to stifle the eggs.

Other standard controls include the use of organic dusts

or sprays such as rotenone, ryania, or sabadilla. Sprinkle the dust in the axils of the leaves where they emerge from the stem. Do it after a rain. If you can find and remove all the eggs, you won't have to spray, but it is sometimes hard to detect the scalelike white masses. The borer itself is easy to find. Remove it. Though the ladybug prefers aphids, that predator will also control corn borers. Send for a box of them, open it, and let them out according to directions. The parasite *Lydella stabulans grisescens*, a fly, is sometimes used in the eastern and middle Atlantic states, and the spores of the fungus *Beauveria bassiana* are found to be effective against newly hatched larvae. The easily obtainable *Bacillus thüringiensis* also works effectively.

The nastiest pest on corn is a fungus called smut that causes first a white bulge, which is a gall, and then, when the spores burst out, a mass of purplish black. Take out and burn any galls you see, but do not rely on your compost heap to consume them. If the fungus happens to survive, it might infect your whole pile. Burpee's Honeycross is said to be resistant to this as well as to earworm and wilt. Order that variety.

Again, good soil is the best preventive of all. One correspondent quoted in *The Organic Ways to Plant Protection*, Emmaus, PA. Rodale, 1966, says, "Several times I have planted a block of corn in my best soil and continued the rows into poorer ground. Borers and earworms have invariably attacked the unnourished plants, while the rest were left strictly alone. I am sure that rich organic soil is the answer to many common problems of plant pests and diseases."

Raccoons absolutely love corn. Wrap up each ear in both a paper bag and a wire net or screening. I hope you have an army of people to help do that tedious job. Keep watch while it is ripening, for then is the time raccoons are especially eager to get at it. After harvesting, put it up where they cannot get at it.

In spring, crows, which do not always cause trouble, sometimes try to dig under the very young plants for the remaining part of the seed kernel you planted, and the very nutritious young sprout. The best way to foil them is to use a good, deep mulch so that the little plants can use up the stored food in the endosperm of the seeds before the crows see them. It may also help to spread netting over the corn

169

patch and pin it down with half coat hangers every 12 inches. We feed the crows once or twice a day at our place, and for years they did not bother our corn. Then one damp, cold year when we planted late, they did come to the patch until we took steps to stop them. In subsequent years they stayed away. I don't know the explanation for this, but I suspect that during the cold, damp year the crows had young coming along.

When you get ready to eat standard corn, remember just this: The sugar begins to turn to starch twelve minutes after picking. Have the water boiling or the pressure cooker heating before you even go out to pick. Cook five minutes or less in unsalted boiling water. All stale corn is second-rate, unless it is Extra-sweet within a reasonable time of harvest.

Roasting is a delicious way to prepare corn. Pull down the husks, but do not pull them off. Remove the silk, butter or oil the kernels, and salt them if you wish. Pull the husks back up, tie them, and roast over coals for 15 to 20 minutes, or in a 350° F oven for 30 minutes or until tender, turning them often.

For freezing corn, be sure you get the ears into the blanching water while there is still sugar in the kernels. Eat frozen corn within a few weeks. There is loss of taste and sugar if you don't. A second method for freezing is to tie up the ears, husks and all, put them in individual plastic bags, and freeze without blanching. Again, the corn should be absolutely fresh-picked. If you can't get fresh-picked standard corn use Extrasweet or Supersweet.

If you have a flour mill, dry all your leftover corn and have it ready to make into fresh-ground cornmeal for hoecakes and hush puppies. And save some cornmeal after grinding for a soap powder for cleaning dishes and pots. It feels soft and smooth on your hands.

Cover Crop

It may be that you have inherited some old worn-out or pesticide-contaminated fields that you want to renovate. One way to go about this is to plow up the field and then plant a cover crop, which is a crop you grow for the express purpose of plowing it under as green manure.

In the summer buckwheat, soybeans, millet, oats, and Sudan grass are suitable, sown in May, though in some areas oats may be sown earlier. Most of them can be plowed under in August. If there is a good yield, the crop should be cut and chopped before it is turned into the soil. Soybeans are excellent for a legume crop, but harvest the beans before plowing them under. (See *Soybeans.*) Other legumes to consider include common vetch, purple vetch, bitter vetch, horse beans, Tangier peas, field peas, fenugreek, and bur clover, depending on your climate. The cover crops that produce the heaviest growth would probably be purple vetch, hairy vetch, horse beans, and Tangier peas.

Winter rye is the favorite winter cover crop; it will also protect bare soil from eroding. This and winter wheat can be planted in most areas between August 15 and September 15 at the rate of 2-½ pounds per 100 square feet, and plowed under the following April. The fertilizing power of these crops will be about 2 percent nitrogen, .5 to .8 percent phosphorus, and 3 to 6 percent potassium.

Cowpeas are well-rooted legumes, valuable where heavy crops have depleted the soil. They make sandy soils more compact and clays more friable because they add humus and regenerate the bacteria. For your own table, soak some cowpeas for several hours in plain water, then simmer over low heat until tender. Add onion and garlic, pork fat or bacon fat, celery, and green pepper.

Cress (Peppergrass)
Lepidium sativum

Garden cress is not as good as watercress, but if you begin every dinner with a salad, as many nutritionists advise you to, you want some variety. Burpee's Curlycress can be grown the year round (in 10 to 20 days), indoors and out. Slow to bolt, too. Excellent for salads and green drinks. Less curly, but also up and edible in 10 or so days are Salad Cress or Upland Cress, available from many seed suppliers. If these cresses go to seed in your garden in midsummer, they will sow the near ground, be up for a new crop in a few weeks, and last until frost. Mild. Wonderful for sandwiches. Very easy to grow, and practically pestless.

Cucumber
Cucumis sativus

We have grown cucumbers in rows, in hills, in the open, in the shade of corn, on and off compost heaps, and have had everything from bad to extremely good luck with them. The worst was when we let the grass get in; the best was when the vines had the most compost and some shade part of the time. One packet of seeds will grow twenty hills, and that's plenty if the vines are kept well picked. We grow only about half a dozen hills with interplantings of nasturtiums, and save the seeds for another year. They are viable for five years. To prolong the season start some seeds in peat pots, and set them out under hotcaps so they will get used to the outdoors as soon as they can stand it.

If you have some big pots to put on a terrace, plant some cucumber vines in one or two. With a good rich soil, an adequate watering system (mostly just remembering to do it), and some sort of support to keep the vines from sprawling, you can have a handsome and convenient potted plant.

If the plant description in the seed catalog mentions that the cucumber is black-spined, that means that it is a pickling cucumber and has little black, slightly prickly knobs on it. A good all-purpose pickle cucumber is National Pickling, recommended for all sizes from very small to six inches long. A prolific small-pickle variety is West India Gherkin, which matures in 58 days.

Any of these will do better on a field that has been used for beans, lupine, or clover the previous year, and on an area scattered the week before planting with at least four-month-old manure as well as compost. Cucumbers need lots of nutrients; if you plant in hills, thin the plants to three per hill, so there will be enough nutrients for all. They grow very fast; be sure to cultivate to make room for the fast-growing roots, unless the soil is very loose to start with. After the plants reach 18 inches, add a high-nitrogen fertilizer. Water at once, or apply just before rain.

Many varieties are available. Standard-sized cucumbers include Spacemaster (52 days), Marketmore (80), Petita (60), with a high yield, and Aurelia (64). Bush cucumbers include Bush Champion (55) and Bush Crop (60). Pickling sizes are available as Picklebush (52), Liberty Hybrid (54), and Saladin

Hybrid Pickler (55). The favorite burpless cucumber is
Sweet Success, which is a self-pollinator. Salad Bush is
recommended for pots, and Cluster for growing on fences.
Keep that one picked and it will go on bearing. Good
bearers, also, are those called gynoecious, meaning all
female flowers. Streamliner (60) is a good example, with a
nice small seed cavity. Try Early Pride Hybrid, which will
also bear over a long period, but will do best if there are
some male flowers around for pollination. Gemini Hybrid
is a favorite, and it is resistant to mosaic, downy mildew,
powdery mildew, and anthracnose. Poinsett is also widely
disease resistant.

No matter which varieties you plant, you will have to keep
watch, even on well-manured, well-composted plots, for
the striped cucumber beetle. As soon as it arrives, dust
plants with wood ashes, rock phosphate, or granite dust,
or use a spray of wood ashes and hydrated lime diluted in
two gallons of water. Some people dust with rotenone.
(The same holds for squash, pumpkin, and melon vines.)
Unhappily, these pests come during dry weather. Lots of
water and good mulches help to keep in the moisture. If the
dust doesn't work in dry weather, and if you have plenty
of water to spare, give the plants a good dousing before
applying the spray. A shortcoming of dusts is that they
sometimes discourage the predators of undesirable insects.
Hosing often does the trick by itself.

Other measures to take would be companionate planting
with onions and garlic, planting marigolds and nasturtiums, and permitting companionate weeds such as lamb's-
quarters and sow thistle to grow up. It also helps to plant
beans, corn, and peas nearby. Blacklight trap lamps have
been used with considerable success on cucumber beetles
at some experiment stations. Also keep the garden free from
debris.

When your cucumbers get long and filled out and green,
pick four to make Breaded Cucumber Slices. Leave them
unpeeled, but wash off dust if you have to. Then slice them
⅛ inch thick, rub each slice with ½ clove of garlic, and
dredge with a mixture of 3 tablespoons bread crumbs, 3
tablespoons flour, ¾ teaspoon salt, ⅛ teaspoon pepper.
Heat ¼ cup soybean or sunflower oil in a skillet and brown
the slices on both sides. Drain on paper towels and serve
right away as a hot vegetable.

If this is too rich for you, braise them, or make soup, or that cold cucumber aspic which is always made from a secret recipe. One recipe I pried out of an English hostess starts with 1 tablespoon of unflavored gelatin, soaked in leftover spinach cooking water for 5 minutes. Then dissolve the gelatin over hot water and add 1 cup of green juice from blended salad greens flavored with 1 teaspoon salt or less, ¼ cup or less lemon juice, 1 tablespoon chives, 3 teaspoons parsley, and a chopped green pepper, all blended together. Add ½ teaspoon fresh-ground white pepper if wanted. Let this nearly set, then add 1-½ cups cucumber chopped fine and ½ cup sour cream or yogurt. Serve on a bed of young mustard greens, watercress, and small kale leaves, with very thin slices of cucumber as decoration.

People no longer believe in soaking cucumbers in vinegar, nor do they think they have to salt and weight them or peel them if they are homegrown. Unfortunately, the store-bought ones that have been coated with paraffin for long shelf life do have to be peeled. That's one additive you do not want to eat.

Cooked cucumbers are somewhat bitter, but they are one variation to use during the season of cucumber surfeit, and are very easy to prepare. Peel, cube, and boil for 5 to 10 minutes, depending on the age of the vegetable.

Dandelion
Taraxacum officinale

Dandelions used everywhere since ancient times as a source of vitamins in early spring tonics, usually made from the roots. In rural areas they are gobbled up as greens by almost anyone who can get out to dig when the days begin to get warm. Some cook them, can them, store them up for the following winter; others eat them raw and relish them in salads. Suburbanites still fight them as lawn weeds, but more and more now eat them when young as well as eradicate them. The old plants are really bitter, and lawn dandelions are never as tasty as those that come up in the fields or the vegetable garden. If you save the crown of buds, and cook it with the leaves, it has a smooth, bland taste that goes well with the stronger taste of the leaves. The roots can easily be peeled and sliced thinly, boiled in two waters, and buttered and salted to eat like parsnips.

To grow your own dandelions, plant seeds in rows 18 inches apart and cover with ½ inch of good soil. Thin the seedlings to stand a foot apart, and use the thinnings for greens. The roots can be used for a coffee substitute if kept to the second year, when they get quite big. Either year, they can be brought into the cellar and planted as you do the roots of witloof chicory (see pages 164–65).

If you want dandelions to eat all summer, start with seeds bought from a seed company, such as the variety called Thick-Leaved. From 25 plants you can freeze or can a winter supply and have fresh greens besides. Condition the soil with compost, and apply plenty of wood ashes and rock phosphate, and fish emulsion in water at 2 or 3 percent. For tender hearts of dandelion, let the outside leaves grow and then tie them up for a week to blanch the inside leaves. They will make a delicate and mild addition to your salads. Dandelions are also easy to grow in a window box or patio tub. They can be interspersed with parsley, ten-day cress, tarragon, and other rugged growers. Keep adding nutrients at three-week intervals because the contest between the roots will be considerable.

Dandelion Wine: In one gallon of water, boil 4 pounds sugar until dissolved. While it's still boiling, pour the mixture over the peels of 2 oranges and 1 lemon that you have placed in a crock. When the liquid is lukewarm, add 1 gallon dandelion flowers, juices of the fruit, and 1 ounce yeast. Cover, and leave for 10 days. Stir daily and remove any flowers that go bad. Strain the liquid into a clean jar: Secure a piece of cheesecloth over the jar and press down in the center, forming a funnel. Tie on two thicknesses of cotton cloth for the top. Keep the jar in a warm room, and maintain it this way as long as little bubbles continue to rise. When it's quiet, begin clearing. Siphon off the yeast deposit. Cover tightly and set the jar in a cool place for a few weeks; then siphon off accumulated yeast again. Continue this until the wine is clear. This could take three months, but you'll be glad to know that this process improves the flavor. Never bottle too early; corks could fly and bottles burst, wasting the wine. Use champagne bottles, if you can get them; their indented bottoms allow for expansion. Sterilize the bottles in hot water with soda added. Rinse and dry in a warm oven. As you remove each bottle from the oven, plug it with cotton. Place two raisins in each bottle before filling. Leave space for the cork to be pushed in until it's level with the top. Wire the corks (you can buy loops), and store the bottles on their sides in a cool, dark place for six months.

Daylily
Hemerocallis fulva

These hardy flowers, which grow almost anywhere and have practically no pests, are wild lilies in Europe and Asia.

As can be seen in Japanese and Chinese cookbooks, the daylily is an important food in the East, eaten as root,

Edible Stages of the Daylily: Sprouts, Flower and Buds

stalk, bud, and opened flower. They are often served, as tempura, dipped in batter and then fried (see page 159). I braise all parts of them in butter over a slow heat, and serve on toast for lunch, or even breakfast. The small stalks when they come up in the spring provide a delicious, nutritious substitute for asparagus.

If you live out in the country, you may know of a stretch of abandoned land along the roadside where the common browny orange daylily has gone wild. The sprouts on fresh, firm roots from that patch, if they are available to you, are just as delicious in the spring as those in your own garden would be. The bud and flower are also excellent. By ordering and planting cultivated daylilies that bloom at different seasons, you can have a good crop coming on from June to September. Many nurseries sell them at fairly reasonable prices. For a fall crop of young new leaves, cut back some early bloomers to the ground in late August; they will spring up again soon afterward.

Edible Flowers

People have long been using nasturtium seeds as a sort of pickled caper, but the leaves, too, are good as a tart addition to salads. The flowers, somewhat milder, add a beautiful touch to a salad; I use them throughout the blooming season. Marigolds and calendulas, with sharper flavors, can also be added, and they are both excellent to lend yellow color to sauces and custards. Violet leaves in the spring make a tasty, mild substitute for spinach, and the flowers are decorative and tasty, too. Chive flowers in June add a fine tang to a salad. Blue borage flowers add a cucumberish flavor. And stuffed squash zucchini blossoms, as well as daylily blossoms, make an attractive dish. (See *Squash* for the suggested variety, and use male blossoms, not female.)

Dill
See Herbs, pages 180–202.

Eggplant
Solanum melongena

If you have rich, somewhat sandy soil and can start seeds in a hot bed or indoors over an electric coil or heat tape, you might have some luck growing eggplant. Start with seeds in early April, or whenever for you is eight weeks before the safe time to set out small plants in the garden. Soak seeds for half an hour first. Plant them in small individual peat pots or Ferto-pellets, then transfer them to bigger peat pots which you later plant in the ground, pot and all. Do not let them wilt by day or get chilled at night. Do not plant them out where peppers or tomatoes were grown the previous year. Cover with a basket or hotcap if necessary. A dusting with rotenone or wood ashes now and then when the plants are still young will help protect them. One packet has about thirty-five seeds, so you would get more eggplant than you'd need if they all germinated. The seeds stay viable for four years.

Perhaps the best way to grow this rather difficult plant is to try your luck with eggplants started by a professional at a greenhouse. Six or eight plants will be plenty for a small family. Set them in a one-foot hole, with a good shovelful of compost worked into the bottom. The recommended variety is Black Magic Hybrid with a maturing rate of 72 days after setting them out. An earlier one is Burpee's Early Beauty Hybrid, which matures in 62 days after setting out and is very prolific. An oriental type of eggplant, Tycoon, will mature in 60 days; the long, tapered Agora in 70 days. A small one, Little Fingers, will come in clusters. Other small ones are Bride (75), and the striped Masumi (65). Two yellow or whitish-yellow varieties are Easter Egg and Thai. There is also a Thai Green.

After the soil is warm, mulch deeply to hold up the fruits. Pick all the fruits as soon as they are plump and glossy, with their seeds small. Your crop will last for several weeks. Do not let the fruit get overripe and pulpy.

The results of growing this difficult plant can be so delicious that the struggle is worth it. The best recipe I know includes a cubed eggplant and a finely chopped onion, sautéed in butter until the eggplant and onion are soft. Then add salt, a tablespoon of chopped fresh basil, one or two beaten eggs, and a handful of grated cheese. Add these all at once unless the cheese you use won't melt easily, and stir only until the egg is thickened and the cheese soft and runny. It is impossible to give exact proportions because the size of the eggplant will vary. You have to practice to get the mixture soft and smooth, and not end up with lumpy egg or stringy cheese. When done just right, this is a good hearty vegetable entrée. Use a little white wine to keep things moist if the juice from the eggplant is not enough. Variations on this dish, somewhat less of a gamble, are a custard with onion and eggplant, and a yogurt, wheat germ, and eggplant sauce which can be used with lamb or soybeans.

Endive
See Chicory, pages 164–65.

Florence Fennel
See Herbs, pages 180–202.

Garlic
See Herbs, pages 180–202.

Geraniums
Pelargonium

Grow lots of them, and after you have one plant, you can easily make slips by cutting off lengths of stem with several nodes, leaving them exposed to the air overnight to form a callus at the place of the cut, then putting them to root in wet sand. After they are well rooted, transplant them to good potting soil. In summer plant geraniums around your garden, on the outer edge and near corn or other vegetables that attract Japanese beetles. White geraniums are especially repellent. If there are hard freezes where you live, take up all plants in the fall to keep indoors over the winter. Make the slips in the spring or summer.

Grapes
Vitis vinifera

Have wild grapevines if you can; they are sturdy and, except for Japanese beetles, fairly pest-free; and they make wonderful jelly and conserves. Otherwise get some two-year-old Concord grapevines to start out with. These are fine blue grapes, excellent for grape juice and jelly. They stand the cold, as do the red grape Agawam and the white grape Niagara, which ripens at about the same time as Concord. Buy sturdy stock from a reliable nursery, and plant the vines in a warm, southsloping place, against a building or fence, but not near trees.

In the North the early grapes include Ontario, Seneca, the blue Van Buren, and Fredonia. Very hardy are Hardy Worden and Alden. Midseason varieties include, besides Concord and Niagara, the good, hardy red grape, Delaware. For late grapes try the blue Sheridan, which keeps for weeks, Catawba, the red grape that also keeps well, and Golden Muscat. The late black, seedless grape, Glenora, is quite hardy. Of course there are many, many varieties grown in the West. Good selections for home gardeners might be Thompson, Cardinal, Pierce for hot areas, and such old-timers as Concord and Niagara.

Plant in 12- or 14-inch holes, of about 16 inches in diameter. Mix bone meal, compost, and granite dust with good loam for planting. Whether you plant in spring or fall, prune the tops in the spring to a single cane with two buds. Grow several vines of each variety, and look forward to harvesting the second year. You might get up to twenty pounds per vine once they get established.

Sometimes it is necessary to put a net over the crop if the birds find the grapes before you are ready to pick. Grape leaves are very attractive to Japanese beetles. I have never found that they did much harm to our vines, but it is obvious that any deprivation of leaf area robs the plant of some of its food. Pick off the beetles and try a garlic-onion-water spray if they persist.

We have not yet tried hardy seedless grapes, but they sound very attractive. Recommended varieties are Interlaken, New Himrod, and Pink Aurora, which is not really seedless. Interlaken is said to be good to combine with Concord, for it ripens three to four weeks earlier. Any time after the leaves come out you can begin to get the benefit of rice, soy grits, onions, and rosemary wrapped in grape leaves and simmered in a casserole until the leaves are tender. We use 1 cup of cooked rice, ½ cup cooked grits, 1 tablespoon wheat germ, 1 tablespoon milk powder or soy milk powder, ½ cup chopped, sautéed onion, and 1 table-spoon crushed rosemary. Mix well and wrap in grape leaves, putting about 2 or 3 tablespoons of the mixture on each leaf, depending on the size. Pin with toothpicks. Use chicken broth or tomato juice for the liquid in the casserole. Bake at 325° F for 40 minutes, or until the leaves are tender. Also nibble some young tendrils. They have a sweet-sour taste.

Herbs

On many occasions you will be glad that the methods of organic gardening demand plentiful crops of herbs. You will begin to clip herbs to add to salads and other foods while the herbs are still young and tender. Many you will plant here and there among your vegetables, and on the outer borders of your garden as pest repellents. Many you will harvest on a warm, clear, sunny day in summer when your herbs are in top condition just before blooming.

Prepare the soil as you would for vegetables, and let it settle a while before planting. Some seeds can be helped along by letting them soak on a saucer in the kitchen before planting. Others can be started in the cold frame. Some come up well in full sun; others need to be shaded when young. But if you follow the general rule of shielding young plants from very hot sun, and from drying out, you will have pretty good luck.

If you are inclined to grow too many herbs, and too much of each, harvest them anyhow, and give them away or take them to the organic food store. They also do well on the compost heap and, in fact, the Bio-Dynamic gardening group systematically incorporates camomile, nettle, and several others into each heap.

The "basic compost herbs" are chicory, nettle, camomile, dandelion, yarrow, valerian, and (though not an herb) the ground bark of oak trees. Specific virtues claimed for these herbs are for chicory, an alkaline salt and silicic acid; for nettle, a sulfuric content that regulates potassium, calcium, and iron; for camomile, a power to mediate between the silicic acid of the cosmos and of the earth; for yarrow, a guiding power for potassium because of its affinity for sulfur, and its ability to draw substances from the atmosphere into the soil and the compost heap; for valerian, a power to help phosphorus compounds be assimilated; for oak, to aid the health of plants by its calcium content.

Pests are rare on herbs, but if you get red spider mites or aphids, wash the plants with soap or insecticidal soap and water, or hose them down; if they are attacked in the home apply a dried tobacco and water spray, rotenone, or pyrethrum. But plants that are sturdy and well nourished probably won't get such pests.

In planning, choose both pest-repellent and culinary herbs, including basil, chervil, sweet marjoram, thyme, rosemary, and tarragon, and the old standbys chives, parsley, summer savory, and dill. Remember that rosemary, the thymes,

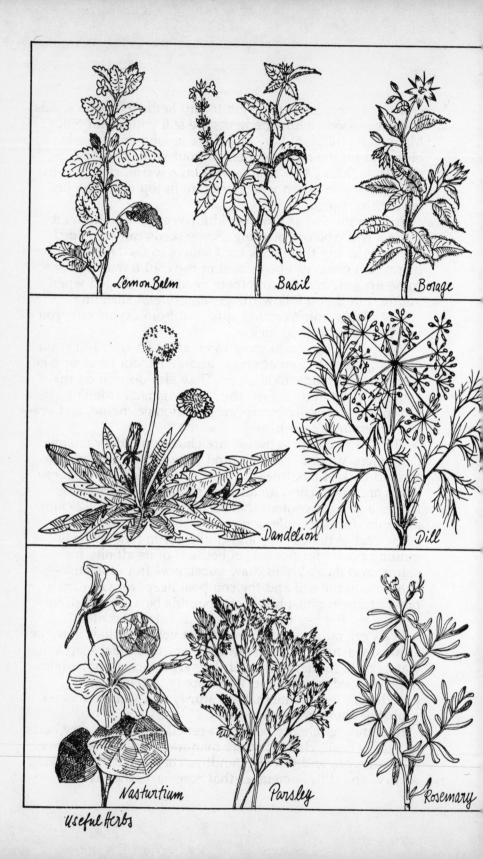

Lemon Balm

Basil

Borage

Dandelion

Dill

Nasturtium

Parsley

Rosemary

Useful Herbs

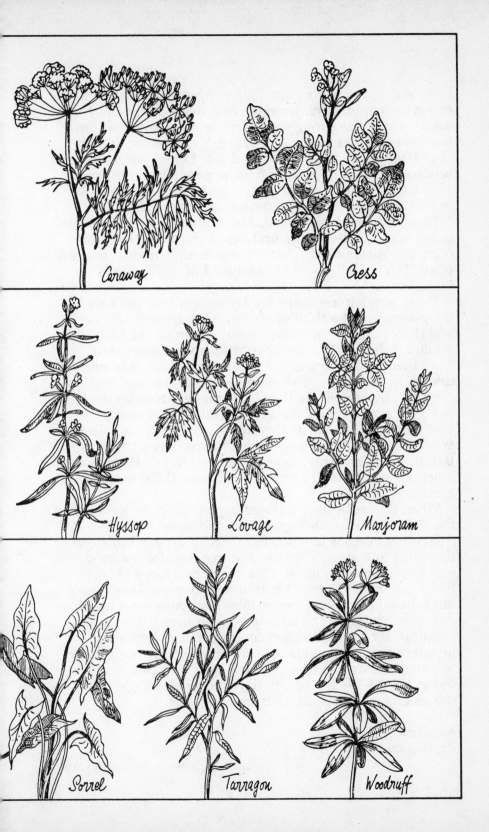

Caraway

Cress

Hyssop

Lovage

Marjoram

Sorrel

Tarragon

Woodruff

sage, and winter savory are quite pungent, and slightly less
so are the mints, basil, tarragon, and sweet marjoram. Not
usually eaten but strongly pest repellent are feverfew, tansy,
marigolds, and as I have said above, nasturtiums; though I
have a recipe for marigold custard and I often put nasturtium
seeds and blossoms in salads. Some perennial herbs, such
as chives, thyme, rosemary, sage, and lemon balm can be
potted and kept on the windowsill or under lights.

Perennials outdoors will also be ready to use the first thing
in the spring, after the ground thaws and the new shoots
come up. A semihardy plant such as marjoram can also be
planted in the fall if you live in a mild plant-hardiness
zone.

When you harvest herbs for drying, cut only the tops of
the plants, about a third or quarter of its growth. (Parsley
and chives can be cut farther down.) Then tie the herbs in
small bunches, or put a rubber band around them, and
hang them to dry in a cool, airy, darkish place. It is quick
drying, in the shade, that preserves flavor, texture, and
color. If the weather suddenly gets muggy, transfer the herbs
to a very slow oven, about 200° F. Watch them often, and
take them out as soon as they are dry, for they can lose their
flavor if left in for too long. If that happens you might as
well throw them away, unless you want to mix them in with
other, strong-flavored herbs for herb teas. (Mint would be a
good coverall.)

When the herbs have finished drying, strip the leaves from
the stems, pack in small glass jars, and store.

Freezing herbs is less satisfactory then drying, but steeping
them in white vinegar for two or three months is a good
way to preserve the flavor. One of the best ways to keep
herbs is to make various kinds of herb butters. They give a
much better flavoring to vegetables than butter and herbs
added separately at the last minute; the herb flavors have
had time to be extracted and concentrated. If left undis-
turbed, a tightly closed jar of herb butter in the refrigerator
will keep for six months. Once the jar is open use it up for
sauces, sandwich spreads, to flavor scrambled eggs, or to
rub on chops, steaks, hamburgers, or roasts.

Angelica
Angelica archangelica

Easy to grow in any good soil,

perhaps in part shade, and perhaps in a slightly moist place. The tender leaf stalks can be chewed as a substitute for candy, put into cakes, or used as candied angelica for cake decoration. Let it resow itself, for it is a biennial. Nichols in Oregon (see Appendix) has seeds and plants.

Anise
Pimpinella anisum

A fragile annual with a licorice taste. If you sow it outside, do not thin or move it, for it cannot stand upset. Put it in the sun, and harvest it for the seeds the minute the first seeds are ripe. Spread in a warm, dry, shady place on papers to dry out. Use for desserts and drinks.

Basil *(green or purple, called ornamental basil)*
Ocimum basilicum

Easy to grow in flats, but hard to start outdoors in the hot sun. If you plant it in the ground, see that the first shoots are well shaded and well watered. It is a native of India, and a very useful herb. It can be harvested all summer from the bottom leaves. Use the cut tops to dry out for winter use, and add oil to the basil to enhance the flavor. Basil is a delicious addition to eggplant and sliced tomatoes, and indispensable in soups.

Several varieties of basil are available, including the handsome purple one and a very nice dwarf variety. The Cook's Garden in Londonderry, Vermont, carries nine varieties, including Sweet Genovese, Mammoth, Opal, Lemon Basil, Cinnamon Basil, and both Purple and Green Ruffles Basil.

Borage
Borago officinalis

This annual herb, much loved by bees, is used as leaves or as a flower in drinks such as lemonade and Pim's Number One Cup. No wonder it has had a fine reputation for curing melancholy, reviving hypochondriacs, and cheering students. It can be found, if you want to hunt, around old dumps and abandoned houses, probably as an escapee, for it reseeds readily. The young, tender leaves have a cool cucumbery taste for salads, and it will add potassium and calcium to your diet (or to your compost heaps). Press out some juice for freezing, to add to jellies, wine bowls, and candies.

Bouncing Bet (Soapwort)
Saponaria officinalis

Brought here by our forebears to help with the washing. The juice, says an old herbal, "scoureth almost as well as Sope." Old people with secret skills clean up and return the color to faded damasks and tapestries with the aid of this herb. It has also been used to scour one's inside, for example, "against the French Poxes" and "the hydropical waters." The gaily flowering bouncing Bet grows wild along the river in our town, and has been brought into several gardens to add its pink blossoms to the summer display. It is easy to grow and charming to have around, but it does need watching because it spreads very quickly. It can be bought from many nurseries. Use its leaves as a laundry aid. For soap, tie together ten stalks of bouncing Bet in bags. Boil in soft water until a soapy froth appears and the water turns greenish. First soak the fabric in cold water, rinsing it until it is clear of dirt. Place the fabric on a board over the bath and work in the soapy froth, using a sponge and moving in a circular motion. Keep applying as long as there is any dirt at all. Finally, wipe foam away, and dab off with towels. Dry in well-ventilated, shady area. (See *Horsetail*, page 194).

Burdock
Arctium lappa

Though the burs of this big biennial plant are hideous to get in your hair, or in your dog's fur, the root, sliced and boiled, is very good, and its food content highly valued—especially by those on a macrobiotic diet. If you want to grow it, you can find it on almost any vacant lot or along almost any old railroad. It is hard to dig, unless it is growing on very loose soil. In Japanese markets in this country the root is known as gobo. One of the best ways to cook it is to fry it as tempura after it has been boiled tender. The young shoots are good in early spring, but you must peel them, for the rind is quite bitter. Just eat the inner pith.

Camomile

The Roman variety is *Anthemis nobilis*; the German is *Matricaria chamomilla*. Both make a good soothing tea, and a bleach for blonde hair. They are pest repellent, and if you sponge camomile tea on bare arms and legs, biting insects will usually be repelled. Sprigs and flowers soaked for a couple of days make a good spray to control damping-off, the fungus that attacks tiny seedlings. Grow it from tiny seeds (Roman is perennial, German is annual). And leave seeds exposed to light to germinate. Camomile is said to lend strength to cabbages, onions, and drooping plants. (See *Feverfew*.)

Caraway
Carum carvi

An herb for seeds to put in your breads and cakes and, in fact, to reproduce the Seed Cake which Molly Bloom eats on Bloomsday. The young leaves and shoots can be used for salads to give a strange tang and also to quell cabbage-cooking smells. Like parsley, this is a biennial, so count on planting seed every other year, or plant annually in a permanent garden, in the same row, between the plants already there. Dress with compost.

Molly Bloom's Seed Cake: 1 cup butter, 1 cup sugar, 4 eggs, 2-½ cups sifted flour, ½ teaspoon baking powder, 2 tablespoons Irish whiskey, and 1-½ teaspoons caraway seeds. Cream the butter and sugar until white and fluffy. Add the eggs one at a time with a dust of flour each time to prevent separating. Beat well after each addition. Fold in sifted flour and baking powder, add seeds, and then the whiskey. Pour into an 8-inch cake pan lined with waxed paper. Scatter some caraway seeds on top and bake for 1 hour at 375° F. Reduce the heat for the last quarter hour to prevent burning.

Catnip
Nepeta cataria

Why not? Lots of people, also, like it—for tea and as a seasoning. Eighty days to mature, and it grows 1-½ to 2 feet tall and is perennial. Burpee has seeds. Not fussy about soil. Good pest repellent. Excellent for compost and green fertilizer.

Comfrey
Symphytum asperum

An herb found in many an organic garden, because of its nutritional values for humans, beast, and soil. Send away to a specialty house for pieces of root, and plant them in good loam with a pH of 6 to 7, at about 6 inches deep. The excellent root system of comfrey taps and brings up many minerals. Its fast, heavy growth chokes out weeds, even when planted 3 feet apart. It should be cut 2 inches above the ground, about five times a season. In the late spring, when the shoots are tender, begin the first harvest for salads.

Since comfrey is rather prickly, you will want to shred the leaves very fine before adding a mild French dressing. Other leaves may be put in the blender with other fresh greens to add minerals and vitamins to the green drinks you make. Or pour boiling water over some young leaves to steep for 12 minutes for an herb tea. Rolled, tied comfrey leaves added to (and later removed from) stews or soups can add nutrients.

If you wish, you can freeze or can young comfrey leaves for use later. For canning, process for 30 minutes in sterilized jars. For freezing, cook first. You can also dry young comfrey leaves in the sun or in an oven at 125° F. Dried, pulverized comfrey makes a fine addition to the herbs you put in your salads the following winter. Recent reports have mentioned possible carcinogens in comfrey, and Nancy Bubel and others have given up eating it.

Coriander
Coriandrum sativum

This delicious herb, now often called by its European name, cilantro, is very easy to grow, and easy to use in salads and sauces. The soil need not be especially rich, and the moisture certainly should not be constant. In fact, coriander is commercially grown in Morocco. Plant it in the spring, but wait until a dry spell when the soil is well dried. Keep it weeded when it's young, and begin to use the leaves as early as you wish. Bees and wasps are attracted to the flowers. When the seeds come, harvest them right away or they'll start reseeding the area.

Coriander is used in many kinds of dishes, from meats to

desserts. I also add some to homemade curry. And leaves or seeds to guacamole.

Dill
Anethum graveolens

This mild herb will grow in any average open area with a little compost dug in along the row, as long as the soil is not acid. A packet of seeds will sow 10 feet and give you plenty of delicate leaves to have fresh in salads, and some seeds for pickles later. The crop matures in 70 days. Keep the plants watered during times of drought to discourage pests, and spray with a garlic-onion blender mixture if you see that red spider mites are getting on them. If your climate is not too severe, plant some seeds in the fall so that they will come up early the following spring. Some people boil dill instead of caraway with cabbage, turnips, and cauliflower.

Dill makes a good trap plant for green tomato worms. In recent years I have not planted it because we have had so many volunteers coming up in the garden. Sometimes there are enough to save our own seeds for another year.

Fennel
Foeniculum

Here is a pleasant herb to have for salads—if you like anise as a taste. The leaves and tender stalks can also be eaten boiled, with or without a cream sauce, though the bulbs are the part usually cooked. If left alone, wild fennel (*Foeniculum vulgare*) will mature in 90 days and grow to 5 or 6 feet, come to seed, scatter seed, and grow up just about everywhere the following year. Therefore, cut back the stalks two or three times, but toward the end of summer let some self-seed. Black fennel is a very handsome plant and tastes just about the same as wild fennel. Try fennel tea, made by pouring a cup of boiling water on a teaspoon of bruised fennel fruit or seed.

Another kind, Florence fennel (*Foeniculum dulce*), has whitish stalks like celery which you harvest as a bulb, and braise. Get the variety called Mammoth to sow in spring when the weather is still cool, spacing 6 to 8 inches apart. In Italy, where the bulb is usually braised, it is call *Finocchio* and has often been used to stuff keyholes to keep out ghosts. Otherwise it has been cooked with fish, used in fish sauce, its seeds added to sausages and soups, rolls and breads, cooked with beet greens, and ground to a medicinal powder for comfort to the stomach. Most seed houses carry it.

Feverfew
Chrysanthemum parthenium

A prolific tangy herb, feverfew is very useful as a repellent. It has pleasant little white flowers that look like small daisies. Herb and flower houses carry it; or dig it up along the roadside, where you often see it growing in the gravel. It looks like camomile, and is often confused with it.

Garlic
Allium sativum

Just about the most useful plant an organic gardener grows, both for its excellent taste and because of its potent and efficacious antibiotic and repellent qualities. It has an incredibly ancient history of use by the peoples of Europe from Siberia to Sicily. In some polite circles it has been thought vulgar, partly because the peasants in various cultures regarded it as an aphrodisiac, and its smell on the breath was always the giveaway. As early as the sixteenth century it was used as a mole repellent ("to make them leap out of the ground"). For modern pest control plant cloves of garlic around your peach, apple, and pear trees, and here and there among your vegetables. Grow a row so you'll have plenty for your own use in the kitchen, and enough to make sprays and to transplant more of the cloves whenever needed.

Garlic does best in well-prepared, enriched soil. Divide bulbs into single cloves and bury them 2 inches deep, though as a repellent you may decide to put some nearer the surface. Weed the garlic plants well, dust the rows with soot, wood ashes, or compost, and be sure you plant in full sun. A 1971 report from the University of California at Davis said that the antibiotic in ten parts per million could be effective in controlling pests in your tomatoes or corn.

Also available now are bulbs for Elephant Garlic. The common varieties can be counted on to grow five to seven new cloves from each clove planted; elephant garlic grows five cloves, and will be five times larger. Plant its cloves 2 inches deep and harvest when the tops die down in about three months.

The virtue of garlic is in its sulfide of allyl, an oil present in all members of the onion family. It is so good a protection against unwanted bacteria that in wartime it has been used as a disinfectant (on a swab of sterile sphagnum moss). It is very health-giving and is liked by cattle, dogs, fowl, gorillas, and wild animals who seek out colonies of wild garlic. Perhaps you have tasted spring milk that is redolent of the garlic the cows ate.

Make garlic butter for bread and vegetables. Put slivers of raw garlic in steak before grilling. Steep some in vinegar and add to mayonnaise. Cook eight cloves to add to mashed potatoes.

Horehound
Marrubium vulgare

The leaves of white or common horehound are used for flavoring candy and making teas. You can buy the seeds from Burpee's or Nichols (who also sell plants) and save a few of the 18-inch plants for perennials. Horehound likes poor, dry soil and does well if sown in spring or increased by root cuttings.

Black horehound (*Ballota nigra*) is a good fly repellent and efficacious, so they used to say, "if you are poisoned." Whereas white horehound has a pleasant odor, black horehound has a foul smell.

Horseradish
Armoracia rusticana

If you can get hold of a few pieces of root, you can start right out on your horseradish plantation. Put it in rich soil with manure dug 18 inches into the soil, water it well, and you'll have all you need in short order. Until the Germans invented horseradish sauce in the eighteenth century (to eat with Friday fish), it was used for medicinal purposes only. The best way to have a year-round supply is to dig some roots to winter-over in a box of damp sand. This herb is a violent spreader. Watch it carefully. Also, wear gloves whenever you handle it.

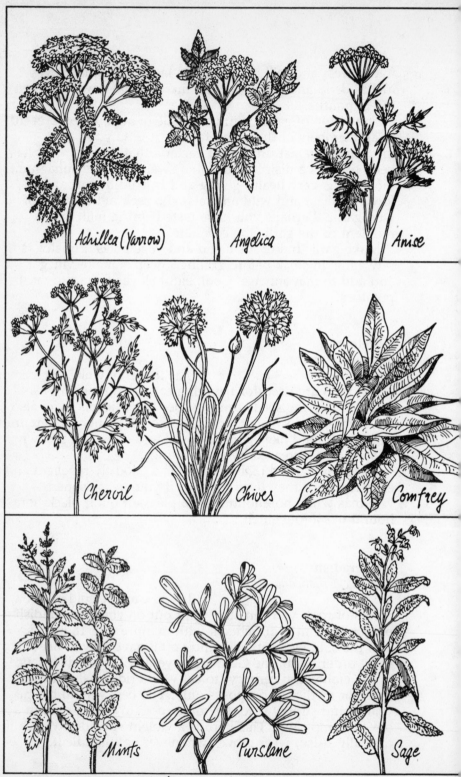

Achillea (Yarrow) Angelica Anise

Chervil Chives Comfrey

Mints Purslane Sage

Unusual Herbs and Weeds

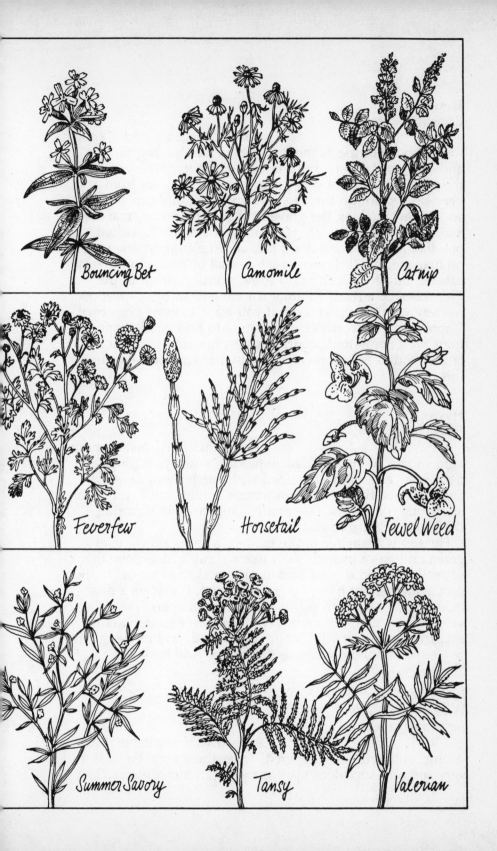

Bouncing Bet

Camomile

Catnip

Feverfew

Horsetail

Jewel Weed

Summer Savory

Tansy

Valerian

Horsetail
Equisetum hyemale

This is "scouring reed," known throughout Europe as the best means for cleaning pewter and other metal pots, for it takes up into its own system the silica which most other plants reject. It comes from a very early point on the evolutionary scale, and can still be seen growing along the gravelly edges of streams, marshes, and roadsides. There are two forms: the many-branched one that looks like a horse's tail, and the straight one with no branches at all. I once saw horsetail offered in a nursery catalog, but if you can't find some plants yourself in the gravel beside a road, I think an accommodating all-purpose nursery would help you out if you want to grow your own Chore-Boy. It's worth experimenting to find good proportions for a spray to discourage slugs, for example, whose tender bodies would be repulsed by the scratchy silica in this plant.

Hyssop
Hyssopus officinalis

This rather bitter-tasting herb with square stems is added to pickles, poultry stuffing, and meat pies, especially combined with parsley and sage. Some believe that it "slayeth worms in man" and will "heal all manner of evils of the mouth." It is used in flavoring the liqueur Chartreuse.

Hyssop is attractive in the garden, for it is almost evergreen and has a growth habit like a shrub's. Bees love this plant. In the old days it was used to make lawn mazes, and propagated either by cuttings or by seed. It prefers a dry, light, warm soil, with plants spaced a foot apart. This is a very strong, pungent herb. Try a little piece in stew. For catarrh, combine it with white horehound, and infuse it with two cups of boiling water to the ounce. Add honey.

Jewelweed
Wild Touch-Me-Not
Impatiens cupensis

A good wild vegetable if eaten young, buttered and peppered, or creamed on toast. It is a very soft and succulent plant, growing in moist places. The

American Indians used it to make a juice to rub on itchy spots. It contains a fungicide, which was isolated at the University of Vermont by Thomas Sproston, Jr. Euell Gibbons had high praise for the juice of this plant as a prevention for poison-ivy rash. Use its liquid fresh, or make it into ice cubes and store in the freezer to apply when you have been or will be exposed to poison ivy.

Marigold
Tagetes minuta or *Calendula officinalis*

Either fresh or dried, the flowers of marigold have been used since olden days for soups, drinks, and custards. To apothecaries, the virtues of this plant included its powers against the pestilence, its ability to draw evil humors out of the head, its efficacy against intestinal troubles, and its curative properties when rubbed on scabs. Down into the eighteenth century marigolds were used for lotions and ointments and for binding up skin afflictions.

Marigolds are especially valuable as a control for nematodes. Plant them for this year's pests, and also where you expect nematodes to attack the roots of your plants the following year. Most effective of all varieties is *Tagetes minuta*, a tall Mexican variety that will assist you greatly if you can locate seeds for it. I plant marigolds in among the vegetables, around the tomatoes, and on the outer edges of the plot, along with nasturtiums.

The name marigold in Spanish (caléndula), which sounds like the word calendar, reflects the old belief that these flowers can be found blooming somewhere in every month of the year. Other uses of marigolds have included yellow hair dye, and medicine for cuts, inflammation, heart trouble, and warts. It is a very hardy, pestless, unfussy plant, and should be grown plentifully in every organic garden. It can be planted outdoors in the ground, and slightly thinned when it gets to be 3 inches high. It can also be started indoors any time in March or April, and be ready to set out after all danger of frost. It is sensitive to frost, and in the fall will turn dark green and brown at the first drop below 32° F. In mild climates it will self-sow and grow up all over. Save its seeds. If you live in a colder climate, leave one plant of the tall variety in a big pot in the house. Fertilize it well and it will turn into a huge houseplant. On a pinholder in a houseplant, marigolds will root and last for weeks.

Marjoram
Origanum majorana

This plant has been used in many way for many centuries. In general, it is a perennial and will winter-over in the ground if it gets a good start. It favors a limy location and will grow to 18 inches when the soil is just right. Mine always grows much smaller, both the mild annual kind in the garden, sweet marjoram (*Origanum marjorana*), and the pungent kind with dry purple flowers that grows in the fields, the perennial wild marjoram (*Origanum vulgare*). The wild kind is not good in salads and stews, but it makes an acceptable tea.

For sweet marjoram, the delicious native of Portugal, harvest the leaves as needed throughout the summer, and then the whole stalk just before flowering to make dried herbs. It is excellent in salads, omelets, soups, and stews.

Milkweed
Asclepias syriaca

For several years I had to go out to look for milkweed, but now it has arrived in our garden, and I am glad of it. From the first early shoots right through the time of flowering, there is always something good to eat on the milkweed plant. The tips come back if you cut them off, and for several months they make tender tidbits. The flowers, though somewhat flabby and sometimes bitter, do make good tempura. They are very pretty on a platter of mixed tempura herbs and weeds. The pods can be cooked, and if you let some go to seed, the silky wings will fly all around and settle down in the grass, in the garden, and along the edge of the road to bring you new plants the next year.

In order to avoid the bitter taste, which might annoy you, cover the part of the plant you harvest with boiling water, boil for 2 or 3 minutes, then recook in a second water. I find that milkweed cooked in the pressure cooker, then drained, gets nearly as good results. It is best, however, to throw out one or two waters to get rid of the alkaloid, which is not good for you, and is quite bitter. I always cook only the top 3 inches, with a good buttering or oiling with soy oil, and lightly salted. They taste to me like a cross between asparagus and spinach—though if the bitter principle is not drained out, they can taste more like cooked dandelion. The young pods, picked while still very tender, are a gourmet delight. They are easy to freeze for winter use.

Mint
Mentha

You can grow spearmint (*M. spicata*), peppermint (*M. piperita*), apple mint (*M. rotundifolia*), and others. Though mint likes moisture, it will do well in any good soil, and it may spread through the garden into the fields and all sorts of corners.

It is very helpful to keep a section of your mint beds well weeded and loosened so that you can dig some up on short notice to move to a trouble spot in the vegetable garden as a pest repellent. An infestation of aphids, for instance, can sometimes be curbed by introducing mint along the row. After hosing the infected plants, set in the slips of mint, and leave them there for as long as you want. Mint is rugged and does not mind being hauled around. Mint sauce, jellies, juleps, and garnishes are all easy to make.

Nettle, Stinging
Urtica dioica

For a year I tried to make up my mind to cook and eat some stinging nettles, for I thought if Euell Gibbons did it, why couldn't I? Yet when spring weather came, I let the crop get large and go past its tender stage without making an effort to put on my gloves and harvest it. Maybe some other year. Who knows? Sir Albert Howard recognized that the deep probing roots of the nettle make it valuable as a soil improver, and also a very nutritious herb to throw on the compost heap or to feed the hens. It is full of nutrients for the brave soul who will pick, cook, and eat it. Until recently, it was used in Scotland for thread fiber, and many a household had nettle sheets and nettle napkins. Obviously the stingers had been removed.

To cook nettles, have the water boiling, and throw in the tender tops of the young plants. Do not use much water. Cover and cook gently for 20 minutes. The leaves can also be blended in water for a good spray—either alone or mixed with garlic, marigold, or mint. You never see pests on nettles. Therefore, follow the hint from nature, and spread bits around on those plants that you want to protect.

Some old remedies include whipping arthritic sore places with branches of nettle. Nettles also provide a kind of rennet to curdle milk.

Parsley
Petroselinum crispum

A well-known herb, and a good thing, too. Its high vitamin C content, especially in the stems, can keep the scurvy away for anyone who will bother to keep a row of pots of it on the windowsill all winter. It also has lots of iron, so it wards off anemia, too. It is easy to grow in the garden, easy to adapt to flower-pot life, easy to plant outside again in the spring. You can grow the curly-leaved variety, which is often used as a garnish, or the darker flat-leaved variety, often called Italian parsley, which is more aromatic. The soil temperature for parsley should be 60° F or over for good germination when you plant the seeds, and the pH should be about 6. Parsley takes quite a while to grow up, so don't get discouraged. Since it is a biennial, it will bolt the second year, but there will still be plenty of side leaves, and I use the blossoms for tempura. Its oil, called apiole, comes from the seed. Its roots are dried for tea, and so are its leaves.

Do not play around with wild parsley. It may turn out to be poison hemlock, or what the English call fool's parsley. The look may be deceivingly the same, but the root and the smell are quite different. If you feel tempted, bruise the leaves and smell the juice. Once you've smelled parsley, you'll know true parsley again. Only take what smells that good.

Purslane
Portulaca oleracea

A good weed. It will be all over your garden, growing low to the ground, with round smooth leaves, so don't bother to plant it. The young shoots are good in salad, almost as full of iron as parsley; the older ones can be cooked like spinach. Used in old times as a mouthwash.

Rosemary
Rosmarinus officinalis

A good bee plant that will grow quickly and be a perpetual emblem of remembrance, as Shakespeare said. It is used in incense, for sprinkling on buttered crackers for hors d'oeuvres, to make lutes, to ward off the evil eye, and for Christmas decoration along with holly and ivy. In a warm protected place in England rosemary can reach tremendous heights and live for twenty years. It is a half-hardy perennial in this country, needing very warm soil (about 90° F) to germinate, and growing to usable size in 85 days. It likes dry, poor soil, and north of Virginia should be moved indoors in winter to a cool place of 50° to 60° F. The pH should be over 7. Use lime if your soil is acid.

Sage
Salvia officinalis

There are various kinds, including golden, pineapple, and purple-leaved, but the perennial called broad-leaved is the most satisfactory for the home gardener. Start a row, thinned to 6 inches apart, from a packet of seeds, and then move the plants around to convenient spots in your garden, where they can remain as pest repellents. They will grow about 12 inches high.

For chicken stuffing, says a 1780 cookbook, "Take parsley and sage without any other herbs. Take garlic and grapes and stop the chickens full and seethe them...and mess them forth." How does that sound? Sage makes a soothing tea, especially if milk is added. It is excellent in sausages, and can be eaten raw as a welcome refresher. The kind of sage called Clary (*Salvia sclarea*) was a preserver of the clear eye, it was thought in old times, and was taken in a way "fried with eggs in manner of a Tansie" (see below). This evidently means a tempura, for other old recipes mention dipping sage leaves in a "batter made of the yolkes of egges, flour, and a little milke, and then fryed till crispe."

Sorrel
Rumex scutatus

Get the broad-leaved French sorrel, plant it in early spring in moist, rich soil, and thin when 2 to 3 inches tall. Begin cooking the thinnings with chicken broth, and make a delicious, tart soup, adding onions and other greens as you wish. The raw leaves are also good in salads and sandwiches. To preserve the leaves, fry them slowly in plenty of butter, and then cool in a jar and keep in the refrigerator. This method is very good for many aromatic herbs. You can also chop some uncooked and green and add them to melted butter to store for preservation.

Summer Savory
Satureia hortensis

Matures in 60 days, for a dried herb, but can be snipped earlier to make *fines herbes* with basil, chervil, tarragon, and rosemary. It is an annual raised from seed, and should be thinned to 6 inches apart and well watered. It goes especially well with English broad beans and soybeans. A good way to preserve it is in an herb butter (3 tablespoons to ½ pound of salted butter). Keep it in the freezer or refrigerator.

Tansy
Tanacetum vulgare

The young leaves, mixed with eggs, were known as a "tansy"; this was often eaten as a Lenten dish, believed to be good for cleansing the "bad humors." For centuries a tansy tea has been used for stomach cramps. The great value for the organic gardener is to plant it in clumps around the garden to ward off flying insects, especially those coming in to lay eggs. It has a fine, strong, very pungent odor, and is a tall, handsome, feathery-leaved plant. Near the door, it repels ants.

Tarragon
Artemisia dracunculus

A delight to the gardener and cook. Its cousin, *Artemisia redowski*, called Russian tarragon, is a bigger, handsomer plant with a much milder taste and bigger, juicier leaves. If you buy seed, it is this Russian kind you get. The so-called true tarragon, which comes from places like Tartary and Chinese Mongolia, produces no viable seeds and has to be propagated by root cuttings. These cuttings, often called French tarragon, are tender and fussy and should be ordered in the spring or early summer so they will establish themselves well before the winter. By ordering early, you also give yourself a chance to reorder if the first planting fails. True tarragon grows about 2 feet tall, and spreads about 2 feet. Russian tarragon grows 3 or 4 feet and spreads 6 feet.

To make a good tarragon vinegar, soak leaves of French tarragon in white or cider vinegar for one or two weeks. Add fresh leaves to salads and sandwiches, and cook some with chicken. True tarragon can be satisfactorily dried. The mild, fresh, almost tasteless leaves of Russian tarragon are good in salad, sandwiches, and cooked with chicken, but the stronger true tarragon is much better for drying.

Thyme
Thymus vulgaris

Often used for a pot herb, or combined with honey as a cough syrup. Very tangy and nice in stews, meat loaf, and most soups. The thymol in it is an active ingredient in cough syrup. Bees love thyme, and it makes a very interesting honey. Strong enough to repel many pests. There are many varieties.

Woodruff, Sweet
Asperula odorata

Grow a little to put in your May wine, and to drive off moths when you strew it around the closet. It is cousin to an escapee called lady's bedstraw (you may have it as a troublesome weed), which was used in old times as a cheese rennet and to put in a mattress to make a woman fertile. The Greeks used woodruff, steeped in oil, to anoint the weary traveler who came to study herbs with the wise men in Greece. (Herb study, gardening, alchemy, even Christianity, were inextricably interwoven in people's minds throughout the Middle Ages, and it was believed that only the pure in heart could succeed in any of them. Such ideas put a damper on the exploitation of gardening for commercial gain and developed the meditative, devoted gardening expert who studied the virtues of plants and the interrelations of plants and people. This gardening expert often discovered values and secrets now well explained by modern physiologists.)

Wormwood
See Artemisia, page 132.

Yarrow
Achillea

A white kind grows wild, and you can order varieties with yellow, white, or red flowers, called achillea or milfoil, from the nursery. Yarrow is quite tangy and beneficial as a protection plant. Bring some into your garden and watch the pests fly the other way.

Jerusalem Artichoke
See Artichoke, Jerusalem,
page 133.

Kale
Brassica oleracea acephala

Kale gives very good cabbagy greens for late fall and early winter. The greens also make a lovely, crisp relish when the leaves are picked very young, to put as a decoration on an hors d'oeuvre tray. Vates, dwarf blue curled kale, is the best to grow, and since it matures in 55 days, you can keep on sowing it well into July. Plant after peas, for instance. A slightly more delicate kind, called Siberian, matures in 65 days. In zones south of New Jersey you can keep kale in the ground all winter, so you can sow it until September. Not a bit fussy about soil, but a heavy feeder, especially when young and growing fast. For best results use both manure and lime when preparing the ground. Do not plant near cabbage. Siberian and Dwarf Siberian as well as Dwarf Vates are other varieties to grow, and in recent years the ornamental kale has become available. This one comes either red on green or white on green, and is very handsome.

The pests that might attack kale are flea beetles, aphids, and the female Herculean beetles which come to lay eggs. Good provision of nutrients, good mulch, and herbs planted nearby will help kale plants. Recommended are mint, thyme, catnip, hyssop, and rosemary. In the rare case of a terrible infestation, try rotenone.

Start harvesting from spring plantings early in June. Eat raw or cooked. There is a good supply of riboflavin and of vitamin A in kale, with more in the green parts of the leaf than in the midribs and stems. To retain kale's good supply of vitamin C, wrap the vegetable upon picking and store in the dark in a crisper drawer. If you boil it, use very little

Fruits and Vegetables high in Vitamin C

water to keep in the 90 percent of the vitamin C you can save. Macrobiotic, yoga, and USDA recommendations all stress that cabbagy and other green-leaf vegetables should never be cooked beyond the point where they are still crisp. Sautéing in oil first is recommended for all these succulent vegetables.

Kohlrabi
Brassica oleracea gongylodes

This member of the cabbage family needs more calcium for its growth than any other, and dolomitic or calcific limestone should be applied to the area to be planted, at the rate of 75 pounds per 1,000 square feet, a week or so before sowing the seeds. In the right climate you can get an early crop by planting in March or April, and another crop before frost by planting about the first of August. When the bulbs are well developed, dig them and eat. They grow aboveground, so you can easily see when they are ready.

A good variety is Early Purple Vienna, flushed with pinky purple. It matures in about 55 to 60 days. Another variety, Early Purple (56 days), takes longer and grows larger. In the North, good varieties include Grand Duke (45) and White Kohlrabi (55). If you harvest some when the bulbs reach about 2-½ to 3 inches in diameter, you will find them quite different from the vegetables you let grow to large size. A packet of seeds will sow 40 feet, and the plants should be thinned to 6 or 8 inches apart. Sow every two weeks to the end of July and keep moist, especially with a mulch, for best flavor. The seeds are viable for three years. They are good sliced very thinly and eaten raw.

Japanese beetles can be a problem, but use the standard tricks to cope with them. Introduce into the ground, especially in the lawn, at 3-foot intervals, a teaspoon of *Bacillus popillae* or milky spore disease (see Appendix), which is fatal to the larvae of these beetles, but to no other creature. Ladybugs and praying mantises also might help, for they eat larvae. Remember that moles and skunks eat the larvae, too.

Leek
Allium porrum

This delicious mild member of the onion family is complicated to grow, but absolutely unmatchable for soup, and braised hot or cold and eaten as the Greeks do. Anyone who likes onions also likes creamed leeks on toast—though unless very tender they can seem stringy.

Buy plants or start seeds yourself outdoors. Plant seeds thinly, ½ inch deep, after the frost is out of the ground, or indoors in a flat, or in a cold frame. When they are 6 to 8 inches high, dig them all up, cut back about half the top

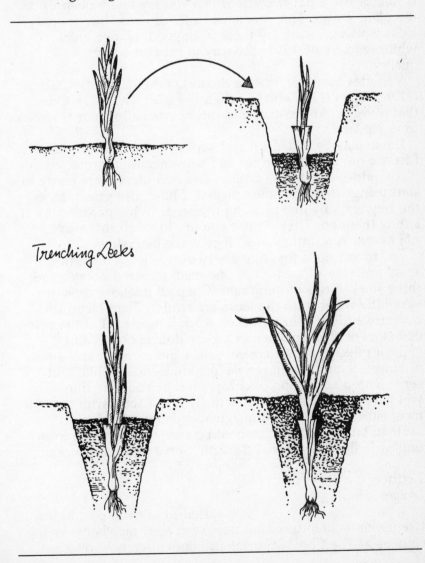

Trenching Leeks

growth, and replant at a distance of about 6 to 9 inches apart in 6-inch trenches, which you fill up as the leeks grow. Plants bought from a nursery are handled the same way. Leeks are not fussy about their soil, but if you give them a good dressing of compost, keep them moist, and fill the trench gradually but persistently, they will grow big and sweet. To keep the stem white all the way up to where the leaves branch, keep on banking with earth after the trench is full, or use a paper collar which you gradually push up as the plant grows. This seems like a lot of work, but the only leeks worth growing are those with good, tender, thick, white stems, and this is the way to get that superior quality.

Varieties available include Broad London (130 days), Titan (110), Electra (125), and the slightly earlier Tivi (115). One that is very cold resistant and can be used all winter is Artico from Holland.

Leeks may be balled up and kept in a box over the winter. I have even balled them up and kept them in a protected place outdoors over the winter, and had them there ready to start using when the snow melted. I have also grown leeks the lazy way, by just planting the seeds in the garden and letting them go. They do not amount to much that way, I can assure you, but even so they make marvelous soup.

The proportions for soup are two large leeks or eight small underdeveloped ones, one medium-sized potato, and three small sprigs of marjoram. Chop all fine and cook in very little water until the leeks are tender. Then blend this mixture, adding a little chicken stock if needed. Put the rest of 2 cups of chicken stock in a glass double boiler, add 2 cups of milk, ½ cup of cream, salt, white pepper, and a pat of butter. Simmer until the flavors are blended, chill, and serve with a sprinkling of chives on top. You may think you have a vichyssoise, but actually it is a soup with the most elusive, mild flavor imaginable. For creamed leeks, sauté in butter, simmer, and add a cream sauce made from unbleached white flour and cream. Serve on toast.

Lettuce
Lactuca sativa

I used to say you could grow twenty kinds of lettuce, but now such seed merchants as the Ogdens at The Cook's Garden in Londonderry, Vermont, are importing seeds from around the world; so you can grow about sixty, if you include the little round red radicchio, the Italian favorite, various chicories, and lamb's lettuce or mache. In the Northeast the best varieties to try are Giulio and Marina. Plant in early June for harvest in September until frost. You'd probably find them all good.

Since a packet of seeds grows too many plants at once, the only way to avoid overplanting and crowding is to time them, plant thinly (preferably mixed with radish seeds), weed, transplant, and then plant a few more as long as the weather is somewhat cool. In general, lettuce seeds are viable for six years. Lettuce doesn't germinate and grow well in hot weather. In the old days, herbals presented four kinds: garden, curled, the cabbagy kind, and Lumbard lettuce. Often used for a boiled green, it was believed to be more digestible that way, though we know today from nutritionists that the minerals and vitamin C in fresh, uncooked lettuces are preferable.

Lumbard lettuce is loose-leaved, the cabbage kind is romaine or cos, and the curled is escarole. Early settlers believed in starting a meal with lettuce, but they also recommended it for nibbling after dinner, too, to "stay the vapours of wine from rising up into the head." They also knew what the great English herbalist Nicholas Culpeper said, that the Moon owns lettuce, and that it in all ways "cooleth and refresheth," and has a very good effect "upon the morals." It was served then with unblanched endive, chicory, and purslane, in a sauce of vinegar, oil, orange or lemon juice, salt, pepper, and sugar—which certainly still sounds familiar as a dressing.

A partially shady place can be used for head lettuce as long as the soil is loose and rich. Leaf lettuce does well in full sun. Most lettuce seeds germinate more readily if covered very lightly or just watered in. Since it is very shallow-rooted, you need only rake in an inch or so of compost, and add some along the rows when the lettuce is up and properly thinned. This is one plant you can safely water in dry weather without injury to the roots. Do it early in the day so that the sun will dry the plants well before evening. In fact, the roots of lettuce are so near the surface that it is the first plant to wilt during a drought. This shallow-root habit also makes it advisable to do any transplanting at the end of the day, after the sun has gone down. The rows need only be 12 inches apart, but the plants should be spaced 8 to 12 inches apart for best heading. If you plant small areas of lettuces all together and without rows, according to the French intensive method, keep the plants dry and all the slugs picked off.

Experiment with different varieties for several years to find out what suits you best. I like Oakleaf lettuce very much, both as a fresh young lettuce and as a mature plant later in the summer. The young leaves wilt rapidly, so use it as soon as you pick it. Slightly more sturdy are the Black-Seeded Simpson varieties and a 40-day favorite of mine, Salad Bowl. This is slow to bolt, so you don't have to race to eat it up before it develops a tough stem. A pretty variation is the reddish Ruby lettuce, which is very tender, too. The new improved Red Sails is a good lettuce for iron and vitamins A and C, and it is slow to bolt. We do not grow iceberg lettuce, but I believe that the kind called Great Lakes is reliable. A butterhead lettuce called Matchless is very good. We grow Bibb, Summer Bibb, and Buttercrunch, and find them all excellent. We also enjoy the patented crinkly lettuce from Burpee called Green Ice (45 days), which is slow to bolt and slow to wilt after you pick it.

The catalog of The Cook's Garden divides its lettuces into spring, summer, and winter varieties. It also lists some they call Cutting Lettuce, including Salad Bowl, Matchless, and Oakleaf. Among spring lettuces are Bibb, Black-Seeded Simpson, and Ithaca, and also such new French varieties as Ballon, Rein des Glaces, La Brilliante, and St. Blaise, a romaine type. These can all be planted as soon as the ground can be worked.

The summer lettuces are more heat-tolerant, probably slower to bolt, and worth planting at intervals, if well watered. They include Buttercrunch, such French varieties as Kinemontpas, and one well adapted to the South, Craquerelle du Midi (literally, Southern Cracker). For winter varieties (to be planted in late summer to grow in the cool fall months) you can get North Pole and also the red Rouge d'Hiver, Rougette du Midi, and the very hardy Brune d'Hiver, which can overwinter. A big, crisp lettuce is the 76-day cos or romaine lettuce, with tall, dark green leaves growing upright and forming 10-inch heads with white hearts. It is more crisp than the delicate Oakleaf lettuce, but it makes a good contrast in a mixed salad.

The most long-lasting in our garden is the curly endive, or escarole, which has a 95-day maturing period. We pick and eat it long after the first frost in the fall. A less curly kind, Florida Deep-Heart, is also good until fairly late in the season. Its leaves are quite tough and withstand adverse weather. Sow these big plants in rows 18 inches apart, and thin to 18 inches. Lettuce of several kinds should also be started in your hot bed or cold frame, beginning your plantings in March or April and keeping them up until the end of May. You can start them over a heat coil, move them to a cold frame, and eventually outdoors to the garden. Transplanting from a cold frame is often easier than thinning and transplanting in the garden, especially if you use such modern aids as Ferto-pellets and peat pots. Always thoroughly bury such containers so they will stay moist. Otherwise when they dry out they block and kill small roots.

A recommended cos is Green Towers; a good romaine is St. Blaise or Paris Island. These take about 70 days to mature.

For radicchio, a small red head is characteristic of Red Verona, and also of Red Treviso. Both are rather tricky to grow.

Marjoram
See Herbs, pages 180–202.

Muskmelon
(Cantaloupe)
Cucumis melo reticulatus

These sensitive warm-weather plants want only light, rather sandy soil. Where it is cool, they must be started indoors in peat pots; they won't withstand transplanting that disturbs their roots. Put them out in hills, with rich compost or aged manure added for fertilizer. Since cucumber beetles attack melons, it is a good idea to cover the young plants with jars, boxes, hotcaps, or other tents when young, and to be ready to apply wood ashes or ashes mixed with three times as much colloidal phosphate. Apply several times a week, and always again after rains. Frost will ruin melons, so if you live where there are September frosts, cover the vines with bushel baskets or other protections if cold is predicted. To keep the soil warm, many gardeners use black plastic mulch.

Varieties featured in recent years are Bush Star (88 days) for small gardens, and Harper's Hybrid (80), Kansas, and Quick Sweet (60) for Northern gardens, or Sweet 'n' Early (75). Other favored varieties include the heirloom Pike (85), very sweet and tolerant of more clayey soils, Sweet Dream (79), disease-resistant Saticoy (90), and Superstar (86) with good big fruits. Be sure to cut up or shred the rinds for the compost heap; they are rich in phosphorus and potassium.

Mustard Greens
Brassica juncea

Mustard greens are relatives of cabbage and all those *caulis* plants. The mustards grown for seeds are other varieties. I don't know what keeps Northerners from growing mustard greens—either indoors or out, the young, tender leaves make a fine addition to a salad, and the cooked greens are a good variation from spinach. I grow a flat in the kitchen, and it is very handy to have there. Sow the seed a little at a time, to keep the crop coming. Outdoors, this can be done until the weather gets quite hot.

Recommended varieties are Southern Curled Giant (50 days), Fordhook Fancy (40), Tendergreen (35), Savanna Hybrid (20 days for a young green), and the curly, long-lasting Southern Giant (50), which easily self-sows. They self-sow in my garden, and I tear off a leaf or so quite often to put in salads. If you want one that tastes quite a lot like spinach, try Tendergreen, which is more heat and drought resistant than the others, and grows fast. Let a few plants go to seed in order to harvest the seed for future crops, but be sure to pick them before the pods open, and in dry weather.

Homemade Mustard: In a mortar pound 1 tablespoon chopped parsley, 1 tablespoon chopped tarragon, 1 tea-spoon chopped chervil, and ½ cup mustard seed. (Of the store-bought mustard seed, the black is more pungent than the white or brown.) The grinding can also be done in the blender, but the flavor may seem more dull. Put this through a sieve and save the powder that comes through. Then slowly add 1 tablespoon oil, preferably corn oil, and 1 tablespoon vinegar. Stir and keep covered. Instead of vinegar you can use a tart juice such as currant juice. Use up homemade mustard quickly, and then make a new batch, for it does not keep well.

Nasturtium
Tropaeolum

There are several varieties that will do well as companion plants in your vegetable garden. Be sure to include some yellow-flowering ones as repellents for aphids, which have a reaction to yellow. Nasturtiums can be sown outdoors in May, after the ground is warm, or started inside in individual peat pots. They do not like cold, damp ground, but they blossom very well in poor soil, so plant them along the edges of the garden where you have not put very much enrichment and compost. Where the soil is rich, they go to green leaves, which, though pest repellent, too, are still not as serviceable for the gardener as the plant that gives blossoms and seeds for eating.

For varieties try Golden Globe, Golden Gleam, Double Gleam, Whirlybird, Primrose Gem, and collections such as Mixed Double Dwarf, Mixed Dwarf Single, Tall Climbing Fordhook if you have trellises, and Dwarf Jewel Nasturtiums, which are especially prolific in bloom. Plant them between the vegetables for pest repellents and in places where you don't plant marigolds and the other useful flowers.

Okra
Hibiscus esculentus

Familiar in southern and western gardens. It is possible to grow okra in the Northeast, too, especially if planted so that it grows in the heat. Soak the seeds for twenty-four hours and then plant them 1 inch deep in good, friable soil, well drained. The seeds will stay viable for two years. The soil temperature should be 80° F or over, the pH 6 to 8. If the soil gets cold and wet, the seeds will rot. In a spell of bad weather, change any plans you have about planting it outdoors, and start okra indoors or in a cold frame or hot bed. Be sure it gets plenty of nitrogenous nutrient such as rotted manure and compost or leaf mold, preferably applied a month before planting. Okra will grow big and bushy, so plant in hills 3 feet apart, keeping the seeds several inches apart. In nonorganic gardening books, the distance recommended is 12 inches apart, but it is obvious that with a nutrient program like that practiced by the organic gardener, it is only sensible to leave room for big growth, especially of woody plants like okra.

Varieties to try include Annie Oakley (50 days), Clemson Spineless (55), Emerald (58), and a new red one called Burgundy (60). There are also white okras, such as White Velvet.

When the pods begin to mature and get to be a few inches long, start harvesting. Remember that they should be only half-grown when picked. If you keep okra picked, and fertilize with manure tea or another rich fertilizer after the first crop, a second crop will come right along. Use the pods as many times as you can for the splendid Louisiana gumbos—shrimp or chicken. Freeze if necessary. And eat some as a boiled vegetable dipped in hollandaise sauce if you don't mind the slipperiness. A fine source of vitamin A, calcium, and phosphorus. The seeds of okra are almost as rich in protein as soybeans.

Onion
Allium cepa

The globe onion can be grown from seeds, from purchased plants, or from sets (the small bulbs that can be bought from seed merchants). With good soil they all will mature for home use during a summer season, but at different times and with somewhat different qualities.

If your topsoil is deep, loose, humusy, and a bit sandy, onions will do well in it. You can start with sets, of the Ebenezer type, planting them where you want the final onions to be. If you use a row, put them about 3 or 4 inches apart, unless you plan to eat some very young, and cover with ¼ inch of soil. One pound will plant a 50-foot row. In five weeks you can pull them as scallions. Later in the summer, harvest the crop.

The plants to send away for are Ebenezer or Sweet Spanish. Plant them about two weeks after you put in the sets. Ebenezer onions are especially good for winter storage, so don't dig too many for summer use. Those you grow from seed will come along last, for it takes 130 days, more or less, for them to mature properly. Harvest onions after the tops die down, and be sure to dry them as much as possible in the warm sun.

Onions come as either short-day or long-day plants. The short-day (suitable for growing in the South) are less pungent, described as "sweet," and not long-keepers. The most famous of the sweet onions, Granex Hybrid, is known by the place-name, Vidalia, in Georgia. It is usually ready in July, and needs to be used right away. A similar sweet onion, suitable for Northern gardens, but just as perishable as Vidalia, is called Walla Walla. Also perishable are Sweet Spanish, White Sweet Spanish, and Sweet Spanish Yellow.

Spanish onions were developed for better-keeping qualities; the improvements also resulted in more pungent onions. Two onions bred for long-day climates are Tango Hybrid and Avalanche Hybrid, both 100 days. Two bred for short days are Early White Supreme Hybrid (90) and Vidalia Granex (80); also Early White Supreme (90), a new onion in 1988, said to be sweet and large. Other pungent varieties besides Ebenezer include Excel, Yellow Bermuda, Copra, Tango Hybrid, Fiesta, and the early-maturing Buffalo, which keeps only until about Christmastime. An onion which is pungent at first but which mellows during storage is Sweet Sandwich. Red onions to consider are Southport Red Globe, Redman, and Benny's Red, which does not keep well.

Bunching onions or scallions are available as Evergreen Hardy White, sometimes called Evergreen Long White, White Lisbon, and Ishikuro. The small, very mild little onions called shallots are available as Dutch Yellow, Giant Red, or just French Shallots. Allow 120 days for maturing.

Sets, of course, send up shoots ready to use quite a bit earlier than the tiny first shoots of onions from seeds.

The perennial chives are a joy to have near the kitchen door for frequent use, especially when in bloom in June, as they offer delicious, tangy blossoms to put in salads and other dishes.

The great convenience of growing onions is that there they are in the garden, full of flavor, and ready to pull in some form or other all summer long. If you plant so-called multiplier onions, you can have them even in early spring. The ones grown from seeds can be pulled for a substitute for chives at any time after they emerge from the earth. You don't have to grow all three versions, and many people settle for only one.

The hazard for young onions grown from seeds is weeds. Therefore it is sensible to grow them in a part of the garden that is fairly free from weeds the year before. You can plan to have them follow carrots, beans, or corn. Keep them weeded, and do not allow any caking of the ground. The little roots are very easy to injure, so weed or cultivate with the greatest care.

The pest to watch out for is the onion thrip, a tiny fly that lays its eggs at the axil of the leaf and whose nymphs suck the plant sap. A soapy spray or rotenone (4 percent) helps to fight this pest. Keep an eye out also for the onion maggot, the larva of a gray fly like a housefly, which works down into the onion bulb. An oily-soapy spray on the ground will help against this pest. The editor of *The Organic Way to Plant Protection*, Emmaus, PA. Rodale, 1966, recommends that you spread your onion plants all around the garden to fight this maggot, instead of planting them in a row. Good advice. By so doing, you also offer protection to plants whose pests are repelled by this aromatic species. We put onions all around the garden to repel rabbits and wood-chucks. We also use pungent flowers, wood ashes, and sometimes (after many experiments) blood meal.

The one method of onion growing we have settled on, after many experiments, is growing from seeds. They are cheaper, and very little trouble, and we cut down on bringing in diseases on purchased plants or sets.

Pak Choi
See Cabbage, Chinese,
pages 155–56.

Parsley
See Herbs, pages 180–202.

Parsnip
Pastinaca sativa

               This vegetable is called a cool-weather, long-season plant, because it grows well in northern states and is able to live over the winter, so you can start digging it the minute the snow melts off. Parsnips are easy to grow and very nutritious. For years I thought I did

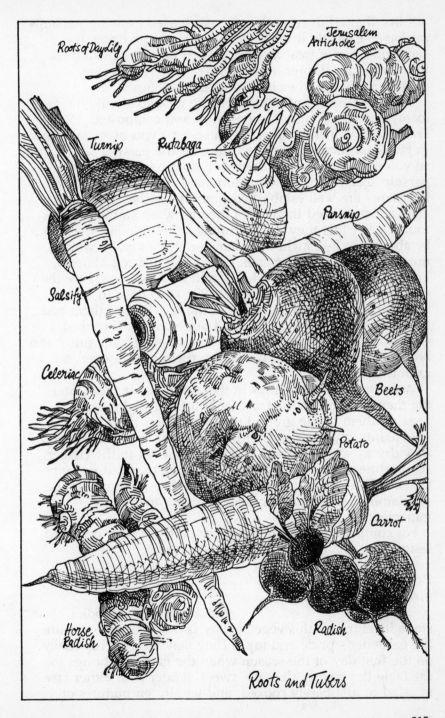

Roots of DayLily

Jerusalem Artichoke

Turnip

Rutabaga

Parsnip

Salsify

Celeriac

Beets

Potato

Horse Radish

Carrot

Radish

Roots and Tubers

not like them, but recently we have started growing parsnips for harvest mostly in the following March, and now it seems like a rare treat to have braised parsnips fresh from the ground for dinner in the spring, or slivers of raw parsnip with a sandwich for a springtime lunch.

To get straight, unforked roots the ground should be loamy and loose, dug 8 inches deep and composted. Plant seeds ¼ to ½ inch deep at the same time you plant radishes. In fact, mix some radish seeds in with the parsnip seeds, so you will know where the row is coming, for it takes parsnip seed a long time to germinate and come up. After the plants are well established, thin to 6 inches apart and cultivate and weed them until they grow up so their leaves touch. After this they are no trouble at all. We like them to be about 2 or 2-½ inches in diameter at the top, so we do not fertilize them very much. Cobham Improved Marrow, Tender and True, Harris Model, and Hollow Crown are the varieties that are best. These take 95 to 105 days to mature.

Be sure to try some parsnips in the fall. Parboil them and then finish the cooking in melted butter or oil. If cooked very slowly and for quite a long time, they become nutty and browned. There is enough sugar in them to give them a carameled quality.

When you leave parsnips in the ground over the winter, dig them as soon as the frost melts and eat right away. Leaving them in the ground too long makes them turn to new plants and their tops grow. If you let them sit indoors, they dry up and get corky and tasteless even in the crisper compartment. Everything else I can think of about parsnips is good. In a cup of parsnips there are five more milligrams of vitamin C than the daily requirement, and plenty of minerals.

For companionate planting, grow parsnips near peas and beans.

Pea
Pisum sativum

An old gardening book I have starts its entry on this vegetable by saying: "Green peas are the gardener's pride and joy." They may well be, especially on the first day of the season when the gardener brings to the table the young, delicate, sweet, tender peas either raw in salad or just barely cooked, and within ten minutes of picking them in the garden. Other peas in comparison taste weeks old, overcooked by half an hour, tough, tasteless, and worn-out. Besides, very fresh peas are highly nutritious.

Peas like coolness, so get them into a well-prepared, moist soil as early as possible. If you use wires or brush sticks to support them, or trellises for Sugar Snap Peas, put the supports up early to be ready for the seedlings when they emerge. Make a trench along both sides and plant your peas in alternating spots on either side of the support. Fill these up with 6 inches of compost which you will push aside in order to plant the seeds 1 inch deep. Rows 12 inches wide are frequently used by modern gardeners. And remember that peas are legumes and should be treated with legume inoculant to boost the bacterial count. The seeds are viable for three years. Put in extra nitrogenous matter, such as cottonseed meal, fish emulsion, fish meal, or something like peanut, sugar, or cocoa wastes. Also add some lime. Get the soil ready a week before planting if you can. But never tramp down soil that is wet and heavy; you could ruin it for the whole season.

Varieties of climbing peas to use are Little Marvel, which matures in 63 days, and Alaska, which comes even earlier, at 55 days. For a very tall pea, you can try Alderman, which comes later, at 74 days. All are heavy bearers. For bush peas, try Burpeeana Early, at 63 days, and for a late pea, Fordhook Wonder Wando, or Lincoln, at 67 days. Wando is the pea best suited to warmer climates or late planting. But keep the soil moist so the peas will germinate. Other favorites are Freezonia (63 days), Titania, with very long pods (63), Green Arrow (70), and the earlier Maestro (60). The odd pea plant, just about leafless and self-supporting on its tendrils, is Bikini. You can eat the tendrils, too.

Be sure to include at least a packet of edible-podded peas, also called sugar or snow peas. They are as tender as green beans, and are cooked the same way, but they taste like peas. You eat the whole pod. (To induce this flavor of the pod when cooking your other peas, snap off the end of each half of 10 or 15 pods and strip off the inside membrane, which is the course one. Cook in the pot with the peas.) The snow peas to grow are Dwarf Gray Sugar, Burpee's Sweetpod or Super Sweetpod, which have thick succulent pods.

For a midget edible-podded pea, use Dwarf Gray Sugar, whose pods grow to 2-½ inches and mature in 65 days.

The plants only grow 2 to 2-½ feet high, and are suitable for window boxes, roof gardening, and patio pots. After removing the dust, eat them, pods and all, as soon as the little peas can be seen inside.

The most recently developed peas, Sugar Snap Peas, are easy to grow, if trellised. They are prolific and delicious, with a crunchy sweetness. Except for the bush variety, Sugar Daddy, they need to have their strings removed before using, either raw for a dip, sliced in salads, or cut up and cooked like regular peas. Varieties include the original Sugar Snap (70 days), the one with long pods, and the big Snappy (63). Breeders have also developed bush types, which are small ones that do not need a trellis: Sugar Ann, Sugar Bon, and Sugar Daddy are among those recommended.

A few seed houses provide the French petit pois varieties such as Frizette (65 days) and Precovil (60). You'll need a trellis for Frizette; since it stands cool weather well, plant some in the fall.

Pea seed is bulky, so you need a pound to sow 100 feet. A packet will sow only 15 feet, hardly enough to get more than a few pickings. It is advisable not to plant in succession, but to plant early, late, and midseason varieties all at once. The reason for this is that peas need cool weather to germinate well. If, however, it stays cool in your climate to the end of May, try some succession plantings, too.

For companionate planting, try carrots in the next row, or even between the plants in a row of peas. Onions and parsnips go well between plants, too, and so does lettuce. All will benefit by the strengths they will derive from root association, and possible interchange below the soil of an antibiotic protection or some sort of growth-promoting substance, whatever it may be. They may even work to repel pests from each other.

If you keep your peas picked as they mature, you may well get a bushel for each 100 feet of row. Burpee's Sweetpod, if the soil, composting, and season are favorable, might yield two bushels per 100 feet of row.

A very good way to serve the first young peas is to steam them for a few minutes over rapidly boiling water and then, when they are tender, to drop them back into the warm pot after you have emptied out the water. Add butter and some heavy cream, and let it heat through. Serve in small, warmed bowls, and eat with a spoon. Served this way the peas are not only delicious, but the warm liquid keeps them hot longer. Plain boiled peas dumped on a cold plate chill before you get them to the table.

An even better way, we think, is to add raw young peas to the early summer salads we make from young lettuce, young radishes, and raw young spinach leaves. We use a very light soy oil and white wine salad dressing with this, and only a little salt for seasoning. Anything stronger would mask the flavors. Save the pods and make pea pod soup, with cream and two sprigs of mint.

Green peas are a very fine source of vitamin E (2.1 mg per cup). There are only three vegetables with a higher count— navy beans, sweet potatoes, and turnip greens. Peas are quite high in all the B-vitamins, vitamin A (680 I.U. per cup as compared with 3,500 in broccoli, 1,110 in tomatoes, or 9,500 in turnip greens), and vitamin C (20 mg, comparable to asparagus or baked white potatoes, but only a tenth of what you'd get in turnip greens, mustard greens, or Brussels sprouts). Peas are also a good source of fiber, right up there with lentils and soybeans.

Peach
Prunus persica

If the right varieties are chosen, peaches can be grown almost anywhere in this country. They all have special temperature requirements for both summer and winter. The cold period in winter must be low enough and last long enough to bring the trees out of their rest period with no damage to tops or roots. For example, Elberta, a very popular variety, needs more cold than Babcock. The best summer temperature is an average 75° F.

Locations east of large bodies of water, such as Lakes Erie and Ontario, and the eastern slopes of the mid-Atlantic states' mountains, are good for peaches. A body of water or the good air circulation of a downhill slope help to protect the trees. Early spring frosts in valleys can kill the buds in spring.

Varieties for the North include Fingerlakes S.H., which is quite hardy. So is Reliance, which is said to be able to stand −20° F. Farther south not only Elberta, but also Red Haven, Belle of Georgia, and Golden Jubilee are now often grown. New Rich Haven will ripen 18 days earlier than Elberta. Most nurseries selling fruit trees carry both standard and dwarf sizes. In California, Desert Gold, Springtime, and Blazing Gold are grown. For a peach tree in a pot select Compact Redhaven.

The usual time to plant peach trees is in the spring, as early as the ground can be prepared. They'll do best in a light, somewhat sandy loam, well aerated especially in the North to protect the trees by cutting short the growing season. Prune off any overlong or broken roots, and set the tree in a large hole with the union line at soil surface. Fill the hole, tamp down, and water. Wrap the trunk. Water the tree all summer every eight to ten days. Mulch and keep down weeds. By the third year, blossoms and fruit will appear. Keep pruning off suckers as the tree grows. Do not allow the tree to bear very heavy crops. Loss of flavor and size, and winter weakness are hazards if you do. Also take steps to control borers, peach yellows, and brown rot. Oriental fruit moth and plum curculio spread the fungus for brown rot. Circle the tree with tanglefoot and plant garlic around the base for borers. Keep the area clean, knock out and catch the curculios, or keep free-ranging chickens to eat them up.

Pear
Pyrus

Pick a place to plant pears where the soil is deeply enriched and well drained. Use a legume cover crop around the base, or mulch heavily. Do not use high-nitrogen fertilizers. Pears require cross-fertilization, so select two varieties that blossom at the same time. The standard sizes are long-lived, handsome trees if you control fire blight. Dwarf sizes are very popular among home gardeners. My favorite pear is Bartlett, and it is a good pollinator except for Seckel. For Seckel, choose Kieffer, hardy in the same zones. (Actually, Kieffer is often self-pollinating.) Other good pears to look into are Clapp's Favorite, a sweet, very hardy and productive pear which, unfortunately, is quite susceptible to fireblight. Resistant to that disease is a pear developed for the South, Ayres, a cross between Anjoy and Garber. Another resistant pear is the hardy Lincoln, good for both North and South. And I've been seeing in markets recently Max-Red Bartletts, grown in Washington. This variety is susceptible to fireblight and needs a pollinator (again, any except Seckel).

We have lost one tree to fireblight, and it is beginning to show up on our Bartlett. The cure for this dreadful disease, which is carried around by insects, is to cut off the infected limb well beyond the part infected, and burn it. You know it is infected because the spurs, then twigs, then a whole branch begin to die. If you are starting afresh, by all means buy resistant varieties. That would not include the handsome, mild Anjou, grown both in the West and North, but does include the practically immune Kieffer.

Pepper
Capsicum

Sweet or hot. Grow both, one for food and one for hotness and the excellent pest-repellent spray you can make out of a hot pepper in the blender. But since peppers take more than 100 days to come to fruit, it is unwise to include them in your garden plans unless you are willing to buy the plants, or start them indoors or in the hot bed.

A very prolific, nicely fleshed sweet pepper is King of the North, and another is Burpee's Sunnybrook. One of the very earliest (60 days after 8 or 9 weeks indoors) is Merrimack Wonder, good to use in northern zones; another is a Japanese variety called Canape. Three varieties recommended as resistant to the mosaic virus disease are Yolo Wonder, Bell Boy Hybrid, and Keystone Resistant Giant. A very satisfactory variety is New Ace. A prolific tapered variety is Gypsy Hybrid. Extra large are Gedeon Hybrids and Whopper. A good yellow pepper is Golden Summer Hybrid, and the purple one is called Purple Bell. The old variety, Bell Boy, is still available. For a long-season green pepper which later turns deep red, try the French variety called Cadice. Sweet Banana is a novelty pepper, tapered, and turning from green to yellow to orange.

For hot peppers to use in pickles, and for an excellent spray, you have your choice of Hungarian Wax, which turns from yellow to red; Rumanian Wax, and Mexi Bell, with sweet flesh but hot ribs; mildly hot Zippy, the earliest, and either Tabasco or Jalapeño. Most of these are ready to harvest in 65 to 75 days, but Zippy only takes 57. For the best cropping pick off the "crown set," which is the first pepper to ripen at the crown when green, so that the plant will produce more fruits. Also, keep well watered and weeded. And don't ever plant leggy seedlings. Feed once a month with manure tea or some other mild fertilizer. The new waterfilled tube cages will help peppers, or just a chicken wire cage with clear plastic surrounding it. Peppers are sensitive to temperature; days of 75° F and nights of 60° F are ideal.

Peppers are good for those seeking sources of vitamin C, with more in the red than in the green. They have from 120 to 180 mg in each average-sized fruit. Also for vitamin A: 700 to 3,000 I.U.; for thiamin: 30 to 70 mg; and for phosphorus: 28 mg. Harvest some green; wait until others mature and turn red.

Eat the pepper fresh. If you wait until it is limp, just about all the vitamin C has gone out of it, and much of the other food value. But fresh or stale, the calorie count is only 25, as careful weight watchers have already found out. As usual, the nutrients are more plentiful in the uncooked vegetable, but you can get tired of raw pepper after a while. Then a stuffed pepper is a welcome change. These are often baked, but simmered in a covered casserole they are just as good, and more mellow. Try a stuffing of ground beef or veal and ham, mixed with the yolks of eggs. Supplement or substitute brown rice and soybean grits, if you prefer.

Plum
Prunus

Generally plums grow best where peaches grow. There are ever so many species of *Prunus*, including plums, from the wonderful Beach Plum, *P. maritima*, which grows wild on Cape Cod, to the familiar sweet plum grown for prunes, such as the varieties Agen or French Prune of the European plum, *P. domestica*. Some are grown for jams, such as Damson and Reine Claude (Green Gage), which are self-fertile, but do need other pollinators close by. Both European and Japanese-American hybrids produce plums familiar in our markets. Varieties of the two groups do not cross-pollinate well. Among Japanese types are many crosses introduced by Luther Burbank, such as the red ones, Beauty and Burbank, or the purple Santa Rosa. Grow two, or better, three of these. Try the prolific Bruce with Santa Rosa.

European varieties to consider for the home garden include Earliblue, good for the North; Stanley, good for both

Northeast and South; the September plum Bluefre; the popular Italian Prune, grown in both the South and West, as well as the long-lived French Prune. A charming yellow plum is Yellow Egg. Especially hardy for colder zones are Pipestone, Toka, and Superior, all good pollinators for each other.

As with apples, you need to be very careful about injuring the spurs (the little twigs on which the fruits grow) on wood that is two to four years old. Standard-sized trees fill 20 feet of space; dwarfs only 10. Dwarfs are grafted on Nanking cherry roots, an Asian cherry shrub.

The plum curculio is the pest to dread most. Chickens, again, are the best control. Humid weather is one of the greatest hazards.

Potato
Solanum tuberosum

If your garden is big enough, you want to grow potatoes. Even if it isn't, you want to grow potatoes; and since I've grown and harvested one in the kitchen window, I do not hesitate to recommend them for roof gardens, window boxes, and patio-pot plants, as well as for the garden. I know sweet potatoes make good houseplants, too, but I doubt the harvest. Nursery catalogs in 1988 began to advertise potato barrels, which will be filled with potatoes that will grow right there in the barrel in 6 inches of soil, compost, and peat, after you plant some eyes. The illustration, of course, shows the barrel chock-full. I haven't tried one.

The organic gardener who mulches deeply just lays each whole or cut piece of potato right in the mulch, and waits for the new plant to grow. Sometimes this mulch is hay; sometimes it is last autumn's leaves piled up 3 feet high and left to weather down over the winter. You can also put seed potatoes on leaves and then cover them with hay. On sprouting, the roots seek the earth below and the plant leaves seek the light; the tubers, which constitute the crop, grow right in the mulch and rarely get scab or other soil-borne diseases. (Scab is a fungus disease that makes ugly brown spots on the skin of the tuber.)

For anyone preferring to plant in the soil, choose a well-drained, fine-loam area, somewhat sandy if possible, and dig a good trench 10 inches wide and 5 inches deep.

Old, matured compost mixed with dried, old cow or sheep manure can be dug in during the previous autumn or a week before planting. But it must be old; fresh manure will injure the potatoes. Since potatoes like acid soil, with a pH of 5 to 5.5, do not use lime or anything that will develop alkalinity and thus encourage scab. If your soil is not slightly acid, it is certainly best to plant potatoes in the mulch.

For 100 feet of row use about a half peck of potatoes, cutting them into four to six pieces. For good economy you can save eyes from the potatoes you eat in the spring. Cut them out with a small piece of flesh attached, wrap them in paper or plastic, and store in the refrigerator until planting time. Ordered seed potatoes should also be kept in a very cold place until planted.

Plant both early and late potatoes. Put in early ones as soon as all danger of frost has gone; plant late ones until the end of May. A few can be poked in during June, to see what happens. The average yield is supposed to be about three bushels per 100 feet of row. With careful practice and good composting you can double this. If you aim for a crop of ten bushels for a family of four, plant two or three rows, depending on your degree of fertilizer and mulch.

You know before you start that if there is one vegetable you thoroughly enjoy, it is a small, new potato, fresh from the garden, boiled whole in its jacket, and dribbled with butter. If you haven't yet had this experience, I can assure you that there is a taste of bliss ahead. When the flower buds show, begin to poke into the soil to find these little potatoes. You will be glad you did. Harvest the bigger ones later when the tops die down. After the early ones are dug use the rows for late plantings of beans, kale, or turnips to get double use of your space. Late potatoes will provide space only for a cover crop.

This wonderful New World plant (from Peru) is a member of the *Solanum* family, which also includes the tomato, eggplant, and nightshade—as you can tell from the similarities of flowers and leaves. The plants and fruits of the vegetables we eat have little of the poisonous substance solanin—except in the early sprouts and growing tips. Avoid growing tomatoes, potatoes, and eggplants close together because as members of the same family they attract the same diseases and pests. Also avoid using the same ground in successive years. Plant a legume instead.

For varieties to choose, the early potato called Irish Cobbler is very reliable. Other early varieties include Norgold Russet, Norland, Red Pontiac, and White Rose. Pontiac and Red Pontiac are suitable for the South. For later varieties, Katahdin and Kennebec are good. Other late ones to consider are Viking, which is of regular size and rather early, but grows to jumbo size as a late potato; Sebago; and a new Idaho potato, Butte. The strange violet potatoes are Improved Peruvian and Purple Gem. And there is a new round white, very disease-resistant one from Gurney called Elba. Sequoia is resistant to leafhoppers; Kennebec, Saco, and Essex to late blight.

For pests, try some of the following: hose off aphids, and sprinkle the plants with homemade onion spray; pick off Colorado beetles and egg cases from the undersides of leaves; use homemade basil spray and mulch deeply for potato bugs—the mulch will thwart their climbing when they emerge from the soil; sprinkle bran to stop beetles; introduce praying mantises or ladybugs; introduce milkweed as a trap plant for leafhoppers; wrap plants in plastic nets for leafhoppers; and use the resistant strains of potatoes. Barn swallows can eat a thousand potato beetles in a few hours. Some people use poisons like pyrethrum, tobacco, or ryania. Unless you have a big patch with an unusual attack, you probably will not need to resort to such sprays. Another possibility against the Colorado potato beetle is *Bacillus thüringiensis*, cleared for this usage by the United States Department of Agriculture. Twenty-three insects are affected by this disease. If you think of using it, consider the fact that there are at least that many species of birds who eat insects and might depend on some of them. In the South, keep all grass out of the patch, for potato wireworms breed there. Also in the South precede the potato crop with a crop of soybeans or some other legume in the same soil. Keep the land well cultivated both years.

To protect your plants from blight, keep everything clean and dry. If blight gets into your potatoes during the cool, humid days of fall, leave them in the ground for two extra weeks. That way the spores will all die down before they get a chance to float out from the stem to the tuber when you disturb the plant and stir up the spores while digging. Keep all tools, shoes, paws, and hoofs clean, and burn all culled plants. Never let the plants get wounded in hot weather. Never use soil or stock that you know was recently infested.

Store potatoes in a safe place with a temperature around 40° F. We put ours in bushel baskets in the cellar. The mice like that. Perhaps a better plan, which we have not used, is to swaddle them in leaves and dry litter in a big hole in the ground. But wouldn't the mice like that, too? Probably the best strategy is to build a screened cage in a cool place, or even to screen over your bushel baskets.

Does anyone need to be reminded anymore that the skins of potatoes should be eaten? Peeled, boiled potatoes have lost 47 to 50 percent of their vitamin C by the time they are cooked. And if you mash them, 10 percent more gets away from you. In addition, if you have soaked them, you have lost some of the vitamin B group, too. There are so many excellent recipes for potatoes that it seems silly to add any cooking hints aside from those warnings. I'm still not able to eat raw potatoes because I have a notion they put my teeth on edge, but grated potatoes, fried very quickly immediately after grating, can be quite good. I also slice them very thinly (with the skins on) and bake the slices in a 350° F oven in a little oil until crispy. A very easy recipe.

For variations on old favorites: Instead of using milk and butter for mashed potatoes, use yogurt and chives, or yogurt and thyme, watercress, sorrel, or mustard leaves. For leftovers, make patties to fry or broil, and add wheat germ, leftover soy grits, mashed wheat berries, or ground nuts to make the potato stiffer. Use ½ cup of any addition to 2 cups of leftover mashed potato. Coat each patty with wheat germ or soy flour, and add some ground marjoram or rosemary. Sometimes go back to the plain baked potato. Rub it first with a little butter or vegetable oil after washing off the bits of soil, and put it in a hot oven—400° F or even 450° F. Do not let it overcook, and prick it with a fork to let in a little air when done so it won't get soggy. In this form it preserves more of its nutrients than in any other. It is not fattening unless you douse it with butter or gravy. If medium-sized it will provide you with 33 mg of vitamin C, about the same as in a large tomato, and 1.5 mg of iron, about the same as in a large egg. If you go to the trouble of peeling, soaking, boiling, and ricing this potato, you will have thrown away 83 percent of the iron, and absolutely all of the vitamin C. To save the vitamin C otherwise lost when a potato is cut open, chill it thoroughly first. And if you do have to cut a potato ahead of cooking time, put the pieces immediately in an airtight bag and return to the refrigerator.

Potato, Sweet
Ipomoea batatas

This is a very nutritious warm-climate vegetable, rich in vitamin C and very rich indeed in vitamin A. You can sprout your own in water, or buy plants as most people do. Sow in soil not too rich or you will get plants with stringy tubers and too much green. The soil should preferably be sandy, but heavier soils will grow them, too. To promote easy harvesting, put the plants 12 or 15 inches apart in furrows. Add some well-seasoned compost in the bottom of the furrow, then put on some soil, and after planting, mound up the soil into 10-inch ridges to prevent the roots from going down deep in the soil. Since these plants grow best in warm weather, don't put them out until well after the last frost, say a month. Push the roots down in and water well. They survive droughts well, and in fact, prefer hot, dry weather.

Centennial (100 days), Jewell (110), and Porto Rico (100) are good varieties to try. Centennial has been tried in the North, and it will produce little tubers of a fine orange color in about 90 days. You can get a bush Porto Rico, rather reddish orange, for small gardens. Some people call orange sweet potatoes, yams, but they are not. Yams grow in the tropics.

Pumpkin
Cucurbita pepo

Halloween, pumpkin pies, and an occasional stewed pumpkin when you have no winter squash are the usual reasons for growing this big husky plant. Shredded raw pumpkin to add to a salad or to fry quickly until crisp is another kind of pumpkin you may not yet know about, but when you do, you will be glad of the taste it offers.

Culture for the pumpkin vine is usually the same as for squash, in hills spaced 4 feet apart or in a row thinned eventually to about that distance. Interplanted with corn, pumpkins will do fairly well, seeming to be helped by the shade of the corn plants. Otherwise plant on the edge of the

227

garden so they'll run onto the grass. A packet of seeds will plant five or six hills, and with fertilizer and good watering this amount might well be enough for all your needs. The seeds are viable for four years. The new bush pumpkin, which takes less room than the older varieties, is called Cinderella, and it is quite a surprise to see pumpkins grow as summer squashes do on a squatty bush. This variety matures in 102 days, as compared to the 115 days for the old varieties such as Connecticut Field. The fruits weigh up to 10 pounds, as compared to 20 pounds for Connecticut Field. For a medium-sized pumpkin, very round and stylish, try Youngs' Beauty. Smaller ones include Jack-o'-Lantern and Baby Pam. Among the giants are Big Moon, Big Max, and the huge Atlantic Giant, which people grow for contests.

Any of these pumpkins are among the great bargains of the garden. You can get a packet of seeds for 75 cents or a dollar this year, and from these seeds you can get several hundred pounds of food. What's more, they store very well with almost no loss of food value; and don't forget the very nutritious seeds, easily dried in the sun or in a warm, dry kitchen. They are as good as sunflower seeds and almost as nutritious. You get from each serving of baked pumpkin 3,400 I.U. of vitamin A, 37 mg of vitamin C, and a big provisions of minerals. It is a mystery why Americans shun this excellent food. If it tastes flat to you, add herbs or spices.

Radish
Raphanus sativas

Easiest vegetable of all. Radishes are easy to plant, for the seeds are large and manageable. The red ones come up and are ready to eat in 21 days, white icicle varieties in 30 days. Even the winter radish, Round Black Spanish, is ready in 55 days after a late sowing in July or August. The tops are edible, too, though rather ticklish when raw. Seeds are viable for four years.

The varieties we like for red radishes are the quick-growing Red Boy and a very round, smooth radish called Cherry Belle. Both are solid and pleasant, and if you slice some very thin and fry them two minutes in oil, they are soft and mild and taste a little bit like turnip. These two varieties have short tops and can be grown indoors as well as outdoors. Try them in the kitchen or on the terrace. A slower-growing variety, Champion, has tops that sometimes get quite large. The tops are tougher, but they make a cooked green if you want variation. A fast-growing one, Saxa, will be ready in 18 days; a so-called "supersweet" radish is French Breakfast, red and white.

For white radishes, there is one 25-day variety called Burpee White, and the 30-day White Icicle with roots that grow up to 5 inches. A midseason one is the very satisfactory White Strassburg, a 40-day radish. One which has the virtue of holding for several weeks in the ground without becoming pithy, as most others do, is called All Seasons.

You won't have to thin radishes if you space them well while planting, or if you intermix them with carrot seeds or herbs when you plant. Just pull them as they mature, and eat them up. You must thin them wherever they grow too thick from careless planting, for then no roots develop well, and all you have are greens. One excellent place to plant radishes is among the hills of cucumbers as companion plants. They also go well with squashes.

Because they are pungent, radishes are bothered very little by insects, and actually drive away cucumber beetles from squash and cukes. But they do occasionally get root maggot, especially near corn and cabbage. In fact, radishes are used as a trap crop to attract maggots away from corn and cabbage. The best deterrents are never to plant in soil that was infested the previous year, always to give the soil good deep preparation with plenty of compost, and to start out with a large dose of wood ashes.

Cut and soaked radish roses may be pretty, but you lose a good portion of their nutriment if you treat them this way. Cut off the tough lower root, and some of the top, and put them in your salad or on your snack dish whole. Leaves fried in hot soy oil or butter will be cooked in two minutes or less. Drain them on a piece of bread. Since they dry out very rapidly, they are fragile and break easily. Best used as a garnish.

Rhubarb
Rheum rhaponticum

This useful perennial was once found only in apothecaries' gardens, but is now grown alongside many home vegetable gardens for use as sauce

Kohlrabi

Endive

Swiss Chard

Rhubarb

Parsley

Dandelion

Chinese Cabbage

Comfrey

Carrot Tops

Relatively Pestless Leafy Vegetables

and in pies and conserves. Buy six or eight roots and set
them out in a rich, well-prepared bed. Do not harvest the
first year, and pull out only a few stalks the second year.
You can also start rhubarb from seeds, and again plan not
to harvest until the second year. The varieties to choose are
MacDonald, Valentine, and Victoria. MacDonald has big
red stalks, of a good flavor. Rhubarb can be divided every
eight or ten years by digging up the plants and cutting the
root in several pieces before replanting.

When the plants comes to flower, cut out that stalk. It uses
up food that might better go to the roots to feed the new
leaves the following spring. In the fall give the plants a good
spread of extra mulch, and manure them well. If you want
to dig some roots in order to have winter rhubarb, take them
up in late fall and store them in sand. Leave outdoors until
after the first hard frost, and then put them in the cellar.
Never permit dock to grow in the neighborhood of your
rhubarb, for it will entice the rhubarb curculio pest to come
into the area. And never eat the leaves of rhubarb; they
will make you sick.

Every spring I make several batches of Aunt Mary's
Rhubarb Conserve, invented for the White Turkey Restaurant. Take 6 pounds of rhubarb stems, cut to 1-inch lengths,
and combine with 6 pounds sugar, 2 pounds seedless
raisins (cut up), 1 pound walnut meats (cut up), 4 oranges
(cut up, skin and all). Mix well and boil for an hour. Put in
sterilized jars and cover well.

Do not peel or scrape rhubarb stems when you prepare
them for conserve, pie, or sauce. That's just throwing
nutrients onto your compost heap that you might as well eat.

Rocket, Rockette,
or Arugula
Eruca sativa

This pleasantly pungent green
is a great addition to the garden, especially for the tangy,
tasty leaves it provides for salads. It is very easy to grow,
not being at all fussy about soil. Best results come from
careful thinning, and the leaves taste best when young.
The one pest I have noticed is the leafhopper, and garlic
spray will usually take care of it. If cabbage worms go to
the leaves use Dipel or Thuricide, the *Bacillus thüringiensis*
biological control. Arugula is a very hardy plant, with-

standing several frosts in the fall. You can dig up some plants to grow indoors for several more weeks or even months. To increase your supply, plant successively during the summer.

Turkestan Rose
Rosa rugosa

Though you may not want to introduce this species of hedge rose into your vegetable garden, seriously consider it for other parts of your place for the sake of its very nutritious rose hips or seed pods, an excellent source of vitamin C. Anywhere you want an accent or a border plant or a hedge, it will probably do well. This rose can be ordered from most nurseries that specialize in ornamental shrubs, roses, and decorative hedges, though it is sometimes not advertised by name. It may be called everlasting hedge rose or something like that, but when you write refer to it as *Rosa rugosa* anyway. Stern's Nurseries, for example, call it by name. It has lots of unspectacular crimson-pink flowers, from June until frost. Cultivation is easy, the only requirement being a good, rich soil. These roses are relatively pest-free, not nearly so pestered as the hybrid tea roses. Pick off the few rose bugs you may see. Harvest the rose hips when they're first fully plump—unless you want to leave them for the birds.

For food value, note these interesting comparisons: vitamin C, 2,000 I.U. in rose hips as compared to 50 in an equivalent amount of oranges or orange juice; vitamin A, 5,000 I.U., compared to 200 in oranges; protein, 1.2 percent; and carbohydrate, 17 percent as compared to .9 percent and 11.2 percent in oranges. To get the full vitamin C benefit from oranges they must be fresh. In roses, the vitamin C persists, even in dried, powdered form, though the hips should be chilled as soon as gathered to prevent rapid deterioration by enzyme action.

When they are cool, and ready to prepare, remove the stem end and the blossom end of the seed pod, and for each cup of hips have ready 1-½ cups of boiling water. Simmer for 15 minutes, and let stand in a glass or pottery vessel for 24 hours. Strain and bring the extracted juice to a full rolling boil. Add 2 tablespoons of lemon juice for each pint of rose hip juice, put it up in sterilized jars and seal. Never use aluminum or copper for storing or cooking these fruits, any more than you would for tomatoes, rhubarb, or other acidic foods. Use the juice to make cobblers, jellies, candies, puddings, and to spruce up drinks.

For rose hip jelly, add a box of commercial pectin, or homemade apple pectin, to a quart of juice, and bring to a boil. Add an equal amount of sugar, bring to a high boil for a minute and then skim and put in sterilized jars.

To dry rose hips, split them in half, spread pieces on a baking sheet and toast them slowly in a 200° F oven until they get crisp. Do not remove the seeds. The pulp from making juice or jelly can be dried also. It makes quite good tea, but eat the grounds, too, to get all that vitamin C. Dried rose materials keep well, if kept clean and dry.
Rose hips from any variety of rose can also be used in all these ways.

Rosemary
See Herbs, pages 180–202.

Rutabaga
See Turnips, pages 246–49.

Sage
See Herbs, pages 180–202.

Salsify *(Oyster Plant)*
Tragopogon porrifolius

This unusual and highly nutritious plant can be a good source of food over the winter, for it is easily stored. It is a root vegetable, and takes about 120 days to mature. Part of the crop may be left in the ground the way you leave carrots and parsnips to be ready to dig in the spring, or during the winter if you protect them so you can get at them. (See page 158.) They grow to about 8 inches in length and have a diameter of 1 to 1-½ inches. They do taste oddly like oysters, especially when well buttered.

The variety to get is Mammoth Sandwich Island, and sow the seeds ½ inch deep in rows 2 feet apart in May. Thin them later to 3 feet apart for the individual plants. They grow best in light, rich, well-composted soil, and will do well if occasional side dressings of old manure are applied down the rows. Two ounces of seeds will plant 100 feet of row, which will give you a big supply. The seeds are viable for only a year.

A very good stew with salsify is made by melting 4 tablespoons of butter in a skillet; in it, lightly brown 1 cup of diced raw veal. Then add 1 sliced carrot, half a medium-sized onion, sliced, 1 tablespoon chopped parsley, 1 tablespoon tarragon, and 1 tablespoon marjoram. Next add 1 cup of hot chicken broth. (Soy milk powder and the liquid of greens may be substituted for the meat and broth.) Cover and simmer for 2 hours. Meanwhile clean and simmer ten salsify plants, and when nearly done, transfer them to the other pan, leaving them there long enough to gather up the flavors. In about half an hour add the juice of a lemon and 3 tablespoons butter cut into small pieces.

Savory
See Herbs, pages 180–202.

Scorzonera, or Black salsify *(120 days)*

This variant of the salsify or oyster plant has been grown in this country since the eighteenth century. It is rarely seen nowadays, but if you want a pleasant novelty for a dip at a party, try this easy-to-grow vegetable. It is not really black but a dark red or dark blue-green, and white inside. Though it prefers light soil, it will grow even in heavy soil. It is especially helpful planted among carrots, about 1 inch deep, for it is said to repel carrot fly. Feed the soil some extra potash. The best way to cook this tasty root is to parboil it and then brown it in butter. Or you can shred it and serve it with hollandaise. sauce.

Soybean
Glycine max

Should be a staple in any organic garden. Though the soil and cultural needs are about the same as those for bush green beans, the maturing time can run from three to five months, so adjustments must be made if you live in a cold climate. For midseason varieties, you can plant any time between April 10 and June 30, if your last frost is on March 20 or thereabouts. If it is as late as April 20, however, you might plant between May 15 and

June 15, thus allowing for the earlier frost at the other end of the season. If your last freeze averages any later than April 30, you are on your own—you may succeed in growing soybeans and you may not.

The zone having an average last freeze around April 30 is a big one, for it not only stretches across the country in the moderate belt, but also comes up the Atlantic coast from Virginia to eastern Maine, with a few extra pockets on the Hudson River and around the Great Lakes. To extend the season you can use hotcaps, large cold frames, or a row cover of heavy plastic or spun polyester. In northern areas grow Giant Green, which matures in 90 to 95 days, and avoid the longer-growing varieties such as Hokkaide and Imperial, which take up to 115 days. Bansei is a midseason soybean, taking 95 to 100 days. If you can harvest them, these midseason beans are versatile for eating green, frozen, or dried. Recently developed shorter edible soybeans include Envy (75 days), earlier than lima beans actually, Maple Arrow (77), and Fiskeby V (70), ready to eat by the end of August in northern areas. Another new one is Butterbean (90). For black ones, try Panther (120) or Black Jet, available from Johnny's Selected Seeds (see Appendix).

The soil you plant in should be well drained, fairly fertile, well limed, and well mulched. It should also be warm. To hasten warming, you can put out large plastic bags of water along the rows where you are going to plant. They will collect the heat of the sun, and hold at least some of the warmth overnight. They are so big they cool off slowly. You can profitably start soybeans in peat pots between April 15 and May 15, and set out the little plants at the end of June when it is warm.

A packet of soybeans will plant 25 feet of row. Put the seeds in a furrow about 2 inches deep, and when the seedlings are 2 or 3 inches high, thin them to stand 4 to 6 inches apart. Row covers or cloches help to keep the plants warm. It is important to keep all untreated bean seeds from the cold and the possibility of rot. You may have a problem with weeds. The plants grow very slowly at first, and if the weeds get a start on them, the little soybeans will not have much chance in the struggle for root space, water, nutrients, and light. Then, if you start yanking out the weeds right next to the very small plants, their root hairs get disturbed, even ruined. If you leave the weeds to devour the available nutrients, your beans will be spindly and lower in nutritional value. So get the weeds out before you plant. Cultivate the soil, let the weeds grow up, and then cultivate again and immediately mulch. When it is time to plant, push the seeds down in through the mulch, leaving an opening big enough to let in the light and air that the small seedling will need. The mulch will help preserve moisture, too, of course.

You may have a problem with Japanese beetles. Plant white geraniums among the soybeans, put around milky spore disease, pick off beetles by hand, and let the house sparrows come in to eat them. In the South, for velvet bean caterpillar, you may have to bring in *Bacillus thüringiensis*, which you can get under the trade name Thuricide, Dipel, or Biotrol.

Keep experimenting to see what method works best for you for outwitting the warm-weather, long-growing season needed by this most excellent of all sources of vegetable protein. If you can grow soybeans successfully, you will have added bountifully to your garden produce.

Harvest the green soybeans as soon as they mature, and let them stay on the vines a little longer for dried beans. When green soybeans are cooked 20 or 30 minutes in a little water or milk, they taste like a nutty version of lima beans. But they never get mushy. To make them easier to shell, blanch or steam the whole bean for 4 or 5 minutes, and then you can snap them in two and squeeze out the beans rather easily. They will stay springy, so do not overcook them; if young and just picked, they might be ready in 15 minutes.

Make a succotash, soup, casserole, vegetarian chili, or salad with leftover cooked soybeans. One soup starts with ¾ cup of grated carrots and 5 tablespoons minced onion, sautéed for 5 minutes in 1 tablespoon of soy oil. Then add 2 cups of cooked soybeans, 4 cups of chicken stock or tomato juice, and 1 teaspoon of fresh marjoram, or whatever herb you prefer. The soybeans may be left whole or blended with 2 cups of the stock first.

For particularly good salad mixtures try green soybeans and cucumber with chives; or soybeans, celery, and onions. A high-protein fritter can be made with 2 cups of mashed soybeans, 2 beaten eggs, and 2 tablespoons of grated onion, fried on both sides until brown on a hot greased griddle. You will be getting a protein content of 12.5 percent. Eggs have 14 percent, veal has 16 percent, steak has 19 percent, and chicken 22 percent protein.

If you mature and dry soybeans, the protein content goes up to 35 to 45 percent. Because dried soybeans are so high in protein, they need a lot of soaking and cooking to make them tender. When ground to grits they cook a lot faster.

For whole dried beans, soak them overnight, then put them in the freezer for several hours to make them even more tender. An hour before using, remove and cook them in a pressure cooker for 45 minutes (or boil them for three hours) and serve plain or with gravy. Make the gravy by stirring 1 tablespoon butter and 1 tablespoon whole wheat flour to the liquid drained off after boiling. For additional flavor, some sautéed carrot shreds, finely chopped shallots or onions, and celery leaves may be added.

Cold, dried, cooked soybeans are good in a brown rice and green pepper salad, and, either whole or ground up, they are valuable additions to many kinds of casseroles. They will provide the protein for a vegetable loaf and for soufflés, croquettes, and stuffed tomatoes or peppers. They make good baked beans, with molasses or honey and a piece of onion. A fine dip can be made by mixing 2 cloves of garlic, minced, 2 tablespoons mixed herbs, ½ cup softened butter, and about 1-½ cups cooked ground soybeans. Thin with mayonnaise if necessary. Can be made in a blender.

Soybean sprouts are easy to make, and very versatile and nutritious. They are excellent in salads, for tempura, folded into scrambled eggs or omelets, in mashed potatoes, or stewed in a little water, milk, or tomato juice. To make the sprouts, soak a cupful of dried soybeans overnight in cold water in a large glass container. Flush it all out, put on a cloth cover, and keep in the dark. Flush the soybeans four to six times a day to keep down fungal growth. In four or five days you will have sprouts 2 inches long, ready to use. Bring them to the sunlight for a few hours to green up, then put them right in the refrigerator so that their plentiful vitamin C will not be lost.

Another delicious soybean treat is as salted nuts. After washing dried soybeans and soaking them overnight, drain them and spread them out to dry. When thoroughly dry, deep-fry them for 8 or 9 minutes in a good fat heated to 350 F. Or bake them in oil for half an hour at 350 F. Drain them on paper towels or pieces of bread, and salt them while they are still warm.

Soybeans can also make fine-tasting grits, blended or ground at home from dried beans, or in the food mill at your organic food store. When the soybeans are ground, the protein content goes up to 56 percent, the same percentage as low-fat soy flour (which has had the bean fat taken out). Soybean flour is made as low fat or high fat. It is yellowish, fluffy, and a pleasure to work with, though it must be mixed with other flours to make bread, for it has no gluten. You can make soy milk, too. Soak dried beans for 12 to 24 hours, changing the water frequently. Grind the beans to a fine paste in a food chopper, using the finest blade. Keep adding water—up to three times the amount of beans you have. Boil to a high foam for an hour, and strain through cheese-cloth. Or run the beans through the chopper, add 6 cups of water to 1 cup of beans, simmer for 15 minutes, and strain. Or make in the blender. Use it as you would any milk. If you want it richer, blend in 1 cup of soy oil and 2 table-spoons of honey.

Soy Ice Cream: Put in a blender 2-½ cups soy milk, ¼ cup corn oil or soy oil, ½ cup honey, and a pinch of salt. Blend well, and add ½ cup chopped fruit and ½ cup nuts. Freeze in a hand freezer. (Strawberry ice cream can be made with the basic recipe, omitting the nuts and increasing the fruit to 1-½ cups. For more body, 1 cup of soy milk powder may be added, especially if the strawberries are very large, fresh, and juicy.)

There is yet another soy product, soy curd or tofu, which is used as cheese, sandwich spread, in desserts, and again as a substitute for meat or fish. It can also be frozen, in or out of water. It is a bit more complicated to make than soymilk, but well worth the effort. A good recipe can be found in *The Book of Tofu*, by William Shurtleff and Akiko Aoyagi.

Spinach
Spinacia oleracea

A crop that goes by so fast that you sometimes wonder whether it is worth growing or not. However, if you have the room, plans for replanting, and someone to help you blanch and freeze it when the whole crop begins to bolt and has to be used, go ahead and plant it.

We start adding the tender outer leaves to our salads as soon as they appear, and keep snipping off and adding leaves as the plants grow. Then we have a meal or two of steamed spinach before the day the plants begin to shoot up and bolt.

Since spinach is a cool-weather plant, succession plantings can be made throughout April and into May until the earth gets too warm. You can plant it very early, for it doesn't mind the frost. It is also possible to plant again in late August so it will come again in the fall.

Varieties to try include Longstanding Bloomsdale (48 days) and cold-resistant Savoy (45) for fall. Another long-standing spinach is America. Two recommended hybrids are the crinkly Vienna and the smooth-leaved Melody, bred for home gardens (42). In addition, there is the New Zealand spinach (not really a spinach), which is heat resistant and is called everlasting because when you pick it, it grows again. Try it. You might like its watery taste. Also try the leaf vegetables, Swiss chard, orach, and edible amaranth. Chard seeds are viable for four years.

For spinaches, use very rich, nitrogenous soil and compost, with a pH of 6 to 7. Sow in rows 12 to 18 inches apart and cover the seeds with ½ inch of soil. Thin the plants to 3 inches apart when they get to be 3 inches high. For an ounce of seeds, you ought to get three bushels or fifty pounds in a 100-foot row. Remember, however, that the waysides and your own garden are full of other greens to cook the same way you do spinach (see *Daylily*, page 176, and *Weeds*, pages 250–51).

On the young spinach leaves there may be a few pests to bother you. One is the spinach leaf miner, which goes into the veins, curls them up, and makes the plants look horrid. Pull up any affected plants you see and bury them in the compost heap. Rout out all weed hosts you notice, and bury them, too. A few blights like fusarium wilt can get into the part of the garden where you grow spinach. If it does, allow at least a three-year cycle before you plant spinach there again. Also switch to the more resistant varieties such as Melody and Tyee (53 days).

For a hearty dish, try spinach with cheese. Combine two cups cooked, chopped spinach with 2 cups cottage cheese,

½ cup grated cheddar or Parmesan, 1 teaspoon salt, and 2
eggs. Mix all together until well blended. Put into a
1-½-quart mold or casserole and cook for half an hour at
350° F. When still hot and ready to bring to the table,
sprinkle on more cheese.

Squash
Cucurbita

Squashes are cucurbits, which
make them cousins of cucumbers, melons, and cantaloupes.
Plant several kinds: for summer use, yellow summer
squash and zucchini, cocozelles and straightnecks; for winter
use, acorn, blue, Hubbard, and the excellent buttercup
squashes. Most squash seeds are viable for four years.

If you live where you need to irrigate, you can build a
ditch or moat of about 4 feet in diameter around each hill
of squash and water your plants in that. The roots will get to
the water, and the water will be held from eroding away.
Make sure that the soil where you plant is very loose. If it is
a little acid, the squash won't mind. When possible, plant
at the edge of the garden, but away from the pumpkins so
that when the vines crawl out, they will not get into your
other vegetables. You can also pinch back the wandering
tips, to keep them under control. A ¼-ounce of seed will
sow 50 feet, with one or two yards between the plants when
they become mature. Plant summer squash in April or
May; winter squash in May or June. Choose bush varieties to
save space.

Put in more of the winter kinds than the summer because
they are easily stored and will last you over the winter.
Pick these just before frost. Wash, dry, and rub lightly with
soy or corn oil, and put in a cool, dark place. Do not worry
about any leftover seeds you may have after you plant, for
they will stay viable for a year or so. Or you can eat the
seeds that you do not plant. Do not plant seeds from your
hybrid cucurbits; you'd get a strange crop. (Ditto for hybrid
corn.) All squashes are heavy users of nutrients, so dig big
deep trenches, fill them up with several inches of well-
rotted or dry manure, then compost and add fine sandy
loam before you plant. A good soaking whenever needed
will also help growth, and a careful inspection every morning for cucumber beetles or squash bugs is advisable during
the period of early growth. Interplant with nasturtiums to

discourage such pests.

Spread wood ashes also, or make a spray of wood ashes and water to use on the leaves. When there is a hot spell in June, use wood ashes anyway, as a deterrent. You should also interplant calendulas and marigolds to deter cucumber beetles, and try an onion-and-water or garlic spray if these pests are persistent. Also pick them off and toss into kerosene.

This fine, nutritious vegetable is good raw, boiled, sautéed, or baked. Some of my favorite squashes are Waltham Butternut, the acorn squash Table Ace, the golden Jersey Golden Acorn, Golden Crookneck, Patty Pan (and the yellow type, Sunburst), and the new Butterblossom, bred especially for good blossoms to fry. (See also *Zucchini*.) Both Big Hubbard and Baby Hubbard are excellent old standard varieties of winter squash. Remember to harvest winter squash when it is fully mature, because the cold weather increases sugar in the fruit.

Crosses can occur in squashes. Acorn will cross with Butternut; Buttercup will cross with Hubbard. But Acorn will not cross with Hubbard.

Sumac
Rhus glabra

Scarlet, or staghorn sumac is a tall shrub found along many roadsides. Its fruit ripens to red plumes in the summer, and its leaves turn bright red in the fall. The malic acid in the fruit makes a delicious tart drink and jelly. Wash roadside sumac thoroughly to get rid of pollution deposited on it from passing cars. Cover with water and crush the horns, or fruits, with a potato masher, and strain the juice through a fine-mesh cloth. Very fine mesh. There are prickles to get out. Only fresh young fruits are good. Stale ones are bitter. **Don't confuse** with the whiteberried swamp sumac, which is poisonous.

Sunflowers
Helianthus

There are several varieties of sunflowers. Whatever varieties you choose, it is a good crop to grow, and what you don't harvest for yourself or for winter feed for the birds, you can leave right there in the flower heads and the birds will come to harvest it themselves. It is pleasant to see the first goldfinches fly in to get their fill.

Sunflowers do best in a deep, rich, slightly moist soil but will survive in many different kinds of soil. The seeds can be planted about half an inch deep and about 12 inches apart, or more if you grow the biggest varieties. The seeds are very high in protein, calcium, phosphorus, and several of the B-vitamin group, and have long been relished as a snack. The oil of the seed is a source of both linoleic acid and lecithin. If you plan to grow large quantities, you should add lime to adjust the soil to a pH over 6, say 6 to 8, and apply plenty of manure, rock phosphate, and granite dust with the lime. At harvest time begin to cut the heads off as soon as the outer seeds get ripe—or as soon as the birds start coming in to peck out those outer seeds. Hang the heads in a warm, airy place, and they will continue to ripen for a while. When ripe, rub out the seeds and store in airtight jars.

Varieties to consider are the giant 12-foot perennial sunflower, *H. giganteus; H. annuus,* the common annual sunflower, which can grow up to 12 feet; also a 5-foot one called *H. decapetalus,* a perennial. When you order seeds, ask for Mammoth; it produces lots of seeds on good, firm heads.

It is all right to plant sunflower seeds in a row, but it is also good to scatter them around the garden and wherever else you can find a bit of soil to put them in. They may need staking when they get big. In the garden they cause a lot of shade when full-sized. The big roots compete for nutrients, so add compost.

Sweet Potato
See Potato, Sweet, page 227.

Tarragon
See Herbs, pages 180–202.

Thyme
See Herbs, pages 180–202.

Tomato
Lycopersicon esculentum

A delicious, nutritious, and very inviting vegetable when it comes warm and ripe straight from the vine. Any other tomatoes, even the ones called "hothouse" from the market, have a completely different taste from those thoroughly ripened in the garden.

Tomatoes are a long-seasoned fruit, so it is customary to start them indoors, though volunteers from the previous year and seeds planted very early outdoors, if they can make it, produce husky, heavy-bearing plants in the fall. Some say that tomatoes like to grow in the same place year after year, and certainly if you use marigolds as a nematode prevention, I believe that to prevent disease in tomatoes it is best to plant tomatoes in ground not recently used to grow tomatoes, potatoes, eggplants, okra, or peppers. Be sure the place you select will have plenty of ventilation, and plan to provide quantities of nutrients, compost, mulch, and water for your maturing plants. It is crucial to keep tomatoes watered during dry spells to prevent blossom end rot. But water only early in the day because tomato leaves and stems should be kept as dry as possible. Do not let dogs run near the plants when they are wet or damp, because tomatoes wound easily, and then diseases get into the wounds.

The tomato is one plant that you do not toss on the compost pile unless you are sure it is absolutely healthy. Even its seeds will come through the very hottest of piles. And do not smoke or chew tobacco in among the plants, or handle them after you have filled a pipe and touched tobacco. Tomatoes cannot endure the results of exposure to tobacco, which causes tobacco mosaic virus. Tomatoes are also subject to wilts and blights.

Tomatoes come in two growth patterns: *indeterminate*, the big tall or sprawling ones with large, late fruits; and *determinate*, the bushy ones usually yielding medium-sized, earlier tomatoes, sometimes caged, but not staked. Small-sized (cherry or cocktail) tomatoes come as both sorts. Determinate tomatoes stop growing when the terminal bud has fruited. It is not usual to prune them, though removal of the terminal bud can produce several strong side branches. It is frequently the practice to prune indeterminate tomatoes, whose growing tip will continue indefinitely. Take out the suckers in the axils and remove the growing tip after six trusses have formed. Some people prune the plant down to one stem, but that much removal of leaves can cause sun scald.

To overcome the early cessation of bearing of determinate tomatoes, start some plants fourteen weeks before setting out, instead of the usual eight to ten weeks. When the plants are 6–8 inches tall, begin making cuttings to root in moist sand with a plastic mulch. Plant out when rooted, and continue to make more cuttings at one-week intervals until 60 days before your first fall frost. The cuttings develop rapidly. Because tomatoes will form roots from their stems, always plant them deeply, or even with the stems laid sideways under the earth. They will right themselves in a short time.

To safeguard your plants somewhat against the hazards of disease, get pest-resistant strains. Varieties resistant to verticillium and fusarium wilts are marked VF in seed catalogs. If they are also resistant to nematodes an N is added, and for resistance to tobacco mosaic a T is added. Burpee's VF Hybrid (72 days from setting out) and Beefeater Hybrid VFN are examples. If you have someone else grow your tomato plants for you, ask for resistant strains of this sort. Remember that it takes at least six to eight weeks to get a tomato plant to the size proper to set out in the ground, so order early. But do not press the season; in most areas the end of May is plenty soon to set out tomato plants. People ruin them by putting them out too early. Both air and soil temperatures should be at least 55° F, and preferably warmed beforehand by black plastic mulch, manure buried a foot deep, or exposure to the sun.

Among the recommended determinate tomatoes is a recently developed All-American variety called Celebrity VFNT (70 days). Even earlier is Fireball (60), and an old favorite, New Yorker (63). Among the earliest, grown in northern gardens are Cold Set, which can be seeded in cool (50° F soil), Scotia (60 days), and a short-season variety which prefers sandy soil, Starfire (56). Burpee's Gloriana (55) has also proved satisfactory for cool climates.

Another All-American variety, said to be tolerant to fifteen diseases, is Floramerica, especially suitable for warmer areas. A small hybrid is Patio Hybrid, a determinate variety good for containers. The 50-day Tiny Tim and Early Pear are other small-sized varieties to consider. Any of these can be caged or left unstaked.

The large-fruited indeterminate varieties, suitable for staking or growing on trellises, bear later and produce the juicy, dark red tomatoes Americans love. There are dozens of varieties available, but some of the most popular are Big Boy (78 days), Better Boy (72), and the golden Sunray (80). Consider also the novelty tomato Long Keeper (78), which is rather acid in taste, but if picked before ripe will keep until Thanksgiving; the huge climbing tomato, Trip-L-Crop; the big Supersteak; and the pot tomato Winter Wonder. One with almost solid flesh and few seeds is Pik-Red. The yellow Golden Jubilee (83) is low in acid, as are most of the yellow ones. Rutgers (74) is one of the most repeatedly grown by many gardeners, and has been for a good many years. A popular small indeterminate tomato is Sweet 100, with cascades of little fruit (70 days). And an heirloom novelty is Pruden's Purple (70), with big 4-inch fruits. Another old-timer is the pink Ponderosa, and the habitually staked Bonny Best (75) is still available at Johnny's Selected Seeds. (See Appendix.)

In seasons of drought, when water is so scant that it does not draw up enough minerals for the plants, a calcium deficiency can develop. Be sure that the soil is properly limed, and be faithful about watering the plants daily, preferably at the roots.

The food value of tomatoes is very high. They can supply in an average serving 1,000 I.U. of vitamin A and 13 to 30 mg of vitamin C, plentiful portions of eight of the B-vitamin group, and minerals including cobalt. For the best supply of vitamin C, grow tomatoes on pole supports so the fruits get lots of sun. Any outdoor-grown tomatoes have twice as much vitamin C as hothouse ones. Do not ripen picked green tomatoes on a windowsill in the sun. Keep in sunless full light.

You can cook nearly everything with tomatoes—sauces, soups, spaghetti, stews, juices, and even cake. Toward the end of the season I begin to bring in some green tomatoes to slice and cover with salt and flour, then fry in butter. They have a delicious tart flavor. I also make green tomato relish.

Pick enough green tomatoes to make two quarts of cut-up pieces. Cover the pieces with ⅔ cup of salt and let them stand for a day. Add 1-½ teaspoons each of pepper, mustard, cinnamon, cloves, and allspice, ⅓ cup of white mustard seed, 2 or 3 chopped onions, and a quart of vinegar. Bring to a boil and cook for 15 minutes. Pack in sterilized jars. They are quite crispy, and go well with all kinds of baked beans and loaves.

The first gigantic plant I ever knew was a single tomato plant nurtured and tended so it produced enough fruit to satisfy the needs of a whole family. It was grown against a fence, and had a chance to spread out as it wished. The family tied each branch very carefully with soft strips that would nowadays be cutoff nylon stockings, I suspect. First it was given a huge 6-foot hole, filled partially with half corncobs and half well-rotted but unleached manure. This was covered with fine loam and compost mixed to the right texture for receiving the young roots when the tomato was planted. Because the location was a sandy seaside spot, the plant was also supplied with a length of hose that went down to the nutrient area, and the tomato was watered every day. Since tomatoes are tolerant of a pH range from slightly acid to neutral, no liming was necessary. As you can imagine, this plant thrived. It was so healthy that it repelled pests. And besides, tomatoes have an insecticidal alkaloid somewhat like digitalin in their leaves. Any worms that arrived were picked off, and the leaves were given a protective spray once or twice of hot peppers blended with water with a drop of detergent in it. Today, I assume, the owners of this remarkable plant would have sprayed it with Thuricide, Dipel, or Diatrel so the *Bacillus thüringiensis* could do in the worms.

Turnip
Brassica rapa

These are sturdy vegetables, one variety small, one big variety called Swede or rutabaga. Well adapted for immediate use and for storing into the winter. Turnips can be grown both early in the spring and in the fall, but are considered much better if grown in the fall. This means that you should get seeds in the ground in late July in the Northeast. Do not plant in the spring or they will bolt and get woody stalks. When they first come up there is a tiny flea beetle which bothers the fresh, green growth. It can be controlled by a dusting of rotenone—but try wood ashes first. Turnip seeds are viable for four years.

Keep the rows a foot apart, and thin the plants to stand 4 inches apart. The recommended varieties are Purple Top White (55 days) and Tokyo Cross Hybrid, an All-American winner which is ready for using as greens in only 30 days, and as a small turnip in 35 to 40 days. Tokyo Cross Hybrid is also resistant to virus and other diseases. Other varieties to consider are Market Express (38 days), said to be a fine, crisp baby turnip with dark green tops, and Ohno Scarlet (55), with a vaguely rosy flesh and red-veined green leaves. Since these last two are slower to bolt than the others, they can be planted in the spring. Plant some for their greens, anyway. Snowball is a good white turnip, and a famous Vermont turnip, Gilfeather, is especially sweet and delicious mashed with potatoes.

Turnip greens will give you more calcium than any other—a stupendous 259 mg in an average serving. Next you get phosphorus—50 mg, surpassed by only six others; then potassium, 440 mg, surpassed by only five; vitamin A, surpassed by only two; and vitamin C, surpassed by one other vegetable, and that is parsley. If you happen to eat both turnip greens and beet greens in any quantity on the same day, you run the danger of locking up the calcium intake in salts that form with the beet greens' oxalic acid. If you want to eat two or more greens in one day, combine your turnip greens with lettuce, dandelions, or one of the endives. The more you are willing to eat raw of both tops and root, the better.

Turnips are light feeders, so they should be rotated with such heavy feeders as kohlrabi, corn, or squash. Fertilize them with a moderate application of compost and a little rock phosphate and granite dust, never with heavy manures. Plant scientists have found that turnip plants have some sort of insecticidal chemical compound in their systems that is deadly to aphids, spider mites, and houseflies, as well as beetles. Therefore, it seems only sensible to use turnips as a repellent for those pests, and to interplant them with beans, for instance, which might be bothered by at least two of those pests. Flea beetles are a possible pest. Use rotenone or protect the plants with row covers. Those covers will also protect turnips from root maggots.

The time to dig turnips is before they get big, woody, and bitter. In September, begin to pull away the soil and look at them, or pull one up to test it. You can leave them in the ground till frost, but not if they are going to get big and woody.

Hardiest for winter storage is the one big turnip that is supposed to be big, the rutabaga or Swede, *Brassica napobrassica*. These vegetables get so big they may seem coarse, but they can be very tender and rather spicy if grown and prepared properly. They are longer growing than turnips, so the seeds should be sown in late June rather than in July, in rows about 2 feet apart instead of 1 foot apart. The best varieties are American Purple Top, an old favorite with many because it stores well, Laurentian, or Burpee's Purple-Top Yellow. Two packets of seeds will sow 100 feet.

I think that some of the most interesting recipes for turnips come from southern cooking. One recipe that has a very good cooking liquid calls for a pound of salt pork, ham hocks, or fresh hog jowl, 3 pounds of turnip greens or young rutabaga greens, 4 cups of cold water, 1 tablespoon vinegar, ½ teaspoon crushed red pepper, ¼ teaspoon fresh-ground black pepper, 1 teaspoon salt, and at the end a garnish of sliced sweet onions and sliced hard-boiled eggs. Cover the meat with cold water, add the seasonings, and bring to a boil. Then turn down the heat and simmer for an hour. Add the washed greens, discarding all yellow leaves and stems. Simmer one hour longer, but remove the cover during the last 15 minutes of cooking. When you drain the greens, reserve the cooking liquid and meat. Chop the greens if you wish, adjust the seasoning, and add a little vinegar if it suits your taste. Put the greens in a serving dish and add the meat and garnishes. Either serve the cooking liquid separately in a pitcher or pour it over the greens in the dish, depending on your preference. Serve with corn bread, to be used to mop up the liquid.

Another variation of a recipe from *Tuesday Soul Food Cookbook* (see Appendix) is *Mixed Greens with Corn Bread Dumplings*, a large recipe for six to eight people. Strip the stalks of 2 pounds of turnip greens, 1 pound of mustard greens, and 1 pound of collards or spinach. Wash very quickly in cold water to get the grit out, and put in a big (8-quart) pot. Add 2 quarts of boiling water, 1 pound of salt pork or bacon, and 1 chopped onion. Boil for half an hour before adding the greens. Add 2 tablespoons sugar and some salt if needed. Simmer it all, covered, for 2 hours. For dumplings to drop into the cooking liquid, mix 1-½ cups of water-ground white or yellow corn meal, 4 tablespoons flour, 1 tablespoon salt, and 1 tablespoon sugar. Add 1 cup of boiling water, stirring until the mixture is stiff. Wet your hands, make small balls of dough, and drop them in the pot of greens. Cover tightly while they simmer for 30 minutes.

These recipes, though they do not follow the preferred natural foods methods of quick cooking, do preserve many minerals and food values, for the cooking liquid is always served as part of the dish and never thrown down the drain.

A quick-cooking recipe for turnip roots is to dice them, sauté in soy, corn, or olive oil, cover, and simmer until tender, adding a little water or milk if needed. Some people mash them when done, but that is not necessary. Garnish with chives. Our favorite form of turnip is raw, sliced in matchstick lengths for finger salads. We combine them with raw carrot, raw cauliflower, celery, and raw pepper, and serve them with a garlic-and-lentil dip and a mild cheese dip.

Watercress
Nasturtium officinale

This crisp, refreshing green belongs to the same family as the turnip, but is to be treated entirely differently. We had in our area for many years a good priest who went around planting watercress in clear cool brooks in various places. I go every spring to one or another wild or escaped planting, admire the extent to which it has spread during the year, and pick a bagful to take home to keep airtight in the refrigerator. I do uproot a few plants to put in the low birdbath we have under a juniper, where they keep on growing for a month or more. You could put them in pots, and keep the pots in a tray of water. You can also grow your own watercress from seed in pots, adding a big handful of leaf mold to the soil, and some sand and ground limestone. You can even take some sprigs and root them in a glass of water. Change the water daily.

The best wild watercress bed I know grows on a stream in a limy area, just above a white, lime-bottomed little pond; the worst I know is in a backwater of a little stream that flows by a big storehouse, where there is a great deal of oil and gunk. A few years ago I would pick good cress there several times each spring, but alas, no more.

Good, clean, fresh watercress on bread and butter makes one of the best sandwiches in the world. This herb also adds tang and flavor to the green drink concoction that organic food enthusiasts make in the blender. In this drink they also put weeds.

Occasionally you can find watercress seeds listed in catalogs. Shepherd's, for example, lists a Dutch variety, Waterkress (53 days), and Harris's sells a variety called Improved Broad-Leaved.

Weeds

Organic gardeners do not hate weeds as much as other people do. Some we revere as pest repellents; others we relish as substitutes for spinach, including amaranthus or pigweed, *Amaranthus retroflexus*; burdock, *Arctium lappa* (page 186); cattail, *Typha latifolia*; curly dock, *Rumex crispus*; dandelion, *Taraxacum officinale*; lamb's-quarters, *Chenopodium album*; marsh marigold, *Caltha palustris*; milkweed, *Asclepias syriaca* (page 196); nettles, *Urtica dioica* (page 197); very young stalks of poke, *Phytolacca americana* (the roots and old stalks are poisonous); purslane, *Portulaca oleracea* (page 198); Russian thistle, *Salsola pestifer*; violets, *Viola papilionacea*; watercress, *Nasturtium officinale* (page 249), wild lettuce, *Lactuca*; and wild primrose, *Primula*; as well as members of the onion family like wild leek, *Allium moly* or *A. tricoccum*; and wild garlic, *Allium vineale*. A few bulbs are tasty, such as those of spatterdock, *Nuphar advena*; toothwort, *Lathraea squamaria*; wild lily, *Lilium philadelphicum*; and cattail, *Typha latifolia*—and, according to Euell Gibbons, many other bulbs. Some of the roots are tasty, too. For salads, greens, and juices to add to soups and gravies or to biscuits and muffins, juices to make into jelly, and tender leaves or slivers of root to make into tempura, wild plants are useful and exciting. As long as you know what you are doing, they add much to the variety and nutrition of a gardener's diet. But do not fool with plants you do not know. Consult the books on edible wild plants listed in the Appendix for guidance.

The nutritional values of "weeds" are sometimes phenomenal. For example, the ascorbic acid value of violet leaves and blossoms is way up to 210 and 150 mg per 100 g of plant. Winter cress is also high, with 163 mg in the buds and 152 mg in the leaves. The only higher source of vitamin C is the leaves of wild strawberry. If you eat those, you get 229 mg. Highbush cranberry, a common plant in our area, yields 100 mg, which is very good in comparison to dande-

lion (30), nettle leaves (83), and daylily buds (43). The weeds
with good protein percentages are dandelion buds, daylily
buds, and especially nettle leaves, with 6.9 g per 100 g of
protein. For carotene, the most valuable sources are wild
spearmint, violet leaves, catnip leaves, and winter cress—
both leaves and buds.

Figures like this show that violet leaves will give you in
half a cup the equivalent in vitamin C of four oranges. We
eat the young leaves and buds every spring and like them
very much. To us they seem to taste like a cross between
spinach and asparagus. You can also make violet flower jelly
and syrup. Both should be kept in the refrigerator.

Wild catnip is also high in both vitamins A and C. It
should be gathered in July, or whenever the blossoms first
appear. It is used mostly for tea, for a mild stimulant, and
also a palliative.

Zucchini, or Courgette
Cucurbita Pepo

These are the prolific green, or
so-called gray or black squashes which have become so
popular in this country. Grow them and take care of them
as you do summer squash, and harvest them when small. I
have, however, overlooked some under the heavy growth
of leaves and harvested them when nearly 2 feet long. These
I chop up and use for pickles or zucchini bread. The young
ones we eat raw or sautéed. A good dark green variety is
Aristocrat (40 days), and a handsome golden one is Burpee
Golden (55). The black one is called Black Magic. A novelty
zucchini is Round Zucchini, sometimes sold as Ronde de
Nice (45). The gray is simply called Gray (42). We plant
nasturtiums sometimes among the zucchini plants, as with
other squashes. A hazard is that the big leaves of this vine
can overshadow the nasturtium plants, so watch over
them.

CHAPTER 7

Final Points

Since I first wrote this book in 1971, there have been some shifts in attitude as well as a lot of new discoveries to help gardeners grow plants naturally. People everywhere are more aware of pollution of the air, water, and land caused by the misuse of chemicals and poor agricultural practices. Many are willing, even eager, to do something to protect the environment. And they no longer have any fear of being called faddists for what they believe.

With new understandings have come new curiosities and the desire for guidance. This edition has tried to meet the challenge of the recent developments, and to answer some of the questions still remaining in the minds of gardeners today.

Extension services all over the country are now providing help and information to farmers and gardeners in the program they call "Integrated Pesticide Management" (IPM). The new attitude toward biological control has led to the inclusion in this program of nonpoisonous, nonchemical methods of controlling insect and other pests, as well as modified and limited applications of chemical pesticides, carefully timed and monitored. These are integrated with the biological controls as necessary, and pinpointed to times of crises which, of course, occur most often on tracts of land devoted to a single crop. It is places like that which provide enormous feasts for pests.

Recommended insect controls include ladybugs, trichogramma wasps, spined soldier bugs, and predatory nematodes and mites. Botanical sprays include rotenone, ryania, pyrethrin, and sabadilla. Milky spore disease and *Bacillus thüringiensis* are also recommended by some extension agents. Others recommend pheromone sex lures with sticky surfaces to catch incoming pests. For apple growers there is a red plastic apple with a scent bottle attached, which lures in the apple maggot fly to get itself trapped on a sticky surface. It can't lay eggs that way.

I have often recommended skunks as controls for grubs of Japanese beetles. Keep them coming to your yard and they'll eat their fill. And I recently heard an extension agent at a meeting recommend that you send out your cat for moles, ". . . if he is as good a mouser and mole-catcher as mine." This speaker also recommended that all gardeners interested in the results of the government's twenty-year study of biological control (recently published in a series of pamphlets) ask for them at their local agent's office.

Unfortunately, the now-banned hard chemicals such as DDT and chlordane are still being exported to other countries. Residues do cling to vegetables and fruits sprayed with these substances, and people in other countries get the bad effects, and so do some of us who eat imported produce. It is claimed to be a very small effect, but there it is. The lengthy, awkward process of revising the law has been begun, according to a USDA representative I heard at the same meeting, but it will take a long, long time for this unseemly situation to improve.

People who had objections to pesticide-sprayed food used to be called food faddists. But not anymore. Now we admire people who are nutrition-conscious and concerned about eating clean food for good health. To many, it seems only sensible to want to avoid substances that are not biodegradable and can therefore build up interminably in the fatty tissues of all the creatures in a food chain. One answer, of course, is to grow your own and avoid contaminated food.

Others evidently say: Why worry?

The Romans evidently did not worry (or were totally ignorant) about the progressive lead poisoning which is now believed to have been a significant factor in the decline and fall of the Roman Empire. The people unconcernedly went on piping their water in lead pipes, storing it in lead containers, and eating their meals from lead plates, or so I have read.

One of today's greatest challenges is the problem of waste disposal. Organic gardeners for decades have supported the practice of recycling whatever can be used over again in the cycles of nature. Though it will take some time and some new habits, town after town now asks its citizens to

sort and deposit their wastes for recycling. This effort
frequently includes municipal composting of leaves, grass
clippings, and other uncontaminated plant wastes. I have
heard that there will soon be available a biodegradable plastic
made from cornstarch, which is very good news indeed.

One powerful incentive for farmers and gardeners to give
up expensive chemicals and sprays has been these people's
discovery that biological means can turn out to be a good
deal cheaper. Some farmers have found that the first year
or so following a switch from chemical fertilizers and pesticides to their natural counterparts saw not much of a
saving, but that the new (yet old) methods soon became
cheaper after all the adjustments had been made.

Recent laws have required farmers to take steps to prevent
soil erosion. For a couple of centuries Americans were
cavalier about taking care of the land. They would use up
the good soil and simply move west to better soil, leaving
the old place abandoned. And we know what a miserably
poor living they eventually scratched from the ruined soil.
In fact, among early reformers such as Louis Bromfield and
Edward H. Faulkner, the aim was to recover the fertility of
old exhausted farmland, perhaps worn out by their own
ancestors. They were organic gardeners and they were
called crackpots, but for those who did see the value of their
advice, they were eye-openers.

Other modern human traits contributed to the methods
which neglected the recycling of natural materials. One has
been a preference for new things—a clean new bag of
fertilizer as compared to old manure. In fact, riding a new
tractor to spread commercial fertilizer was more appealing
than shoveling manure. And the quick method appealed,
as compared to the long and usually more arduous methods
of building compost, and the often slow and somewhat
uncertain process of biological controls. Meanwhile farmers
were told over and over that the way to become affluent
was to use commercial fertilizers—and then commercial
pesticides and herbicides. Few farmers or gardeners were
sufficiently schooled in microbiology to understand the roles
soil microorganisms played in the growth of plants.

It was obviously more appealing to use the brute strength
of big machines than to kowtow to mere germs in the soil.
The powerful weapon of DDT was first used in World War II
to kill fleas on soldiers, and mosquitoes in malaria-infested

areas. A friend of mine told me that her husband sent her some DDT from the war zone to use in her cow barn. She also told me that the flies became resistant to it in a matter of about fourteen months, even before the war ended. We imagine that the potency of something like DDT will be comprehensive, forgetting that in nature there can be a few escaping resisters that will produce a whole population of resisters, or that can mutate when feasible.

I find myself saying that it is lucky that nature can take over from proud humanity's tendency to think it can run things itself. The irony is that proud humanity makes the same sort of mistake over and over. In the nineteenth and twentieth centuries people thought that nitrates could be miraculously helpful because they made plants grow big and fast. But now we are discovering river pollution from farm runoff, pollution of the estuaries, acid rain from other nitrate sources, and the hazards of eutrofication in ponds, lakes, and oceans.

Twenty years ago there was a joyous sense of gardening and growing your own food in an age of confusing problems. The organic gardener then had a feeling of adventure and of taking part in a new movement. Today the new organic gardener is much more knowledgeable, much wiser about ways to maintain health and improve nutrition. Today's organic gardener is following what he or she sees as a sensible road to help clean up our environment, to proceed as a partner in nature's schemes, and to reap the benefits of a moderate and straightforward method of gardening. The fun of outwitting the pests is still there, and the intense and private pleasure of watching things grow is possible throughout the growing seasons. And of course, things grown in your own yard have a freshness and flavor unmatched by any market. In the early 1970s an organic gardener had to rely on a few magazines (or really only one), on a few suppliers of provisions, and the books of two or three publishers. Today's organic gardener has resources from any number of publishers and magazines, and most seed companies and nurseries carry provisions for organic gardeners as a matter of course. Some seed suppliers provide only untreated seeds; almost any of the others will provide them on request. It is obvious that the aims and desires of organic gardeners are no longer thought of as strange and quirky, but as worthy aims consistent with the desires of mainstream Americans.

Of course there are people who have no concern for the methods used to grow the food they eat, and no interest in gardening practices. Some may never have heard of soil erosion, or of built-up resistance among insects to chemical pesticides. Many, however, are well aware of mercury or other pollution in fish and shellfish, of nitrates in baby food. As the knowledge of dangers and possible cures spreads, I believe that more people will want to grow their own vegetables, fruits, berries, and nuts in an environment where creatures and plants can thrive and live in harmony in natural good health.

Directory for Seeds and Supplies

SEEDS AND PLANTS

Burgess Seed and Plant Company, 905 Four Seasons Rd., Bloomington, IL 61701

W. Atlee Burpee Company, Warminster, PA 18974

Comstock, Ferry & Co., 263 Main St., Wethersfield, CT 06109

The Cook's Garden, Box 65, Londonderry, VT 05148

DeGiorgi Company, Inc., Council Bluffs, IA 51502

Farmer Seed and Nursery Co., Faribault, MN 55021

Henry Field's Seed & Nursery Co., Shenandoah, IA 51602

Gurney's Seed & Nursery Co., Yankton, SD 57079

Harris Seed Co., 961 Lyell Ave., Rochester, NY 14606

Hastings, Seedsman to the South, P.O. Box 4274, Atlanta, GA 30302

Johnny's Selected Seeds, Albion, ME 04910

Kelly Brothers Nurseries, Danville, NY 14437

Le Jardin du Gourmet, Danville, VT 05828

Liberty Seed Co., Box 806, New Philadelphia, OH 44663

Earl May Seed & Nursery Co., Shenandoah, IA 51603

Meadowbrook Herb Garden, Rt. 138, Wyoming, RI 02898

J.E. Miller Nurseries, Inc., Canandaigua, NY 14424

Nichols Garden Nursery, 1190 North Pacific Highway, Albany, OR 97321

George W. Park Seed Co., Box 46, Greenwood, SC 29648

Pinetree Garden Seeds, New Gloucester, ME 04260 (many supplies and books also)

Redwood City Seed Co., P.O. Box 361, Redwood City, CA 94064

Seeds Blum, Idaho City Stage, Boise, ID 83706

Seed Savers Exchange, Box 70, Decorah, IA 52101 (Membership $12; heirloom species)

Seed Saving Project, University of California at Davis, Dept. LAWR, Davis, CA 95616
(Membership $3; endangered species, etc.)

R.H. Shumway Seedsman, Box 777, Rockford, IL 61101

Stark Brothers Nurseries & Orchards, Louisiana, MO 63353

Stokes Seeds, Inc., Box 548, Buffalo, NY 14240

Thompson & Morgan, Box 1308, Jackson, NJ 08527

Otis Twilley Seed Co., Box 65, Trevose, PA 19047

Vermont Bean Seed Co., Garden Lane, Fair Haven, VT 05743

Vesey's Seeds, Ltd., Prince Edward Island, CANADA, C0A 1P0 or
   Box 9000, Houlton, ME 04730-0814

Walnut Acres, Penns Creek, PA 17862

Wayside Gardens, 1 Garden Lane, Hodges, SC 29695

White Flower Farm, Litchfield, CT 06750

SUPPLIES AND TOOLS

Various supplies, fertilizers, biological insect controls, composting aids, botanical sprays, and so on are available from seed companies. Frequently there are headings like "Organic Gardeners' Page." There are twenty pages of gardener's aids in the *Burpee* catalog, for example. Special possibilities include:

"All and Only" natural organic fertilizer. See *Liberty* catalog.

Beneficial insects such as lacewings, ladybugs, trichogramma wasps, and praying mantises. See *H. Field* catalog, and others.

Bonemeal and rock phosphate. See *Pinetree* and *H. Field* catalogs.

Brookside Nurseries, Darien, CT 06820. Many biological supplies.

Country Home Products, Box 89, Cedar Beach Rd., Charlotte, VT 05445.

DIPEL for *Bacillus thüringiensis* against worm pests. See *H. Field* catalog, etc.—(See also Thuricide and Biotrel.)

Dried Blood. See *H. Field* catalog, etc.

Gardener's Supply, 128 Intervale Rd., Burlington, VT 05401. Composters, composting aids, winter protection for plants, tillers, coldframes, Wall-O-Water plant protectors, organic soil activators, boots, gloves, chippers, scissors, harvest and preserving aids, planting and watering aids, rodent rocks, and so on.

Garden Tillers.

Gravely, Gravely Lane, Clemons, NC 27012.

Mantis Manufacturing Co., 1458 County Line Rd., Huntingdon Valley, PA 19006.

Troy-bilt Rototillers, 9th Ave. & 102 St., Troy, NY 12180.

Greensand. See *H. Field* and *Brookside* catalogs, etc.

Growing Naturally, P.O. Box 54, Pinesville, PA 18946. Biological controls and natural fertilizers.

HAVAHART traps, 148 Water St., Ossining, NY 10562. See also seed catalogs.

Indiana Botanic Garden, Hammond, IN 46325. Soil-testing kit and other supplies.

Insecticidal soap. See *Pinetree* and other catalogs.

Juwel Cold Frames. See catalogs.

Kinsman Co., 775 River Rd., Point Pleasant, PA 18950.

Milky Spore disease (to control Japanese beetles). See *H. Field* catalog, etc.

National Gardening Association, 180 Flynn Ave., Burlington, VT 05401. Assists community gardens, seed service, seed swap, answering service, excellent magazine. (Membership $18, address: Depot Sq., Peterborough, NH 03458 for membership.)

National Gardening Research Center, Box 149, Sunman, IN 47041. Biological controls for insects, weeds, and rodents; seeds for groundcovers, series of Lawn Alive, Compost Alive, Tomatoes Alive, and so on; beneficial nematodes which parasitize insects; insecticidal soap, sapadilla dust, pyrethrum-rotenone-ryania blend.

Ohio Earth Food, 13737G Duquette St., Hartville, OH 44632. Diatomaceous earth, phosphates, greensand, kelp, Erth-rite.

Pinetree seed catalog has offers of many small tools, seaweed products for fertilizing, sprays, sulfur fungicide, compost boosters, testing kits, row covers, and sex lures for insect control.

Companion Plants, Rt. 6, Box 88, Athens, OH 45701. Plant protection.

Ringer, 9959 Valley View Rd., Eden Prairie, MN 55344-3585. Many environmentally safe products, including Safer's insecticidal soap, miticide, and fungicide.

Smith and Hawken, 25 Corte Madera, Mill Valley, CA 94941. High quality clippers, hoes and other tools, ladybugs, agrikelp.

Sudbury Laboratory, Inc., Sudbury, MA 01776. Soil-testing kits.

Sunhat plant protector. See *Burgess* catalog.

Thuricide. See DIPEL.

True Friend Garden Tools, Inc., Box 1278, Cumming, GA 30130.

VORNADO leaf eater, *Vornade Power Products*, 2 Main St., Melrose, MA 02176.

WALL-O-WATER. See *Cook's Garden* catalog.

MAGAZINES

COUNTRY JOURNAL, Box 8200, Harrisburg, PA 17105 (Subscription address: Box 392, Mt. Morris, IL 61054-9956)

THE HERB QUARTERLY, Newfane, VT 05345

HORTICULTURE, 20 Park Plaza, Suite 1220, Boston, MA 02116

THE MOTHER EARTH NEWS, Box 38, Madison, OH 44057

NATIONAL GARDENING, c/o National Gardening Association, 180 Flynn Ave., Burlington, VT 05401

THE NEW ENGLAND GARDENER, Box 2699, Nantucket Island, MA 02584

ORGANIC GARDENING, 33 E. Minor St., Emmaus, PA 18049

Recommended
Readings

The Life of Plants
Bold, H.C. THE PLANT KINGDOM. Prentice-Hall, 1970.

Bonner, James and Varner, Joseph. PLANT BIOCHEMISTRY. 3rd Ed.
Academic Press, 1976.

Corner, E.J. THE LIFE OF PLANTS. University of Chicago Press,
1981.

Cronquist, Arthur. BASIC BOTANY. Harper & Row, 1981.

Galston, A.W. THE LIFE OF THE GREEN PLANT. 3rd Ed. Prentice-
Hall, 1980.

Klein, Richard M. THE GREEN WORLD: AN INTRODUCTION TO PLANTS
AND PEOPLE. 2nd Ed. Harper & Row, 1986.

Machlis, Leonard and Tottey, John G. PLANTS IN ACTION. W.H.
Freeman, 1959.

Platt, Rutherford. THIS GREEN WORLD. Updated. NY: Dodd, Mead,
1987.

Steward, F.C. and Krikorian, A.D. PLANTS, CHEMICALS &
GROWTH. Academic Press, 1971.
———————————————————————. See also his six volumes of
plant physiology.

Torrey, J.G. DEVELOPMENT OF FLOWERING PLANTS. NY: Macmillan,
1967.

Composting
Campbell, Stu. LET IT ROT! Pownal: Garden Way Publishing,
1975.

Golueke, Clarence G. COMPOSTING: A STUDY OF THE PROCESS & ITS
PRINCIPLES. Rodale Press, 1972.

Minnich, Jerry et al. eds. THE RODALE GUIDE TO COMPOSTING.
Rodale Press, 1979.

Sussman, Vic. EASY COMPOSTING. Rodale Press, 1982.

Founders of the Organic Farming and Gardening
Movement
Balfour, Lady Eve. THE LIVING SOIL. Reprint. Universe, 1976.

Bromfield, Louis. MALABAR FARM. NY: Ballantine, 1948; also
Amereon, 1976.

Faulkner, Edward H. PLOWMAN'S FOLLY. Norman: University of
Oklahoma Press, 1943; also Island Press, 1987.

Howard, Sir Albert. AN AGRICULTURAL TESTAMENT. London: Oxford
University Press. Reprint. Schocken, 1972.

Nearing, Helen and Scott. LIVING THE GOOD LIFE. NY: Schocken, 1971.

———————————————. CONTINUING THE GOOD LIFE. NY: Schocken, 1979.

Pfeiffer, Ehrenfried. BIO-DYNAMIC FARMING AND GARDENING. NY: Anthroposophic Press, 1943, O.P.

Rodale, J.I. PAY DIRT. Rodale Press, 1971.

Gardening Guides

Carleton, R. Milton. VEGETABLES FOR TODAY'S GARDENS. Wiltshire, n.d.

The American Horticultural Society. ILLUSTRATED ENCYCLOPEDIA OF GARDENING. Volumes on Vegetables; Fruits and Berries; Tomatoes; Herbs and Species. Mount Vernon, 1974-1980.

Bubel, Nancy. THE ADVENTUROUS GARDENER. Rodale Press, 1979.

———————. THE SEED STARTER'S HANDBOOK. Rodale Press, 1978.

Carleton, R. Milton. VEGETABLES FOR TODAY'S GARDEN. Wiltshire, n.d.

Gillespie, Janet. PEACOCK MANURE AND MARIGOLDS. NY: Viking, 1964, O.P.

Northen, Henry T. and Rebecca T. THE SECRET OF THE GREEN THUMB. Barens, 1942, O.P.

Owen, Millie. A COOK'S GUIDE TO GROWING HERBS, GREENS, & AROMATICS. Knopf, 1977.

Philbrick, John and Helen. GARDENING FOR HEALTH AND NUTRITION. Bio-Dynamic Way, 1975, Garber Communications.

Seymour, John. THE SELF-SUFFICIENT GARDENER. Doubleday, 1979.

Smaus, Robert. THE LOS ANGELES TIMES CALIFORNIA GARDENING BOOK. Abrams, 1983.

Smith, Marny. GARDENING WITH CONSCIENCE: THE ORGANIC INTENSIVE METHOD. Harper & Row, 1981.

Tilgner, Linda. TIPS FOR THE LAZY GARDENER. Pownal: Garden Way Publishing, 1985.

USDA. GARDENING FOR FOOD AND FUN YEARBOOK. USDA, 1977.

Soil

Balfour, Lady Eve. THE LIVING SOIL. Reprint. Universe, 1976.

Donahue, Roy and Miller, John. AN INTRODUCTION TO SOILS AND PLANT GROWTH. 5th Ed. Prentice-Hall, 1983.

———————————————. et al. OUR SOILS & THEIR MANAGEMENT: INCREASING PRODUCTION THROUGH ENVIRONMENTAL SOIL AND WATER CONSERVATION. 5th Ed. International, n.d.

Garrett, S.D. SOIL FUNGI AND SOIL FERTILITY. Elmsport, NY: Pergamin, 1969.

Howard, Sir Albert. THE SOIL AND HEALTH: A STUDY OF ORGANIC AGRICULTURE. NY: Devin-Adair, 1947.

USDA. SOILS AND MEN: YEARBOOK OF AGRICULTURE. Washington, DC: USDA, 1938.

USDA. SOILS YEARBOOK OF AGRICULTURE. Washington, DC: USDA, 1957.

Wakeman, Selman A. THE SOIL AND THE MICROBE. NY: John Wiley, 1931.

Ecology

Barbour, Michael G. and Billings, W.D. NORTH AMERICAN TERRESTRIAL VEGETATION. University of California, n.d.

———————————————. et al. COASTAL ECOLOGY. University of California, 1974.

———————————————. LAB STUDIES IN BOTANY. 6th Ed. University of California, 1982.

Carson, Rachel. SILENT SPRING. 25th Anniversary Ed. Houghton, Mifflin, 1987.

Dubos, Rene. THE RESILIENCE OF ECOSYSTEMS. Colorado Association, 1984.

Ehrlich, Paul R. THE MACHINERY OF NATURE. Simon & Schuster, 1986.

———————. POPULATIONS BOMB. n.t.: Ballantine, 1976.

Keating, Joni. INTERDEPENDENCE IN THE NATURAL WORLD. Trillium Press, 1987.

Kormondy, Edward J. CONCEPTS OF ECOLOGY. 3rd Ed. Prentice-Hall, 1984.

Leopold, Aldo W. SAND COUNTY ALMANAC. Reprint. Oxford University Press, 1987.

Nebel, Bernard J. ENVIRONMENTAL SCIENCE: THE WAY THE WORLD WORKS. Prentice-Hall, 1980.

Odum, Eugene P. BASIC ECOLOGY. S.C.P., 1983.

Pringle, Lawrence. RESTORING OUR EARTH. Enslow Publishing, 1987.

Rudd, Robert L. PESTICIDES AND THE LIVING LANDSCAPE. Madison: University of Wisconsin, 1964.

Sears, Paul B. DESERTS ON THE MARCH. 4th Ed. Norman: University of Oklahoma, 1980.

———————. THIS IS OUR WORLD. University of Oklahoma, 1971.

Storer, J.H. THE WEB OF LIFE. NY: New American Library, 1972.

Thoreau, Henry David. WALDEN. 1864. Many reprints.

USDA. A PLACE TO LIVE, YEARBOOK OF AGRICULTURE. Washington, DC: USDA, 1983.

Wallace, Robert A. BIOSPHERE: THE REALM OF LIFE. 2nd Ed. Scott, Foresman, 1987.

Pest Control and Companion Planting

Brooklyn Botanical Garden. HANDBOOK ON BIOLOGICAL CONTROL OF PLANT PESTS. Brooklyn, NY.

————————. GARDENING WITHOUT PESTS. 1979.

Carr, Anne. GOOD NEIGHBORS: COMPANION PLANTING FOR GARDENERS. Rodale, 1985.

Philbrick, John and Helen. THE BUG BOOK. Garden Way Publishing, 1974.

————————. COMPANION PLANTS AND HOW TO USE THEM. Devin-Adair, 1966.

Pyrethrum Information Center. HOW TO KILL INSECTS THE NON-TOXIC WAY . . . WITH PYRETHRINS. 744 Broad Street, Newark, NJ 07102.

Riotte, Louise. CARROTS LOVE TOMATOES. Garden Way Publishing, 1976.

————————. ROSES LOVE GARLIC. Garden Way Publishing, 1983.

————————. SLEEPING WITH A SUNFLOWER. Garden Way Publishing, 1987.

Rodale et al. ORGANIC PLANT PROTECTION. ed. R.B. Yepsen. Rodale, 1976.

Yepsen, Roger B. THE ENCYCLOPEDIA OF NATURAL INSECT AND DISEASE CONTROL. Rodale Press, 1984.

Herbs

Culpeper, Nicholas. COMPLETE HERBAL. Reprint. Hackensack: N. Wehman, 1960.

Fox, Helen M. THE YEARS IN MY HERB GARDEN. NY: Macmillan, 1953, O.P.

Garland, Sarah. THE HERB GARDEN. Viking, 1985.

Hylton, William H. ed. THE RODALE HERB BOOK. Rodale Press, 1974.

THE HERB GROWER (quarterly), Falls Village, CT.

THE HERB QUARTERLY, Newfane, VT.

Jacobs, Betty E.M. GROWING AND USING HERBS SUCCESSFULLY. Garden Way Publishing, 1976.

Northcote, Lady Rosalind. THE BOOK OF HERB LORE. Reprint. Dover, 1971.

Rohde, Eleanour. HERBS AND HERB GARDENING. N.p., n.d.

Simmons, Adelma. HERB GARDENING IN FIVE SEASONS. Reprint. Gale, 1977.

I N D E X

Black salsify, 234
Blackberries, 55, 143–147
Blueberries, 55, 147
Book of Tofu, 238
Borage, 24
  Borago officinalis, 185–186
Boron, 43, 94, 99
Botany, *See* Plant Growth,
  Plant Structures
Bouncing bet, *Saponaria
  officinalis*, 186
Broccoli, 54, 55, 63
  Brassica oleracea italica, 151–152
Bromfield, Louis, 254
Bromine, 43
Brussels sprouts, 54
  Brassica oleracea gemmifera,
  152–153
Bt, 160
Burdock, *Arctium lappa*, 186,
  250
Burpee Co., 56
Bush beans, 60

C

Cabbage, 54, 55, 60
  Brassica oleracea capitata,
  153–155
Cabbage loopers, 160
Cabbage worm, 13, 154
Calcium, 43, 44, 94, 99,
  112–113
Cambium, 35–36
Camomile, *Anthemis nobilis,
  Matricaria chamomilla*,
  187

Canning, vegetables, 55
Cantaloupe, 209–210
Caraway, 24
  Carum carvi, 187
Carbon, 43, 116–117
Carbon dioxide, 36–37
Carrots, 54, 55, 61, 63
  Daucus carota sativas, 156–159
Catalogs, seeds, 55–60
Caterpillars, 13, 162
Catnip, 63
  Nepeta cataria, 187
Cattail, *Typha latifolia*, 250
Cauliflower, 54, 55
  Brassica oleracea botrytis,
  159–161
Caulis, 165, 210
Celeriac, *Apium graveolens
  rapaceum*, 161–162
Celery, 54, 55, 62
  Apium graveolens, 162–163
Cellulose, 38
Chard, 54, 55
Chemical fertilizers, 8–9,
  12–13, 26, 107, 120
Chemical pest controls, 6–14,
  49, 252–254
Cherries, 55
Chervil, 24, 54, 64
Chicory, 54
  Cichorium intybus, 164–165
Chinese Cabbage, *Brassica
  pekinensis*, 155–156
Chives, 62, 64–65
Chlordane, 253
Chlorinated hydrocarbon pes-
  ticides, 3

Planting zones, 57
Plants,
    endurance of, 27
    experiments with, 20–23
    growth of, 17, 19–20, 26–52
    heredity, 50–52
    structure of, 15, 34–52
    temperatures for, 26–28
    winterizing of, 54–55,
       170–171
    see also specific structures
Plastic tunnel, 32
Plum, 55
    Prunus, 222–223
Poke, *Phytolacca americana*, 250
Pole beans, 60
Polistes wasps, 168
Pollen, 49
Pollen tube, 51
Pollinators, 49
Pollution, *See* Environment
Potash, 114
Potassium, 37, 39, 40, 43,
    92–95, 110–111, 114,
    119–120
Potato, 20, 54, 59, 63
    Solanum tuberosum, lpomoea
    batatas, 223–227
Potting soil, 19,–24
Praying mantises, 13
Prunes, 55
Pumpkin, 54, 55
    Cucurbita pepo, 227–228
Purdue University, 75
Purslane, *Portulaca oleracea*,
    198, 250
Pyrethrin, 252

Pyrethrum, 13, 59

R

Rabbits, 62
Radish, 17–19, 54, 63–63
    Raphanus sativas, 228–229
Raspberries, 54, 55, 143–147
Red Cabbage, 155
Reflectors, 25–26
Rhubarb, 55
    Rheum rhaponticum, 229, 231
Rhubarb Conserve, 231
Ringer Supplies and Tools,
    56
Rock phosphate, 8, 12, 39
Rocket (Rockette), *Eruca sativa*,
    231–232
Rodale Press, 9, 12, 112
Rosemary, 24, 180–202
    Rosmarinus officinalis, 199
Rotenone, 13, 59, 64, 169, 252
Rue, 63
Russian thistle, *Salsola pestifer*,
    250
Rutabaga, 54, 246–249
    Brassica napobrassica,
    247–248
Ryania, 13, 168–169, 252

S

Sabadilla, 13, 59, 168–169,
    252
Sage, 54, 61, 64–65, 180–202
    Salvia officinalis, 199

About the Author

Catharine Osgood Foster was born in Newton Highlands, Massachusetts, and was graduated from Mount Holyoke College, but became a Vermonter by adoption when she started teaching literature at Bennington College and later married a Vermont native, Thomas H. Foster, ornithologist and critic. She has been actively involved in conservation work in the state of Vermont for many years and since her retirement from teaching, she has written a weekly column for the Bennington Banner. The Fosters live near Old Bennington, where they practice what they preach surrounded by trees and shrubs, a garden and a yard with living creatures, who help maintain the good health and harmony of their land.